Wakefield Press

The Engaging State

The Engaging State

South Australia's Engagement with the Asia-Pacific Region

Edited by
John Spoehr & Purnendra Jain

Wakefield Press
1 The Parade West
Kent Town
South Australia 5067
www.wakefieldpress.com.au

First published 2012

Cover designed by Michael Deves
Typeset by Wakefield Press
Printed in Australia by Griffin Digital, Adelaide

National Library of Australia Cataloguing-in-Publication entry

Title:	The engaging state: South Australia's engagement with the Asia–Pacific Region / edited by John Spoehr and Purnendra Jain.
ISBN:	978 1 74305 157 3 (pbk.).
Subjects:	International relations. South Australia – Foreign relations. Pacific Area – Foreign relations.
Other Authors/ Contributors:	Spoehr, John. Jain, Purnendra.
Dewey Number:	327.5

Contents

Contents

Preface

The Engaging State is a book for its time. It is a product of multi-disciplinary effort within the University of Adelaide, which has aimed to deepen understanding of the dimensions and complexities of South Australia's engagement with the Asia Pacific Region. At a time when subnational governments have come of age as international actors in their own right, this book contributes to conceptual and practical knowledge of the evolving role of sub-national governments in international affairs.

Most authors completed research for this book and finalised their chapters before the Hon Jay Weatherill, MP, took office as South Australia's 45th Premier in October 2011, replacing the Hon Mike Rann. Even in his early days as Premier, Mr Weatherill has vindicated the importance of this book through his international engagements as Premier. In January 2012, he launched a South Australia–India economic development directions paper underscoring the rising economic importance of India for South Australia. In the same month he travelled to the United States to consolidate and strengthen South Australia's economic and other multi-layered linkages with the US. His international activism in the first few months after taking office shows a clear commitment of the new state government to further deepen South Australia's engagement with the nations of Asia Pacific through economic, cultural, social, educational and even some political linkages.

Preliminary research for these chapters was presented by the group at the 18th Biennial Conference of the Asian Studies Association of Australia, held at the University of Adelaide in July 2010. The papers have been subsequently refined for publication in this collection. We thank all the authors for their thoughtful and timely contributions to the book.

Our thanks to Lance Worrall, Deputy Chief Executive, Department of Manufacturing, Innovation, Trade, Resources and Energy and a number of departmental staff for helpful insights and comments.

We also thank the Faculty of Humanities and Social Sciences for supporting the project that has underpinned publication of *The Engaging State*. Finally, we thank Wakefield Press for publishing *The Engaging State*, with special thanks to Michael Bollen and Stephanie Johnston.

John Spoehr
Purnendra Jain

Adelaide, February 2012

LIST OF ACRONYMS

AALD	Australian-Asian Leadership Dialogue
ABC	Australian Broadcasting Commission
ABS	Australian Bureau of Statistics
ACBC	Australia-China Business Council
AIBCSA	Australia-India Business Council South Australia
AJA	Australia-Japan Association SA
ANZCERTA	Australia New Zealand Closer Economic Relations
ANZUS	Australia New Zealand and United States
APEC	Asia-Pacific Economic Forum
ASCO	Australian Standard Classification of Occupations
ASEAN	Association of South East Asian Nations
CBD	Central Business District
CGE	Computable General Equilibrium model
CII	Confederation of Indian Industry
CITSCA	Council for International Trade and Commerce of South Australia
DECS	Department of Education and Children's Services
DFAT	Department of Foreign Affairs and Trade
DIAC	Department of Immigration and Citizenship
DTED	Department of Trade and Economic Development - South Australia
EAS	East Asia Summit
EDS	Electronic Data Systems
ELICOS	English Language Intensive Courses for Overseas Students
ETSA	Electricity Trust of South Australia
FTA	Free Trade Agreement
FTE	Full Time Equivalent
GDP	Gross Domestic Product
GFC	Global Financial Crisis

GMH	General Motors Holden
GMO	Genetically Modified Organisms
GRP	Gross Regional Product
GSP	Gross State Product
IAASA	Indian-Australian Association of South Australia
I-O	Input-Output
JABC	Japan-Australia Business Council of SA
JAFA	Japan-Australia Friendship Association
JSA	Japanese Society of Adelaide
MFP	Multi-Function Polis
MIS	Municipal international cooperation
PIF	Pacific Island Forum
PRC	People's Republic of China
SAFC	South Australian Film Corporation
SAFTA	Singapore-Australia Free Trade Agreement
SAMEAC	South Australian Multi-cultural and Ethnic Affairs Commission
SEATO	South East Asia Treaty Organisation
SNGs	Sub National Governments
SRMS	Skilled Regional Migration Scheme
SSRM	State Specific Regional Migration Scheme
TAFE	Technical and Further Education
TAFTA	Thailand-Australia Free Trade Agreement
VET	Vocational Education and Training
WAP	White Australia Policy
WHM	Working Holiday Maker program
WCTU	Women's Christian Temperance Union
WTO	World Trade Organisation

CHAPTER 1

The Engaging State – Australian Subnational Government Engagement with the Asia Pacific Region

JOHN SPOEHR and PURNENDRA JAIN

Australia's links with the nations of Asia-Pacific, particularly of Asia, are strengthening at an unprecedented pace. Economic ties, especially trade, continue to expand exponentially. This comes as no surprise since in 2010 China overtook Japan as the world's second largest economy and as Australia's largest trading partner, and India is now one of the top destinations for Australian exports. About two-thirds of Australia's trade is concentrated in the Asia Pacific region and these days, usually seven or eight of Australia's top ten trading partners are in the Asia Pacific. Direct investment from Asia, especially from Japan and Singapore, remains high. In more recent years Chinese investment in Australia, especially in the mining sector, has also begun to take off and Indian companies, too, are proceeding with modest investment in Australia. Given the expectations inspired by China and India's recent economic growth patterns and Japan's place as the world's third largest economy and still a significant economic power in the region, both trade and investment links with Asian countries appear set to increase even further.

This solid flow of goods and finance is accompanied by – to a considerable extent has inspired – a similar surge in flows of people and ideas. Tourism and exchange/volunteer programs carry significant numbers of people between Australia and Asia alongside commercial and official travellers. Another human flow has much deeper and longer-lasting import: the phenomenal growth of migration from Asia, particularly from China and India, which is reshaping Australia's demographic landscape. One key migration route is eligibility of full-fee paying international students for permanent resident status on completing a recognised study program in Australia. The study program may be a degree or diploma at tertiary or government-funded vocational institutions, or may even be through privately run institutes' vocational courses such as cookery, hair dressing, hospitality and community welfare, or other areas where the Australian government defines skill shortages. While the migrant inflow from many Asian countries has increased in recent years, by far the largest numbers – most of them taking the student route to 'permanent resident' status – are from mainland China and India. The passage and settling in Australia of people from Asian countries has entailed the increasing popularity of foods, cultural events, grocers and other cultural trappings from Asian countries, which helps to promote a culturally richer, more diverse Australian society.

Scholarship of Australia–Asia relations has almost exclusively concerned national level dynamics, detailing economic, strategic, political and socio-cultural links and associated issues in the context of the nations involved. Studies include government and private reports and research conducted by think tanks, specialised centres, individual scholars, diplomats, journalists and political leaders (e.g., Keating 2000; Dobell 2000; ASAA 2002; Wesley 2011).[1] But clearly, when we consider the nature and extent of contemporary engagement between Australia and Asia, much of it reaches beyond the national level and therefore is not considered in depth within the Australia–Asia scholarship. The international roles of other government, non-government, private sector and individual actors who comprise, and produce, this international engagement have not been fully recognised or examined in this geographic context.

This book turns the lens onto one of these 'other' international actors now playing an increasingly important role in Australia–Asia relations. Here our concern is with the next unit of government below the national level, which in the Australian case is state government. Specifically we are concerned with the government of South Australia, the fourth largest of Australia's six states and two territories. Literature on international relations has referred to internationally active governments below the national level with various terms, including sub-national authorities, sub-national and regional actors and meso-level governments. We use the term subnational government (SNG) to refer to all governments below the national government. SNGs therefore include the governments of all Australian states and territories and the administrative units within them.

While little has been published concerning the role of SNGs in shaping Australia's relations with the nations of Asia-Pacific, this is much less true of the international role of SNGs in some other parts of the world. The international relations and international political economy literature contains ever more analyses of the international roles of SNGs – their initiatives, actions, policy responses and motivations in various parts of the world. This is testament not just to more careful, insightful scholarship of 'international actors' but also to the increasing scope, diversity and importance of SNGs in their evolving international roles. Examples discussed in the literature are not just from North America but are also from a large number of European countries, and in recent years from such Asian countries as China, Japan and India as well. It is useful to briefly consider this literature for insights into the nature, purpose and significance of internationally active SNGs to better understand the Australian context and the South Australian case in comparative perspective.

COMPARATIVE PERSPECTIVE

Publications concerning internationally active SNGs, particularly in European and North American contexts, began to appear from the early 1990s. Today the international relations literature has ever more studies of SNGs, forming part of a rich seam of empirical and conceptual analyses that detail the role in international affairs of actors beyond the nation-state and national level players. These actors include government units above and below the level of national government, such as the European Union, ASEAN and other supranational bodies, and SNGs respectively, as well as non-state actors such as non-governmental organisations (NGOs), business groups and other civic and private groups and individuals. The role and significance of these actors has increased substantially in the post-Cold War period marked by increasing globalisation, as international relations and diplomacy enter new terrain and force new scholarship to explain.

An observation by Hocking (2006) expresses this complex picture succinctly: 'diplomacy is becoming an activity concerned with the creation of networks embracing a range of state and non-state actors focusing on the management of issues demanding the application of resources in which no single participant possesses a monopoly'. Hocking employs the term 'multi-stakeholder diplomacy' to capture the international role of diverse non-state actors that shape international outcomes while pursuing their own internationally significant interests outside – and sometimes even inside – their national borders.

Scholarship concerned specifically with internationally active SNGs offers sundry terms that refer to SNGs' international activities, from sub-state diplomacy, paradiplomacy and protodiplomacy to microdiplomacy and constituent diplomacy. In all instances 'diplomacy' denotes the official, government nature of these activities.[2] Other offerings have a narrower reach. For example, Hobbs (1994) refers specifically to 'city diplomacy'. And Brande (2010, 200) acknowledges 'sub- or infra-state foreign relations' but advances the term 'federated state diplomacy' for situations where subnational actors become key players in a nation's foreign affairs including in treaty making processes.[3] For the present study of the state of South Australia in its relations with Asia, the term SNG remains the most appropriate. But as we shall see, while the South Australian state government's international activities involve government officials in international negotiations and relationships, their main purposes are not to pursue international 'diplomacy' as usually understood in the context of foreign diplomats and foreign ministries. Their purposes here are explicitly concerned with working for the people and the state of South Australia – in these instances crossing national borders to do so.

The literature suggests that the trend towards SNGs becoming internationally active has been under way most strongly in Western nations. Yet at present, the erosion of the exclusive power of nation states and national governments in international affairs means that 'sub-state entities across the world today engage in international relations and conduct a 'foreign policy' that runs in parallel, complements, or is sometimes in conflict with their central governmental counterparts' (Criekemans 2010, 1). Increasingly, SNGs in Asia are actively pursuing their own interests abroad, in cooperation with the national government and sometimes independently (Jain 2005). Indeed, the literature, or at least English language literature, may not be keeping pace with action on the ground. Cornago (2010, 24) has observed, 'Chinese provinces are among the most active actors all over the world in the field of sub-state diplomacy'.

At this point we should ask why 'conducting a foreign policy' is now virtually a standard feature among 'sub-state entities across the world today'. There are multiple and complex answers that usually depend upon the distinctive circumstances of each SNG or at least their national context. One reason appears to be central and universal: SNGs increasingly need to support themselves financially. They now pursue international engagements as a vital component of the self-sustainability that national governments are increasingly requiring of SNGs as national budgets are forced to stretch further. While many SNGs have responded by pursuing their own interests abroad through cultural, educational, commercial and other cooperation programs at the grassroots level, one of the major motivations is to gain economic benefit for their locality, usually through promoting trade and attracting foreign investment and increased tourism.

In Europe, a number of regions have opened 'embassies' abroad and negotiate their own trade agreements; some have linked themselves in state-of-the-art transportation networks to attract foreign business. Some local governments are claiming new ground in EU decision-making (Matthews 1997; Newhouse 1997; Bomberg and Peterson 1998). Almost all 50 US states have trade offices abroad, and all have official standing in the World Trade Organisation (Hobbs 1994; Fry 1998). US state governors have been particularly active in this field (McMillan 2008). Similarly, in some Asian nations SNGs are actively promoting their economic interests through overseas trade and attracting foreign investment for their locality (Cheung and Tang 2001; Arase 2002; Jain 2005).

Political considerations – at times mixed with ethical considerations and altruism – may also motivate the international activities of SNGs. Some SNGs see that they have a crucial role to play in a range of global issues such as combating poverty and promoting sustainable development (Shuman 1994). Some, especially in Europe, have become involved in delivery of foreign aid both independently and in conjunction with their national government. Municipal international cooperation (MIC) serves as a mechanism for SNGs to become directly involved in overseas development assistance, providing SNGs of developing countries uninterrupted access to technical assistance and financial support from their partners in the industrialised world (Schep 1995). Some SNGs, particularly in North America, take action against abuses of human rights internationally, through punitive actions such as imposing economic sanctions and establishing laws banning state agencies from signing contracts with companies doing business with the blacklisted nation. The laws imposed by Massachusetts State against Burma are one renowned example (Guay 2000). Many SNGs far and wide try to ensure they have a representative at international forums relevant to their concerns.

What enables and encourages SNGs to set out on an international path? First are factors concerning the constitutional distribution of powers and institutional arrangements between national and state governments. Federations, such as Australia and the US, are characterised by partially self-governing states or regions united by a central (federal) government. Unitary states, such as France and the UK, are governed as a single unit, with the central government as the supreme source of authority, and subnational units as *administrative divisions* able to exercise only the powers that the central *government* delegates to them. Australia's relatively decentralised federal system presents some guaranteed space for SNGs to pursue international activity but also sets restrictions, as we discuss later.

Second, irrespective of their constitutionally regulated relationship with the national government, SNGs have learned to speak for themselves to protect their specific 'local' interests, which may be in conflict with what their national governments recognise internationally as national interests. For example, decisions that national governments make at international organisations like the WTO and the UN or through bilateral agreements can impact profoundly on local economies and their governance. Decisions by the Australian government to establish free trade agreements advantage some states while other states may have adverse impacts on their regional economy.

Third, SNGs have the political will to undertake these activities. They recognise, particularly through the precedents of their counterparts nationally and internationally, that international linkages can enhance SNG independence from their central government, not just in financing (which they see as vital) but also in policy matters. SNGs are generally very eager to achieve greater autonomy, which provides the imperative to search for new areas – activities and overseas locations – where they can generate sources of income for themselves and introduce innovative policies both independently and ahead of the national government. Some SNGs have the constitutional capacity to represent the political voice of local constituents, as the Massachusetts State laws against Burma demonstrate. As explained below, Australian states have quite limited constitutional capacity to take explicitly political action that has national consequences.

Fourth, reciprocally, SNGs lack what national governments cannot escape in their international dealings. Here we refer to diplomatic baggage and perception of it that can disable national governments from undertaking some actions that SNGs can perform effectively, precisely because they are government but not national government. A recent Australian example concerns diplomatic discussion of convicted Rio Tinto executive Stern Hu, a Chinese Australian citizen. While Chinese leaders were reluctant to talk to federal Trade Minister Simon Crean about the controversy, the Shanghai Mayor discussed the issue with visiting Western Australian Premier Colin Barnett (Callick 2010).

A final reason concerns SNGs' mutual awareness and knowledge of what SNGs can do outside national borders. The early efforts of internationally active SNGs provided precedent for their counterparts in the national and international context to follow suit – or reach even further. Internationally active SNGs are now so common, with links between them firming, that SNGs have their own international networks that operate independently of national governments. In some instances these networks have been institutionalised, such as the States and Regions Alliance's role in climate change (Rann and Charest 2010). It is not just that SNGs can learn from each other but also that they can identify with each other, sharing similar dispositions, problems, and capacities/incapacities to solve them. Returning to Western Australian Premier Colin Barnett on his Chinese SNG counterparts, 'Politicians tend to trust each other. They may say something to me that they wouldn't say even to the biggest of Australian companies' (Callick 2010). They understand that SNG commercial and other arrangements abroad are in many respects political, and locate their policies within that context.

The discussion above points to some important considerations concerning pursuit of interests. In international affairs the interests of SNGs may be in conflict with interests pursued by their central governments on some issues. For example, all state governments did not endorse the federal government's ban on exporting uranium to India while it was in place. But the interests of both may also be very much in sync, particularly in pursuit of economic and diplomatic gain that can benefit both locality and nation. This is also likely in international aid delivery and the various educational and exchange programs that generate goodwill. In some cases SNGs' overseas actions can reinforce the centre's political position or even express it explicitly when the centre is unable to. This points to the need for mutual cooperation to achieve mutual benefit for both levels of government. Australia's national policy responses to trade liberalisation, foreign investment, migration, international education and so forth directly affect Australian state governments. It is natural, then, that as stakeholders, state governments want to have their views considered to produce policy that is at least not damaging of Australian state interests and ideally is beneficial for stakeholders at both national and sub-national levels.

The interests of SNGs themselves may also set them in competition with each other to achieve the benefits that international linkages can yield. Overcoming skill shortages in areas of high occupational demand is a case in point. Up until 2011 South Australia had some advantage in this respect with Adelaide being designated a 'region' under the Australian migration program. This gave skilled migrants a discount on the number of eligibility points they had to score to gain entry, increasing the attractiveness of Adelaide as a destination for migrants. Some tension was generated within South Australia by this with complaints from local government that Adelaide 'should never have been allowed to have regional status' as it is 'an impediment to the South-East and the other regions' that face skill shortages (Wills and Littley 2011). It is likely that these competitive tensions will intensify within South Australia and between South Australia and other states while demand for skill remains relatively high.

Two other factors are also very important in shaping what Australian SNGs can and will do as international actors. First, as the discussion above signals, a major determinant of what SNGs do as international actors are the authorisations and restrictions set out in national constitutions and/or the national legal code. In the US, Canada and some European countries, many SNGs have vast-ranging constitutional powers that far surpass those of Australian state governments. For example, US states and local authorities have entered into thousands of accords, compacts and agreements (not 'treaties') with their counterparts overseas and with Washington approval, state governments have even begun to dispatch their National Guard Units abroad to train military and civilian leaders in Warsaw Pact nations (Fry 1998, 5). US state governors engage actively in foreign policy activity as they have institutional powers, budgetary control and electoral support behind them (Macmillan 2008). Belgium's constitution since 1994 even provides its federated states with the quasi-sovereignty to enter into treaties with outside powers within 'the necessary internal competency' (Van den Brande 2010, 200). Australian circumstances are somewhat more restricted. Here institutional arrangements are based on the Westminster system, and do not provide state premiers the kind or extent of executive autonomy to pursue international affairs in the way of their US and Belgian counterparts.

The second factor is Australia's geographical location. Unlike most nations, which share contiguous land borders, Australia is completely surrounded by ocean. This initially reduced both the imperative and the opportunity for Australian SNGs to actively seek links beyond their state and national borders. Yet in the era of globalisation, Australia has become linked much more closely to the region and the world than even a few decades ago. The forces of globalisation and capacities of technology have inevitably activated both imperative and opportunity for Australian SNGs to pursue international activities, perhaps an inevitable consequence since so much of what these SNGs are required to do, can do, and aspire to do is profoundly influenced by what happens outside Australia. Growing economic interdependence as well as links between people particularly through migration, employment, education and tourism make it essential for state and other subnational units to conduct their own 'foreign policy'.

AUSTRALIAN SUBNATIONAL GOVERNMENT IN INTERNATIONAL AFFAIRS

We have noted that Australian SNGs have become active internationally, though not at the forefront when considered against counterparts abroad. For whatever reasons, this development on the part of Australian SNGs has not drawn the scholarly attention it appears to deserve as an increasingly important aspect of Australia's international engagements. Let us briefly consider this minimal literature on Australian SNGs as international actors before turning to our specific case of South Australia.

John Ravenhill's study at the end of the 1990s mapped out the role of Australian SNGs in international activities in some detail in the context of federal–state relations. He observed that Australian states had expanded their international role during earlier years, but through the 1990s 'retreated from some of their international activities and increasingly entered collaborative arrangements with one another and with the Commonwealth government' (Ravenhill 1999, 136). Today state governments maintain their own offices overseas mainly to conduct economic activities. These at times overlap with what the Commonwealth government does and are often in competition with other states.

On an empirical level, two volumes in the mid-1990s presented some documentation on state government international activities (McNamara 1994 and McNamara 1996). But these were not analytical studies, essentially describing briefly the kinds of activities Australian state and territory governments were undertaking in Asia. Since information presented in the volumes was based on materials supplied by government agencies themselves, the author rightly acknowledged the 'incomplete', 'unchallenged' and 'tentative' nature of the reports (McNamara 1996, 58). Even so, these reports are a valuable source for some understanding of Australian SNGs' activities overseas in the mid-1990s. They point to the need for an updated study, especially since we can be reasonably sure that SNGs have stepped up their international programs, particularly economic, in the 15 year interim when Australia's engagement with Asia has expanded and fortified, particularly through economic interdependencies.

Surveys and commentaries on Australia's sister-state relations, especially with China and Japan were also published during the 1990s (Jain 1991; Goodman 1996; Dunn 1996). These sister ties can serve as an important vehicle for economic and cultural activities, but their overall impact has not been examined and it appears that the quality and intensity of sister ties varies from state to state. Other studies (Elliott 1995; Minami 1997; O'Donnell 1994) contributed to our understanding but focused mainly on economic aspects and bilateral examples with Japan, since written in the mid-1990s when Australia's economic partnership with Japan was still booming. As Asia's two new giants, China and India, have surfaced through the 21st century, they both provide areas to which our analytical lens should be turned, given their potential (partly realised) for unprecedented influence on Australia's economic, social and political landscape and the engagement already underway between Australian state governments and their Chinese and Indian counterparts.

ENGAGEMENT IN A CHANGING WORLD

South Australia's engagement with the Asia Pacific region during the latter part of the 20th century continues a long tradition of engagement with politically and economically dominant nations and regions. The character of South Australia's international engagement was profoundly influenced by British colonisation and patterns of late 19th and early 20th century migration, investment, trade and cultural development. Subsequent waves of foreign investment and the development of deep trading relationships with other nations and regions, particularly the United States, Europe and Japan have diversified South Australia's international relationships. As the second decade of the 21st century unfolds the focus of attention is now the Asia Pacific region, particularly as a consequence of sustained high rates of economic growth in China and India which continue to fuel strong demand for South Australian commodity exports. This has been vitally important in the face of the global financial crisis which has dampened demand for South Australian exports from the United States, Britain and Europe as we shall later in this chapter.

Early signs of South Australia's economic engagement with Asia emerged during the 1970s when Premier Don Dunstan visited Hong Kong and Japan to organise trade representation in those countries (Dunstan 1981, 184). Dunstan signalled the importance of building ties with the region, visiting Singapore, Jakarta, Hong Kong and Japan. He established a South Australian presence in the region through various mechanisms. Dunstan recalled, 'In Japan we hired as agents the branch office of Elders GM, the South Australian pastoral industry giant, and other local offices were hired in due course in Hong Kong, Kuala Lumpur, Singapore and Jakarta. The agents were required to keep us informed of local market opportunities, to suggest products or processes south but not supplied, and to service South Australia businesses on their visits to the countries concerned' (ibid, 192).

Over the last two decades there have been various attempts by policy-makers to strengthen economic and commercial ties with the Asia Pacific region. National policy settings, in particular the phasing down of tariffs and more aggressive export strategies, have forced the pace of this in South Australia. Following the lead of the Hawke Government's economic and industry development reforms during the late 1980s and early 1990s, the South Australian Labor Government led by John Bannon looked to Asia as a source of future growth. In the midst of recession it commissioned the US based consultancy firm Arthur D Little to generate a policy blueprint – 'New Directions for South Australia's Economy'.

Released inF 1992, the so called AD Little draft report focused the attention of policy makers on the Asia-Pacific region (Little 1992). The report highlighted the growing importance of tradeable services to meet the needs of the Asia-Pacific region, noting that 'rapid economic development taking place' in the region, 'gives rise to many opportunities for the sale of tradeable services' and the provision of technical assistance with infrastructure development (ibid, 15). The seeds for the growth of one of South Australia's fastest growing service export industries – international student education were sown at this time (ibid, 7). The report urged the State Government to place particular emphasis on the development of trade and investment relationships with the Asia-Pacific region and 'as a matter of urgency … improve or increase' government representation in the region (ibid, 28). Specifically the AD Little Report recommended that the State Government establish representation in Indonesia, Malaysia and Taiwan 'to build closer relationships with government and industry in those countries' and 'to promote South Australian trade and investment and identify opportunities for joint venture and collaborative activities (ibid, 32).

The AD Little Report was sidelined by the calamitous events surrounding the collapse of the State Bank during the early 1990s (Spoehr 1999, 10–11). While the change of government that flowed from the State Bank crisis ushered in a political era dominated by micro-economic reform, the incoming Liberal Government led by Dean Brown made pre-election policy commitments to engagement with Asia through the establishment of an International Business Centre with a particular focus on Indonesia, Singapore, Thailand, Hong Kong, China, Taiwan and Japan (Brown 1993, 10–11). In part, the new government justified its outsourcing and privatisation strategies as tools of engagement with major corporate interests in the Asia Pacific region. The Government's Development Council identified the export of public services to Asia as a priority and established a Government Services Export Panel (South Australian Development Council 1996, 12).

Outsourcing became a major instrument of international economic engagement as well as financial policy in the mid 1990s when the Liberal Government signed contracts for the management of Adelaide's metropolitan water and waste water infrastructure with the French/Anglo/Australian United Water Consortium and the management of the State Governments information technology services to US based Electronic Data Services. To bolster exports to Asia the Government supported the establishment of a Water Industry Cluster of companies focused on export development (Department of Industry and Trade 1998, 14).

Soon after re-election for a second term of government in 1997 the Liberal Government led by Premier John Olsen announced that it would privatise the South Australian electricity industry (Spoehr 2003, 27). The scale of the asset privatisation program was certain to attract overseas interest and it did. By the end of 1999 it had leased Flinders Power, a major electricity generating facility to US-based firm, NRG Energy along with ETSA Utilities, the State's electricity distribution system, to Hong Kong-based Hutchison Whampoa group which included major infrastructure investors, Hong Kong Electric and Cheung Kong Infrastructure (ibid, 46–47). The extent to which these relationships have underpinned net growth in the export of South Australian goods and services remains unclear.

FOCUS ON THE ASIA-PACIFIC

At the end of the 1990s a strategy to target Asia as a major destination for exports and the development of trade relationships was emerging. A network of overseas offices had been established in the region by the State Government including offices in Jinan, Shanghai and Hong Kong, Bandung in Indonesia, Kuala Lumpur in Malaysia and New York (DBMT 2002–03, DTED 2004). Reflecting changes in the priorities of the state Government offices in Tokyo and Jakarta were closed in 2002. Government sponsored trade missions were common in the early 2000s and included visits to China, Japan, Korea, Malaysia and the US. There was a particularly aggressive effort at this time to try and boost South Australian exports to China through a 'Market Awareness Mission' to Hong Kong, Shanghai and Singapore and the establishment of a 'China Cluster' involving the Premier and Lord Mayor of Adelaide leading various delegations to promote South Australian produce and services. The growing focus on the Asia Pacific region was reflected in the number of overseas visits by DTED officers to the region in 2003–04, particularly to Singapore, the Philippines and China.

South Australia's wider commercial engagement with the world was significant during the 2003–04 period involving 'more than 300 business matching appointments between South Australian and overseas companies in targeted countries' (DTED 2004, 21). Additionally around 530 'overseas delegations participated in 66 inbound industry and business missions from overseas markets' (ibid, 22)to South Australia. These trends would continue in the years to come. The newly elected Rann Labor Government regionalised the export push to Asia through the establishment of 'TradeStart' offices in Regional Development Boards.

Over the course of the decade the focus of trade development broadened. In 2009 the South Australian government expanded its network of trade offices, through service agreements with Austrade, to include Chile and Vietnam (DTED 2008–09, 20–21). There were around 24 State Government-sponsored overseas missions during 2009–10 including a high level mission to China led by Premier Rann and another to the Shanghai World Expo in 2010. In the wake of proposed cuts to the State Budget in 2009–10, the State Government announced that it would rationalise its network of overseas offices and operate services through Austrade.

In late 2011 the State Government commissioned a review of overseas offices by Hartley Consulting (Hartley 2012: 7). The review recommended that the Singapore, Chennai and Shanghai office be 'phased out as soon as possible ... in their current form' and that the 'Jinan office remains open pending the outcome of strategic analysis'. Subsequently the focus of the State Government has been on developing strategic relationships with China and India, firstly through the development of 'directions papers' outlining opportunities for mutually beneficial engagement and then the release of strategies for engagement.

TRADE AND ENGAGEMENT – THE RISE OF CHINA AND INDIA

The changing composition, value and volume of South Australia's imports and exports with the Asia Pacific region tell a story of deep engagement and interdependency over the last decade.

Around one third of South Australia's gross state product is generated by international trade, increasingly with the Asia Pacific region. South Australia's engagement with the world has undergone dramatic transformation since colonisation when British investment dominated the South Australian economy (Wanna 1981). Over time American and Japanese investment would play an increasingly influential role in South Australia, particularly through the establishment in Adelaide of General Motors Holdens in 1931 and Chrysler Australia in 1964. These companies remained major players in the automotive sector until the late 1970s when Chrysler sold out to the Japanese auto giant Mitsubishi. Financial difficulties facing the parent company in Japan and sluggish domestic sales in Australia led Mitsubishi to close its Southern

Figure 1: South Australia's trade in goods, 2000–2009

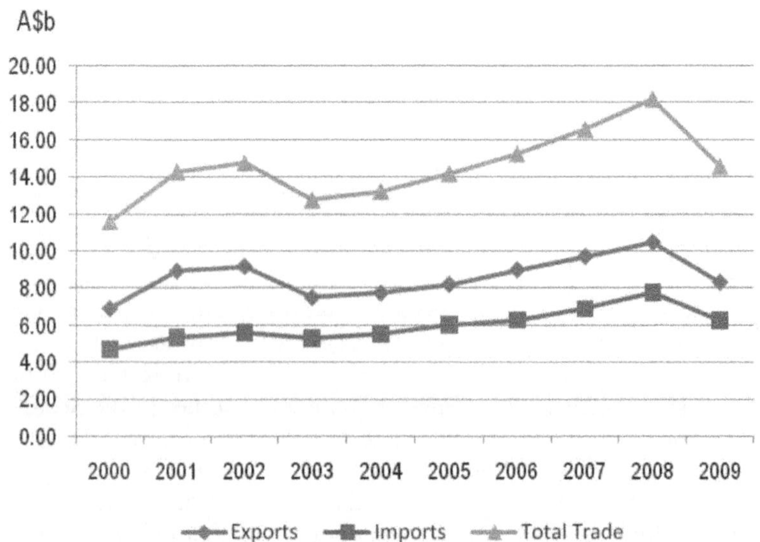

Source: ABS, Catalogue 5368.0 International Trade in Goods and Services

Adelaide based engine and assembly plants in the late 1990s. General Motors Holden is the sole auto manufacturer based in South Australia. By the late 1990s the United States and Japan had become the two largest export markets for South Australia mirroring wider trends in the national economy. Asia became the destination for nearly 50% of South Australian exports (Kosturjak 2001: 247). The fastest growing markets for South Australian exports over the 1990s were China, the United Kingdom, Hong Kong, the USA and the ASEAN group of countries (ibid, 250).

The value of South Australia's trade in goods with the world grew steadily throughout the 2000s. Figure 1 shows that South Australia's total trade in goods rose steadily before declining by around 20 per cent in 2009 in response to the global financial crisis (GFC). Total merchandise trade increased from AUD$ 11.59 billion in 2000 to AUD$ 14.58 billion in 2008.

South Australian merchandise exports grew by around 2 per cent per annum before experiencing a sharp decline of around 20.6 per cent in 2009 in response to the GFC. In 2009 the State's merchandise exports were dominated by alcoholic beverages (17 per cent), Copper (11 per cent), Wheat (7 per cent) and iron ore and concentrates (6 per cent). The State's top 10 merchandise exports over the 2006–09 period are detailed in Table 1.

Table 1: South Australia's 10 principal exports (AUD$ million)

	2006	2007	2008	2009	2009 Share
Alcoholic beverages	1,543.37	2,013.46	1,648.82	1,434.10	17.2%
Copper	1,298.95	1,190.60	1,142.93	905.95	10.9%
Wheat	514.04	346.76	692.35	564.42	6.8%
Iron ore & concentrates	66.87	222.98	406.56	491.30	5.9%
Lead	218.14	576.40	511.09	416.01	5.0%
Meat (excl beef), f.c.f.	309.80	339.07	359.32	415.57	5.0%
Copper ores & concentrates	0.00	2.82	3.20	326.28	3.9%
Silver & platinum	145.66	156.31	186.27	176.79	2.1%
Passenger motor vehicles	1,043.02	912.87	1,655.25	175.93	2.1%
Refined petroleum	221.28	244.96	212.06	155.21	1.9%

Source: DFAT

Figure 2 shows that China overtook the USA as the largest destination for SA's exports of merchandise in 2009, with exports valued at AUD$ 1.18 billion (14.2 per cent of total merchandise exports). The USA was the second largest destination for exports valued at AUD$ 1.07 in 2009 and accounted for 12.8 per cent of total merchandise exports while Japan was third, exporting AUD$ 716 million.

Figure 2: Major export markets

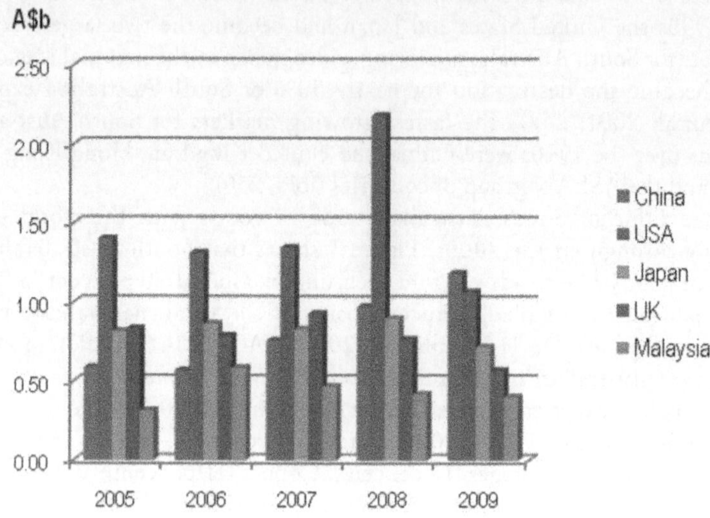

Source: ABS, Catalogue 5368.0 International Trade in Goods and Services

South Australian imports grew by around 3.3 per cent over the decade to 2008 when they rose sharply by around 19 per cent before declining sharply by 19.2 per cent in 2009. South Australia's main merchandise imports in 2009 were refined petroleum (15 per cent), Passenger motor vehicles (7.2 per cent) and rotating electric plant and parts 4.1 per cent. The State's top 10 commodity imports are detailed in Table 2.

Table 2: South Australia's 10 principal imports (AUD$ million)

	2006	2007	2008	2009	2009 Share
Refined petroleum	1,157.3	991.9	1,475.6	933.2	14.9%
Passenger motor vehicles	479.5	504.8	562.1	447.9	7.2%
Rotating electric plant & parts	61.3	146.9	142.4	256.6	4.1%
Goods vehicles	133.9	195.5	230.9	204.9	3.3%
Vehicle parts & accessories	287.0	368.2	343.0	199.1	3.2%
Chemicals & related products, nes	137.9	152.9	197.9	185.5	3.0%
Alcoholic beverages	120.2	175.2	191.0	170.4	2.7%
Furniture, mattresses & cushions	113.3	128.7	144.2	144.5	2.3%
Non-metallic mineral manuf, nes	101.8	102.3	122.3	119.6	1.9%
Heating & cooling equipment & parts	75.3	82.8	94.8	119.0	1.9%

Source: DFAT

Figure 3: Major import sources

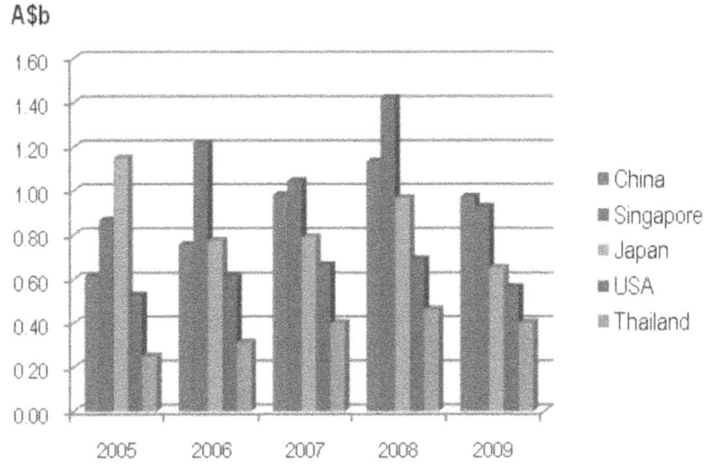

Source: ABS, Catalogue 5368.0 International Trade in Goods and Services

Figure 3 indicates that China has emerged as SA's largest source of imports, accounting for 15.5 per cent (AUD$ 972 million) of total imports in 2009. It is followed by Singapore which accounted for 14.8 per cent (AUD$ 928 million) and Japan (AUD$ 651 million).

Reflecting a decline in global demand for merchandise exports in the wake of the GFC, South Australia recorded a surplus of AUD$ 2.1 billion on its trade in goods in 2009, compared with an AUD$ 2.7 billion surplus in 2008.

South Australia's trade in services has risen sharply from around AUD $2.5 billion in 2000 to AUD$ 4 billion in 2008. This represents annual growth of around 4.6 per cent per annum. Over the last decade South Australia has become a major exporter of educational services as Chapter 4illustrates. South Australia's services exports accounted for 52.5 per cent of total services trade (AUD$ 2.04 billion) in 2009 while imports were 47.5 per cent. Table 3 indicates that the State's major services exports are education services and tourism services.

Table 3: South Australia's major services exports (AUD$ million), 2005–2009

	2005	2006	2007	2008	2009	2009 Share
Education services	509	592	673	813	990	48.55%
Travel services	480	438	484	462	436	21.38%
Business services	82	105	97	115	125	6.13%

Source: ABS, Catalogue 5368.0 International Trade in Goods and Services

Table 4 shows that the State's main services imports were tourism services which amounted to AUD$ 871 million (47.2 per cent) and freight transportation services with AUD$ 318 million (17.2 per cent).

Table 4: South Australia's major services imports (AUD$ million), 2005–2009

	2005	2006	2007	2008	2009	% Share 2009
Tourism services	548	547	635	813	871	47.21%
Freight transportation services	371	387	394	459	318	17.24%
Business services	107	111	118	133	129	6.99%

Source: ABS, Catalogue 5368.0 International Trade in Goods and Services

AUD$ 990 million in exports income flowing into the South Australian economy in 2009, representing growth of around 22 per cent on 2008 when South Australia attracted around 34,000 international students.

Figure 4 shows that China was the major origin for international student enrolments in 2009 (11,970 students) followed by India (6,988 enrolments).

Figure 4: International student enrolment in SA, by origin, 2009

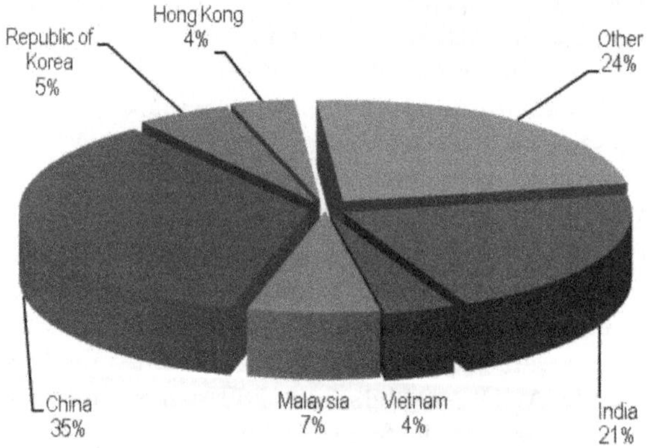

Source: Department of Education, Employment and Workplace Relations, International Student Enrolment Data 2009

SOUTH AUSTRALIA AND THE ASIA-PACIFIC CENTURY

South Australia's engagement with the Asia-Pacific region has increased in intensity and complexity over the last decade, particularly as result of the rapid industrialisation of China and India. While policymakers in South Australia have been aware of the economic transformation that has been taking place in these nations most have been astonished by the high rates of growth that have prevailed. It is widely understood that this has played an important role in dampening the impact of the global financial crisis on Australia. While Europe and the United States struggle to recover from the crisis, China and India remain relatively robust, generating strong demand for South Australian commodities and services. While this demand is likely to fluctuate over the decades to come it in unlikely to sharply decline in the way that demand has in Europe and the US. The global focal point for engagement over the decade to come appears to be clear given these circumstances.

There are many dimensions to South Australia's engagement with the Asia Pacific region that deserve our attention including informal and formal economic, social, cultural and political ties. To date there have been few attempts to systematically document these. It is vital that we develop a more sophisticated understanding of the character and evolution of this engagement, both to understand its implications but also to inform SNG strategies for the development of respectful and productive relationships with nations of the Asia Pacific region.

The chapters that follow provide further insights into South Australia's engagement with the Asia-Pacific region, beginning with a review of recent trends in population flows between the state and the region, the political dimensions of engagement and the emergence of international education as one of the state's fastest growing exports. The remaining chapters focus on bi-lateral relationships with China, India, Japan, South East Asia and the United States of America.

NOTES

1 The Melbourne University Asia Link entirely focuses on Asia-related issues; The Lowy Institute in Sydney houses many experts on Asia and of course there are a large number of Asian studies centres across Australian universities focusing on the studies of politics, society, history and culture along with language programs.

2 A summary of what these terms stand for is provided in Criekemans (2010).

3 This term is employed specifically for the Belgium case because its federated states have the (quasi-) sovereignty to enter into foreign relations and are competent to play an important role in country's treaty-making 'by means of institutionalised intergovernmental mechanisms' (Paquin 2010, 173).

REFERENCES

Arase, D. 2002, 'Japan Sea Regionalism: The Role of Sub-national Authorities', in Markus Perkmann and Ngai-Ling Sum (eds), *Globalization, Regionalization and Cross-Border Regions*, New York: Palgrave Macmillan, pp. 176–88.

ASAA. 2002, *Maximizing Australia's Asia Knowledge*, Asian Studies Association of Australia, place of publication n/a.

Black D. and Sone, Sachiko (eds) 2009, *An Enduring Friendship: Western Australia and Japan – Past, Present and Future*, Perth: University of Western Australia Press.

Bomberg, E. and Peterson, J. 1998, 'European Union Decision Making: The Role of Sub-national Authorities', *Political Studies* 2, 219–35.

Brande, L. Van den. 2010, 'Sub-state Diplomacy Today', *The Hague Journal of Diplomacy* 5, 199–210.

Brown, D. 1993, *Making a Change for the Better*, Liberal Party Policy Speech, 28 November, Liberal Party of South Australia.

Callick, R. 2010, 'Foster Relations with China, Premier Says', *The Australian*, 30 August.

Cheung, P.T.Y. and Tang, J.T.H. 2001, 'The External Relations of China's Provinces', in David M. Lampton (ed.), *The Making of Chinese Foreign and Security Policy in the Era of Reform, 1978–2000*, Stanford: Stanford University Press, pp. 91–122.

Cornago, N. 2010, 'On the Normalization of Sub-State Diplomacy', *The Hague Journal of Diplomacy* 5, 11–36.

Criekemans, D. 2010, 'Introduction', *The Hague Journal of Diplomacy* 5, 1–9.

Department of Industry and Trade 1998, *Annual Report*, Government of South Australia, Adelaide.

Department of Trade and Economic Development, 2004, *Annual Report*, Government of South Australia, Adelaide.

Department of Trade and Economic Development 2008–09, *Annual Report*, Government of South Australia, Adelaide.

Dobell, Graeme 2000, *Australia Finds Home: The Choices and Chances of an Asia Pacific Journey*, Sydney: ABC Books.

Dunn, H. 1996, 'Queensland–Shanghai Relations', in C. Mackerras (ed.), *Australia and China: Partners in Asia*, South Melbourne: Macmillan Education Australia.

Dunstan, D. 1981, *Felicia, the political memoirs of Don Dunstan*, Adelaide, Griffin Press.

Elliott, K. 1995, 'Subnational Activism in Australia: The NSW–Japan experience', MA thesis, University of Sydney.

Fry, E.H. 1998, *The Expanding Role of State and Local Governments in US Foreign Affairs*, New York: Council of Foreign Relations Press.

Goodman, D.S.G. 1996, 'China's Provinces and Australia's States: Sister States and International Mates', in C. Mackerras (ed.), *Australia and China: Partners in Asia*, South Melbourne: Macmillan Education Australia.

Guay, T. 2000, 'Local Government and Global Politics: The Implications of Massachusetts' "Burma Law"', *Political Science Quarterly* 115: 3, 353–76.

Hartley Consulting (2012) *A Review of South Australia's Overseas Representation*, April.

Hobbs, H.H. 1994, *City Hall Goes Abroad: The Foreign Policy of Local Politics*, Thousand Oaks: Sage Publications.

Hocking, B. 2006, 'Multistakeholder Diplomacy: Foundations, Forms, Functions and Frustrations', in J. Kurbalija and V. Katrandjiev, *Multistakeholder Diplomacy: Challenges and Opportunities*, DiploFoundation, Malta and Geneva. (Copy obtained from the author.)

Jain, P. 1991, 'Japan's Urban Governments: Their International Activities and Australia–Japan Relations', *Policy Organisation and Society* 4, 33–44.

Jain, P. 2005, *Japan's Subnational Governments in International Affairs*, New York and London: Routledge.

Keating, P. 2000, *Engagement: Australia Faces the Asia-Pacific*, Sydney: Macmillan.

Kostjurak, A. 2001, 'Trade', *Essays on Regional Economic Development*, Edited by Greg Coombs, Adelaide, Wakefield Press.

Little, A.D. 1992, *New Directions for South Australia's Economy*, South Australian Government.

Matthews, J.T. 1997, 'Power Shift', *Foreign Affairs* 76:1, 61–2.

McMillan, S.L. 2008, 'Subnational Foreign Policy Actors: How and Why Governors Participate in US Foreign Policy', *Foreign Policy Analysis* 4:3, 227–53.

McNamara, D. 1994, 'State Government Activity in Asia', in Trood, R. and McNamara, D. (eds) 1994, *The Asia–Australia Survey 1994*, South Melbourne: Macmillan Education Australia, pp. 38–54.

McNamara, D. 1996, 'State Government Activity in Asia', in Trood, R. and McNamara, D. (eds) 1996, *The Asia–Australia Survey 1996–1997*, South Melbourne: Macmillan Education Australia, pp. 38–59.

Minami M. 1997, 'The Role and Policy of the South Australian Government in the Development of Economic Ties with Asian Nations', M.A. thesis, University of Adelaide.

Newhouse, J. 1997, 'Europe's Rising Regionalism', *Foreign Affairs*, January–February 76:1, 67–84.

O'Donnell, F.M. 1994, 'A Loose Partnership: Business and the Regional State in the Development of Queensland's Relations with Japan', PhD thesis, University of Queensland.

Paquin, S. 2010, 'Federalism and Compliance with International Agreements: Belgium and Canda Compared', *The Hague Journal of Diplomacy* 5, 173–97.

Ravenhill, J. 1999, 'Federal–State Relations in Australian External Affairs: A New Co-operative Era?', in Francisco Aldecoa and Michael Keating (eds.), *Paradiplomacy in Action: The Foreign Relations of Subnational Governments*, Frank Cass, London.

Schep, G.J. et al. 1995, *Local Challenges to Global Change: A Global Perspective on Municipal International Cooperation* The Hague: Sdu Publishers.

Shuman, M. 1994, *Towards a Global Village: International Community Development Initiatives*, London: Pluto Press.

South Australian Development Council 1996, *Annual Report*, Government of South Australia.

Spoehr, J. 1999, 'Beyond the Contract State', *Beyond the Contract State – ideas for social and economic renewal in South Australia*, Adelaide, Wakefield Press, 1–18.

Spoehr, J. 2003, 'Market Power', in Spoehr, J. Ed, *Power Politics – the electricity crisis and you*, Adelaide, Wakefield Press, 27–50.

Van den Brande, L. 2010, 'Sub-state Diplomacy Today', *The Hague Journal of Diplomacy* 5, 199–210.

Wanna, J. 1981, *Defence not Defiance: the development of organised labour in South Australia*. Adelaide: Texts in Humanities.

Wesley, M. 2011, *There Goes the Neighbourhood: Australia and the Rise of Asia, Sydney:* University of New South Wales Press.

Wills, D. and Littley, B. 2010, 'Adelaide's regional status robbing rural areas of skilled migrants', *Advertiser*, 4 July

CHAPTER 2

Population Flows Between South Australia and Asia

GRAEME HUGO

INTRODUCTION

In the postwar shift of Australian economic, political and social attention to Asia, one of the major elements has been an increased level of population movement in both directions. In this respect the 1970s was a significant turning point with the abolition of the last vestiges of the White Australia immigration policy and the subsequent influx of Indochinese refugees who were the harbingers of an increased migration from across Asia which has continued to the present day. The permanent settlement of more than 2 million Asians in Australia since the 1970s, however, is only one dimension of a complex pattern of population mobility which has developed between Australia and the Asian region and which has significant economic, social and political implications.

This pattern of increased mobility to and from Asia has been less evident in South Australia than in other mainland Australian states. This is partly a function of the early era of Asian migration to Australia coinciding with a reduction in the state's relative national economic significance. It may also be influenced by its relative lack of accessibility to the region from Asia. The situation has changed in the last decade with the introduction of a State population policy and the subsequent increase in both permanent and temporary migration. This chapter seeks to examine the contemporary patterns of population movement between South Australia and Asia and discuss some of its implications.

CONTEXT

Not only has global population movement between countries increased exponentially in scale and complexity in the last 15 years, but international migration research and thinking has also undergone a major transformation. Two changes are of particular significance. Firstly, there has been a shift away from an overwhelming concentration of migration as permanent relocation and an increasing focus on migration as a process of transnationalism. This has seen a shift away from the dominance of a narrative of departure, arrival and adjustment to a focus on migration involving the creation of a set of linkages and relationships joining origin and destination and involving multiple players. Accordingly, in this paper the approach is to go beyond seeing migration from Asia to Australia as immigrant settlement to one which considers multiple kinds of mobility between South Australia and Asia. Figure 1 presents a model of the Asia-South Australian migration system. This indicates that permanent relocation of Asians to South Australia are only one element in a complex set of flows. Conceptualising migration in this way emphasises the potential of migration to embed South Australian society and economy in Asia.

Figure 1: A model of the Asia-South Australian migration system

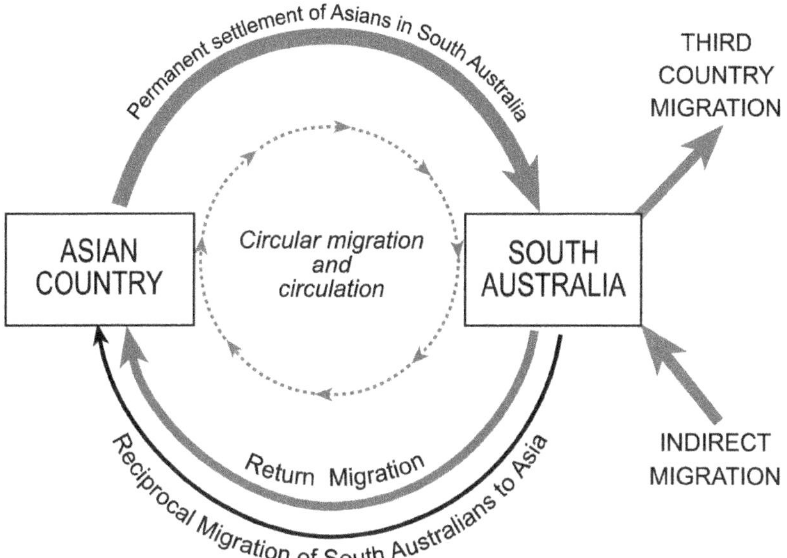

A second and related shift in migration thinking relates to the relationship between migration and development. Until recently the dominant perspective has been that of 'brain drain' whereby nations of origin are negatively effected by emigration because of the selectivity of the movement and the loss of the 'brightest and the best' which compromises development efforts at home. Increasingly, however, there has been a focus on the potential for migration to deliver development dividends at home through remittances, engagement with the diaspora and return migration. Emigration can have both negative and positive implications for origins and the key is to develop policy interventions which minimise the former and maximise the latter. It is important to see Asian migration not only in terms of its impact on South Australia's society and economy but also its effects on Asian countries of origin.

SOUTH AUSTRALIA'S POPULATION

At the end of 2010 South Australia's population stood at 1.65 million – 7.3 per cent of the national total. The state's share of the nation's population has been gradually declining since 1966 when it had 9.4 per cent. Figure 2 shows South Australia's rate of population growth exceeded the national average in the first half of the postwar era but it has been the slowest growing mainland state for most of the last 40 years. The growth rate fell to less than 0.3 per cent per annum in the wake of the State Bank collapse but increased sharply following the introduction of the state's population policy in 2004. Population growth rates breached the one per cent per annum level for the first time in more than two decades in 2006–07 and peaked at 1.2 per cent in 2008–09 before falling back to 1.0 per cent in calendar 2010.

Figure 2: Australia and South Australia: rate of population growth per annum, 1947–2010

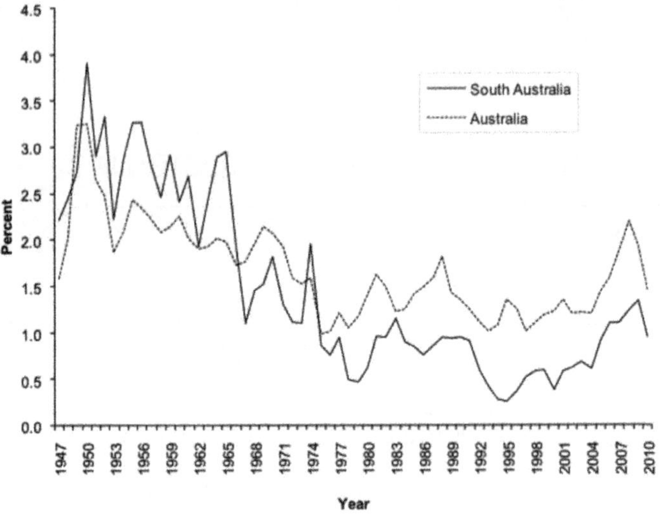

Note: Data are for Calendar Years

Source:ABS 1986 and Australian Demographic Statistics, various issues

In examining Asian population movement to South Australia it is important to consider the state's population policy (Government of South Australia 2004). South Australia was the first jurisdiction in Australia to develop and operationalise a population policy which was embedded within the state's Strategic Plan (Government of South Australia 2007). This policy was developed in response to the release of ABS projections which indicated that the state's population would begin to decline after 2021. A centrepiece of the new population policy was to increase net international population gains (Table 1). In order to achieve this, the SA Government set up Immigration SA, an agency within the Department of Trade and Economic Development. It became active in lobbying the Federal Government to position the state in the State Specific and Regional Migration Scheme to overcome the disadvantages of its peripheral location and lack of migrant communities to attract new immigrants.

Table 1: South Australian Strategic Plan population targets, 2007

Target 1.22: Total Population
'Increase South Australia's population to 2 million by 2050, rather than the projected pop'n decline. Interim target of 1.64 million by 2014'.
Target 1.23: Interstate Migration
'Reduce net loss to interstate to zero by 2010 with a positive inflow from 2010–14'
Target 1.24: Overseas Migration
'Match SA's share of international migrants to Australia with the State's share of the overall national pop'n over the next 10 years. Net overseas gain to be 8,500 by 2014'.
Target 1.25: Fertility
'Maintain at TFR of 1.7'
Target 5.9: Regional Populations
'Maintain and develop viable regional population levels for sustainable communities. Keep share at 18 per cent.'

Source: Government of South Australia 2007

It also stepped up efforts to recruit migrants from selected countries. Until 2011 it was the only state in which the capital city, Adelaide, was eligible for all 'regional' migration programs which gave skilled migrants a discount on the number of points they had to achieve to gain entry to Australia.

Increased net overseas migration gain has played a major role in the revival of population growth in South Australia. Figure 3 demonstrates the steep climb in net overseas migration from a low of 2,765 in 2000–01 to a peak of 17,934 in 2008–09. In line with national trends[1] it fell to 11,745 in 2010.

Figure 3: South Australia: Net overseas migration, 1979–2010

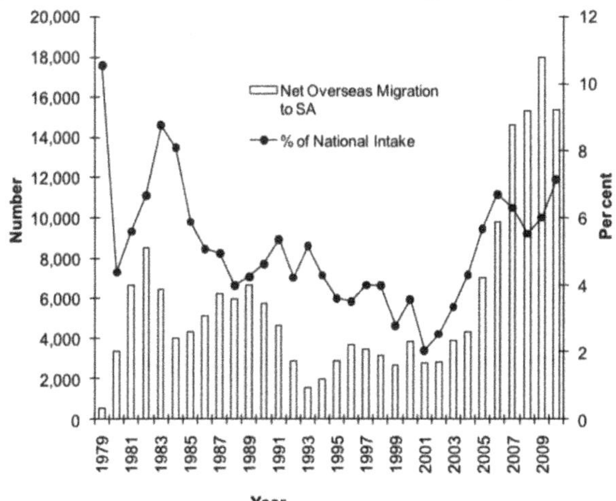

Source: ABS Australian Demographic Statistics, various issues

A key factor in the increase in international migration has been the highly active participation of the South Australian government in the State Specific and Regional Migration initiatives (DIAC 2009). These subcategories are only available for skilled migrants. This set of visa categories introduced progressively over the last decade give particular advantages such as extra points or waiving of particular conditions to potential setters willing to settle outside of the major areas of immigrant settlement. Until 2011, all South Australia, including Adelaide, were eligible for all such schemes and, as Figure 4 indicates, South Australia has been more heavily reliant on this source of settlers than other states. It is noticeable, however, in the diagram that South Australia's dependence upon the SSRM Scheme has reduced over time. This is to be expected as there is a build-up of communities of recent settlers in the state who send back information and encouragement to friends and family in their origin country to migrate to the state. The low levels of immigration to South Australia in the 1980s, 1990s and early 2000s meant that there were few recent migrants in the state so that important social network related migration was very small. This disadvantage is gradually being overcome as migrant communities build up in South Australia.

The origins of permanent settlers to South Australia are shown in Table 2 and it is noticeable that the United Kingdom has been the major country of origin of South Australian settlers. The United Kingdom has long been the traditional main source of immigrants to South Australia (Hugo 1989) and UK immigrants settled disproportionately in South Australia in the postwar economic boom years. The return of the UK to dominance in the state's migrant intake in the mid 2000s partly reflected the concentration of Immigration SA activity recruiting in the UK but also the strength of linkages between South Australia's substantial UK-born population back to their homeland. However, the growth of the UK origin migrants levelled off after peaking at 3,009 in 2005–06 and indeed it is notable that they have lost their ranking as the largest single country of origin of settler arrivals in South

Table 2: South Australia: Settler arrivals, top 10 countries, 2002–03 to 2009–10

Top 10 Countries in 2009–10	2002–03	2005–06	2008–09	2009–10
India	138	909	1578	1983
United Kingdom	785	3009	2291	1897
China	113	879	905	1292
Philippines	134	285	362	519
Sri Lanka	23	85	145	448
South Africa	209	263	329	389
New Zealand	232	373	479	354
Bangladesh	1	16	122	354
Malaysia	91	154	139	331
Korea	34	163	194	324
Other	1897	2963	3151	3486
Total	3657	9099	9695	11377

Source: DIAC unpublished data

Figure 4: Australia: Settler arrivals by state according to whether they are State Specific and Regional Migration Scheme Migrants or other migrants, 2005–06 and 2008–09

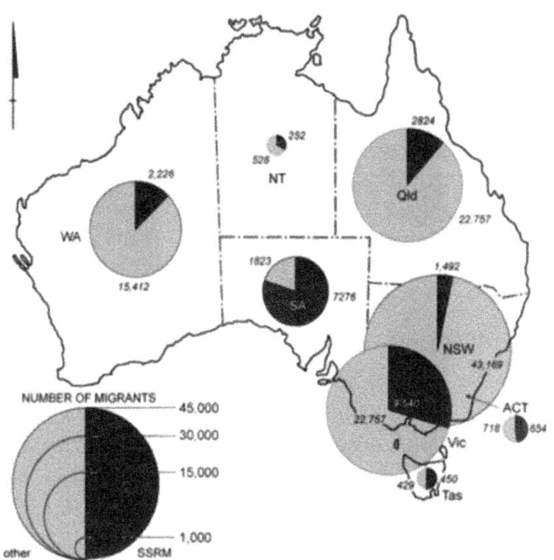

2005–06

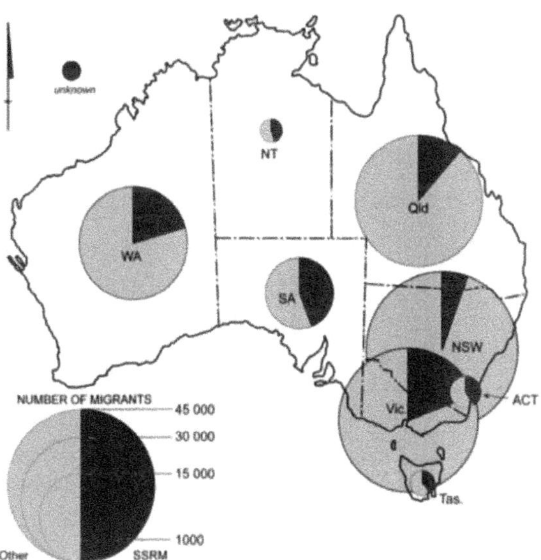

2008–09

Source: DIMA unpublished data; DIAC Population Flows: Immigration Aspects, various issues; DIAC Immigration Update, various issues; DIAC 2009

Australia. It was significant that 2009–10 marked the first year that an Asian country (India) was the largest single source country of immigrant settlers in South Australia. In 2009–10 seven of the 10 largest countries of origin of settlers were Asian. It is also interesting to note that while New Zealand in 2006–07 was the largest single origin of immigrants to Australia as a whole; in South Australia in 2008–09 it was only the tenth largest source, making up 3.1 per cent of arrivals compared with 17.1 per cent of the national intake. However, the most striking trend in Table 2 is the rapid increase in the numbers of migrants coming from India and China, doubling between 2004–05 and 2006–07 and together accounting for 25.6 per cent of the total intake in 2008–09 and 28.8 per cent in 2009–10 compared with 6.8 per cent in 2002–03. This reflects a significant shift in the South Australian immigrant intake and it is examined in some detail in the next section.

PERMANENT MIGRATION BETWEEN ASIA AND SOUTH AUSTRALIA

The modern era of Asian migration to Australia began with the influx of Indochinese refugees in the 1970s. Figure 5 shows that the number of settler arrivals from Asia to all of Australia fluctuated between 25,000 and 40,000 in the decade up to 2004 but since then has accelerated and in 2010–11 North and South Asia accounted for 44.2 per cent of the total migration program (DIAC 2011a, 6) and China (29,547) and India (21,768) were the largest and third largest single countries of origin settlers respectively. It is apparent from Figure 5 that until the initiation of the South Australia population policy in 2004 its share of Asian migration to Australia was very small. In the 1990s the Asia-born population of Australia increased from 687,850 in 1991 to 882,918 in 2001 (28.4 per cent). However, in South Australia the increase was only 24.1 per cent from 32,720 to 40,621. This, however, has changed since 2004 as Figure 5 shows. In fact, in 2009–10 the state took around one tenth of the national settler arrivals from Asia. Hence the upswing in Asian migration to Australia in the 1980s and 1990s was delayed in South Australia for almost two decades.

The recent upturn in the number of settler arrivals from Asia in South Australia has involved each of the major sub-regions of Asia. However, Figure 6 shows that China and India have been especially significant. On the other hand, while Southeast Asia has for a long period provided most Asian settlers to South Australia there has been only a slight increase in recent years.

The migration flows have significantly increased the Asian representation in the South Australian population and this undoubtedly will be reflected in the results of the 2011 Australian Census of Population and Housing which unfortunately was not available at the time of writing. Table 3 shows that between 1971 and 2006 the Asia-born population of South Australia increased tenfold and their share of the state's population increased from 0.5 to 3.9 per cent. On the other hand there has been a decline in the numbers born in UK-Ireland and other parts of Europe. The changing composition

Figure 5: Australia and South Australia: Settler arrivals from Asia, 1994–95 to 2009–10

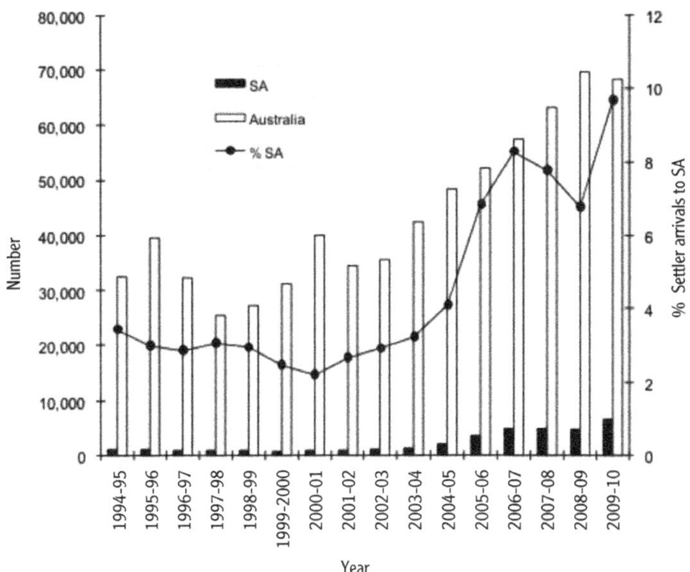

Source: DIAC Settler Arrivals, various issues

Figure 6: Settler arrivals to South Australia, Asia-born, 1993–2010

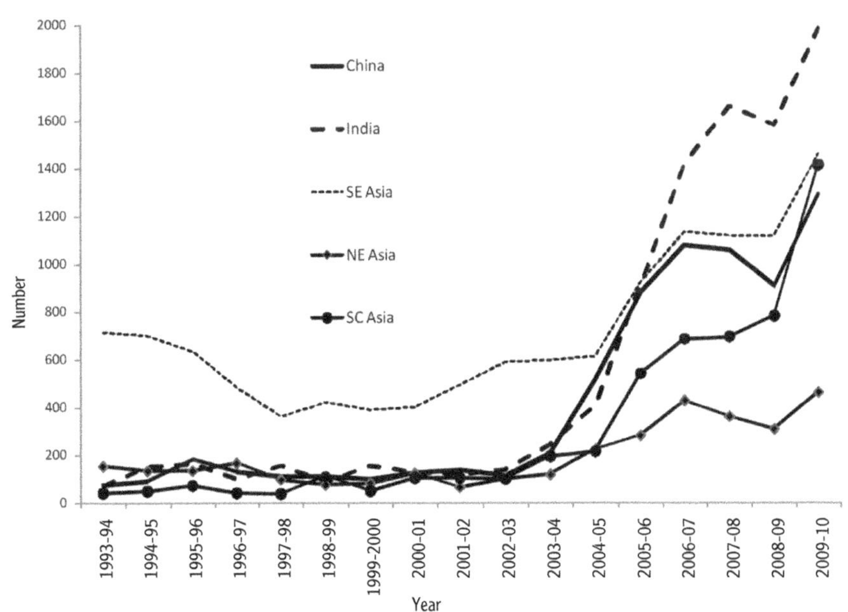

Source: DIAC unpublished data

of the state's population is also reflected in the substantial increase in Africa-born groups although the numbers remain quite small.

Table 3: South Australia: Birthplace of population, 1971, 2001 and 2006

Region of Birth	Number 1971	Number 2001	Change 1971–2001	Number 2006	Change 2001–06
Australia	884,923	1,099,585	24.3	1,110,297	1.0
Overseas	274,352	296,465	7.8	304,666	2.8
UK-Ireland	146,391	127,274	-13.1	122,076	-4.1
Other Europe	111,801	95,663	-14.4	87,335	-8.7
Oceania	3,607	12,980	259.9	13,537	4.3
Africa	1,741	6,740	287.1	11,755	74.4
Middle East	2,581	5,259	103.8	5,673	7.9
North America	2,602	4,579	76.0	5,299	15.7
South America	294	2,711	822.1	3,032	11.8
Asia	5,335	40,284	655.1	55,095	36.8
Percent Asia-Born	0.46	2.9		3.9	
Total	1,159,275	1,396,050	20.3	1,414,963	1.4
Percent Overseas-Born	23.7	21.2		21.5	

Source: ABS Population Censuses

The main countries of origin of Asian settlers to South Australia are shown in Figure 7. It is apparent that there is a dispersed spread across the Asian region reflecting the fact that the state has significant communities from most of the major countries in Asia. This can provide an important basis for developing wider linkages with those countries. To some extent it 'hardwires' the state into the economies of the major Asian countries. It also reflects the fact there is not a single birthplace or ethnic group that dominates in South Australia's Asian population.

While there will have been significant changes in South Australia's Asian population since the 2006 population census, especially in the growth of the China- and India-born populations, Table 4 shows the numbers in the main Asian birthplace groups at the last two censuses. In 2006, Southeast Asians made up more than half of the state's Asian population, reflecting a long history of migration to the state beginning with Colombo Plan students in the 1960s. The largest single group were the Vietnamese with 10,512 persons. However, it will be noted that they increased by only 0.7 per cent between 2001 and 2006, reflecting the fact that the peak of their immigration was in the 1980s. The numbers of Vietnamese will have been exceeded by both the China- and India-born populations by 2011. The Cambodia-born population also has stabilised and has its origins in refugee movement in the 1980s (Stevens 1984). The Malaysian and Singaporean populations have increased significantly and reflect both skilled migration and the influx of students from these countries, many who seek permanent residence. The movement from Thailand and Philippines is different and involves a significant marriage migration element.

Figure 7: Country of birthplace of South Australian Asia-born, 2006

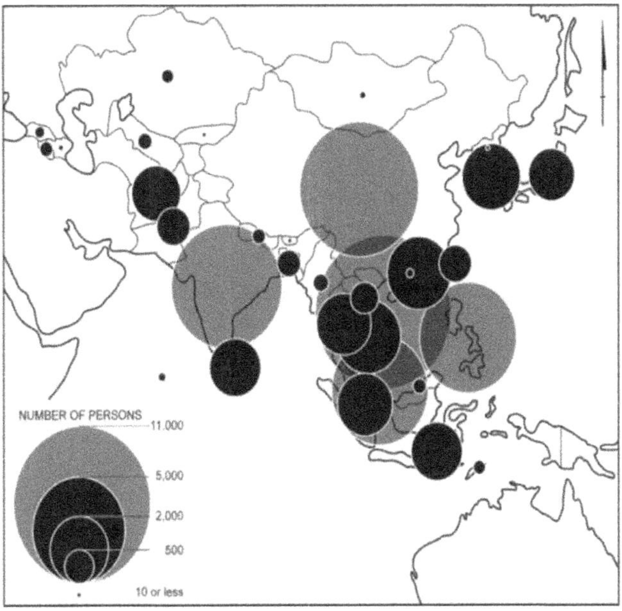

Source: ABS 2006 Census

Table 4: South Australia: Asia-born population, 2001 and 2006

Region/Country	2001	2006	% Change
Cambodia	2,317	2,442	5.4
Thailand	1,327	1,706	28.6
Vietnam	10,441	10,512	0.7
Malaysia	4,162	5,323	27.9
Philippines	4,512	5,431	20.4
Singapore	1,382	1,740	25.9
Other South-East Asia	2,024	2,313	14.3
Total South-East Asia	26,165	29,467	12.6
China (excl. SARs and Taiwan Province)	3,587	8,062	124.8
Hong Kong (SAR of China)	1,802	2,367	31.4
Korea, Republic of (South)	910	1,981	117.7
Other North-East Asia	1,415	1,906	34.7
Total North-East Asia	7,714	14,316	85.6
India	3,688	6,851	85.8
Other Southern Asia	1,685	2,602	54.4
Total Southern Asia	5,373	9,453	75.9
Total Central Asia	1,369	1,859	35.8
Total Asia	40,621	55,095	35.6

Source: ABS 2001 and 2006 Censuses

The increase in China-born was the largest of any Asia-born group in the 2001–06 period, more than doubling. However, there were also significant increases in the numbers coming from Hong Kong and Korea. The third most rapid increase was in the India-born and this rapid growth has certainly continued in the subsequent five years.

The 2001 and 2006 population censuses also asked questions on ancestry and these results reflect another dimension of Asian immigration to Australia. Table 5 shows that while in 2006 the Vietnamese were the largest Asian birthplace group in the state, the Chinese made up the largest single Asian ancestry group. This reflects the fact that much of the migration from Southeast Asia has been of people of Chinese ethnicity. In 2006 the Chinese made up 44.1 per cent of all Asian ancestry people in South Australia.

Table 5: South Australia: Change in selected ancestry groups, 2001–06
Source: ABS 2001 and 2006 Censuses

Ancestry	2006	2001	Percent Change 2001–06
Chinese	25363	18494	37.1
Vietnamese	12493	11544	8.2
Indian	9238	5058	82.6
Filipino	7446	5778	28.9
Indonesian	1274	1001	27.3

Permanent migration between South Australia is, however, a two-way process and there is also permanent movement from South Australia to Asian countries. Figure 8 shows that permanent arrivals are much larger than the flow in the other direction although this too has increased in recent years. This outflow is split fairly equally between Australia-born and overseas-born groups. The Australia-born not only comprises long serving Australian citizens but also the Australia-born children of Asians returning to their homeland. The overseas-born are made up mainly of Asians returning to their homeland. It has been shown elsewhere (Hugo 2008) that return migration is greatest among East Asians and least among South Asians. The backflow represents a significant opportunity to strengthen South Australia's linkages with the Asian countries that former residents have returned to.

There is an increasing flow of the Australia-born out of the country (Hugo, Rudd and Harris 2001) as Australians increasingly engage in international labour markets.[2] The rapidly growing economies of Asia have opened up substantial opportunities for skilled South Australians and the flows to Singapore, Hong Kong, Malaysia, Indonesia and, increasingly, China have grown. While most of these migrants return (Hugo 2009) they also represent a significant body of social capital of South Australian interest in Asian countries that could be better engaged to facilitate economic activity.

The Australian permanent immigration program comprises a number of components – skill, family, refugee and humanitarian, special eligibility and non-Program migrants (mainly New Zealanders). In South Australia those entering under the skilled category made up 70.5 per cent of all permanent additions to the population through migration. Table 6 shows that India, China and the Philippines are among the five largest origin countries for

Figure 8: South Australia Settler arrivals of Asia-born and permanent departures to Asia, 1993–94 to 2009–10

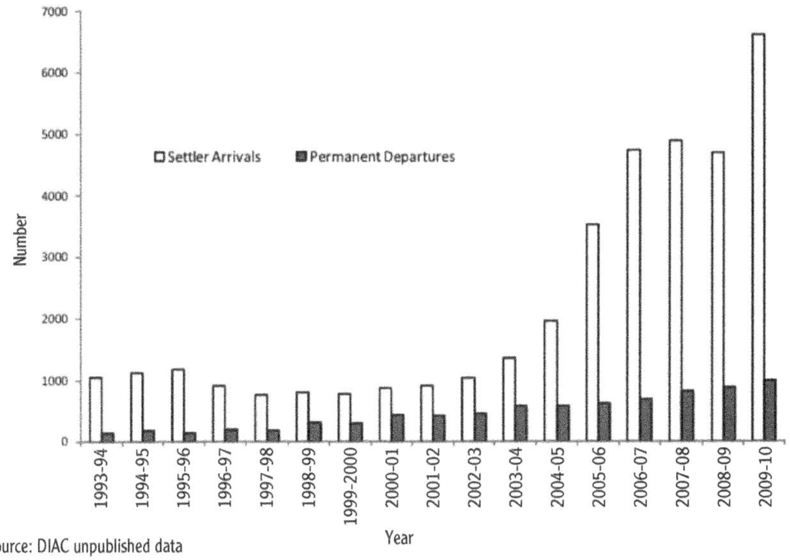

Source: DIAC unpublished data

skilled migrants to the state. The same three countries are joined by Vietnam to be among the five largest sources of family migrants. It is interesting that family migrants accounted for only 18.6 per cent of the state's permanent additions in 2009–10 compared with 28.5 per cent of the national intake. This reflects the lack of a large recent migrant chain migration base in the state due to low levels of migration in the last two decades. It can be anticipated that family migration will increase as skilled migrants settle in the state and seek to bring family to join them. It is notable that Vietnam is a significant source of family migrants since it is one of the few long established Asian communities of significant size in South Australia.

Table 6: South Australia: Visa categories of permanent additions by main countries of origin, 2009–10
Source: DIAC 2011b, 115

Category of Permanent Additions	Number	Main Origins (Percent)
Skill	10,742	India (23.2), UK (19), China (14.6), South Africa (5.4), Philippines (5.4)
Family	2,831	UK (13.2), China (12.2), India (8.8), Philippines (7.7), Vietnam (5.9)
Refugee-Humanitarian	1,098	Bhutan (19.7), Afghanistan (12.9), Burma (11.9)

One distinctive feature of South Australian migration over the last decade is that it has taken more than a proportionate share of refugee-humanitarian settlers due to some particular initiatives of the State Government (Hugo 2011). In 2009–10 the state took 7.5 per cent of the national intake and

Table 6 indicates that three Asian countries were among the main origins of refugee-humanitarian settlers in the state.

TEMPORARY MIGRATION BETWEEN ASIA AND SOUTH AUSTRALIA

One of the most important changes in Australian immigration over the last decade has been the increase in non-permanent migration. This represents a parametric shift from the Australian immigration policy imperative of the half century following World War II which eschewed temporary worker migration in favour of focusing on permanent settlement. Elsewhere it has been shown (Hugo 1999; 2006) that there has been significant growth since 1995 in the numbers coming to Australia and being granted temporary residence in order to work. There has been particular growth in:

- Temporary business migrants (457s)
- Students
- Working holiday makers

Figure 9: South Australia: Long term arrivals and departures to and from Asia, 1993–94 to 2009–10

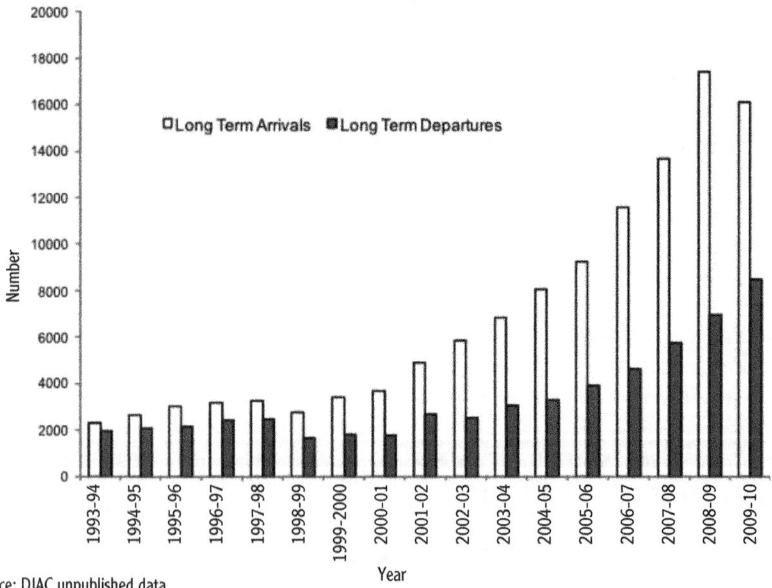

Source: DIAC unpublished data

The temporary residents who intend to stay in Australia for more than one year are picked up as long term visitor arrivals[3] by DIAC and Figure 9 shows that there has been a steady increase in non-permanent long term migration from Asia to South Australia in recent years. Indeed the level of long term migration from Asia increased by eight times between 1993–94 and 2009–10. What is also evident in Figure 9 is that although these arrivals are on temporary resident visas, the number who leave South Australia for Asia is less than half the number arriving. Clearly the state's population growth includes not only permanent settler arrivals but also temporary residents who extend their stay in South Australia, many eventually becoming permanent residents. Hence in any consideration of Asian migration's influence on South Australian population growth it is crucial to include a consideration of long term temporary, as well as permanent, settler arrivals.

The increasing role of 'onshore' immigrants, or migrants who successfully transition from temporary to permanent residence in South Australia's net migration gain and the importance of Asians in this is evident in Table 7. This shows that in 2009–10 a quarter (25.4 per cent) of South Australians gain of permanent 'migrants' was made up of onshore settlers. Moreover, it will be noted that Asian groups make up a larger proportion of 'onshore' migrants who initially enter Australia on temporary residence visas and take out permanent residence than they comprise of offshore immigrants. Hence Table 7 shows that Asian countries comprise 7 of the top 10 origin countries of settlers in 2009–10 and while those 7 supplied 34.5 per cent of all offshore migrants they were the origin of nearly half (48 per cent) of all onshore settlers. China and India were the origin of a third of all onshore migrants.

Table 7: Top 10 Source countries, South Australia, 2009–10

Country of birth	Onshore	Offshore	Total
India	684	1983	2667
United Kingdom	431	1897	2328
People's Republic of China	621	1292	1913
Philippines	277	519	796
South Africa	235	389	624
Sri Lanka	50	448	498
Malaysia	124	331	455
Korea (North & South)	86	324	410
Bangladesh	13	354	367
New Zealand	0	354	354
Other	1343	3486	4829
Total	3864	11377	15241

Source: DIAC 2011b, 115

Since the mid 1990s Australia has introduced a number of visa categories whereby foreigners can come to Australia for an extended period to work but on a temporary resident visa. This contrasted with the pre-1996 situation when such migration was discouraged. The crucial point to be made about this migration is that the categories are focused very strongly on skill – even more so than is the case in permanent migration. Moreover, persons arriving under these programs have higher levels of workforce participation than permanent arrivals. However, South Australia has tended to receive less than its proportionate share of long term visitor arrivals in Australia although it increased from 3.5 per cent at the turn of the century to over five per cent in 2008–09.

One of the most important temporary residence categories is the 457 long term temporary business visitor group the numbers of which increased continuously until 2008–09 when they peaked at 4,670, 4.6 per cent of the national total. Along with Australia as a whole, there was a decline in 2009–10 and the numbers of 457s in South Australia fell to 3,190. For several years the main three countries of origin of 457s have been the UK (790 in 2009–10), India (710) and the Philippines (510). The Philippines has become increasingly significant as a source of 457s in recent years and in 2008 (*Advertiser*, July 2008, 1) it was announced that the state had negotiated a Memorandum of Understanding to receive up to 50,000 workers over the next decade.

There has been some controversy around the 457 visa category in South Australia with a number of newspaper stories (e.g. *Advertiser*, 13 February 2006) which suggest that 457 migrants:

- Are being used to replace Australian workers.
- Are being paid less than Australian workers.
- Have conditions below the minimum acceptable to Australian workers.

Each of these contravenes the regulations of the 457 visa which is only available for occupations in the top four ASCO categories and for which a minimum salary is set. Hence if employers are contravening the conditions of the visa in these ways they should be prosecuted.

One of the major elements in the increased international migration into South Australia in recent years has been an increase in student migration. Along with Australia as a whole there has been a rapid increase in overseas student numbers as education export has become a more significant industry. However, Figure 10 shows that not only have numbers increased more than sixfold since 1999, to 33,731 in 2009, but South Australia has increased

its share of the national intake from 3.2 per cent in 2000 to 5.4 per cent in 2006 although it declined to 5.1 per cent in 2007 and increased to 5.3 per cent in 2009. As with other forms of immigration the state has stepped up activity in attracting students to South Australia with the setting up of a dedicated agency to facilitate this movement (Education Adelaide). Figure 11 shows that Asia is the dominant origin of students and this is adding to the significant presence of Asian origin people in Adelaide. The main origins are China (33 per cent), Malaysia (12 per cent), India (10 per cent) and Hong Kong (8 per cent).

Students are especially important from the perspective of permanent settlement since they have a high rate of application for permanent residence (Tan 2011). South Australia for several years had an advantage in that stu-

Figure 10: South Australia: Overseas student enrolments, 1994–2010

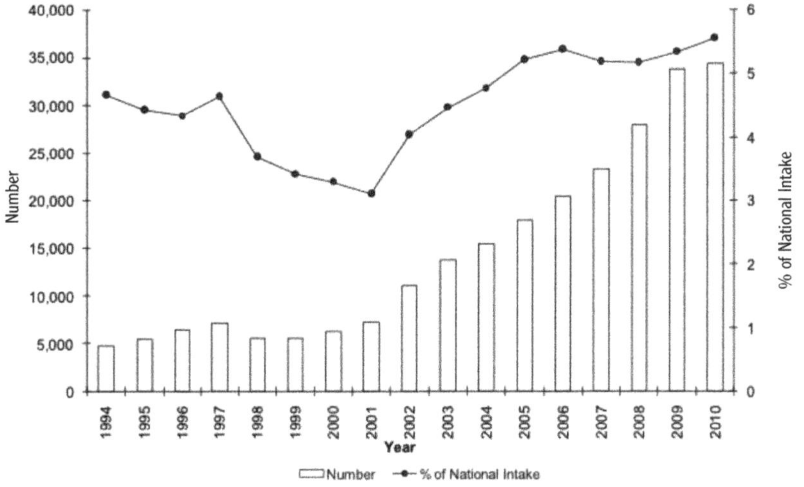

Source: Australian Education International

Figure 11: Onshore overseas students by region of origin, South Australia, YTD June 2006 (Total = 15,295)

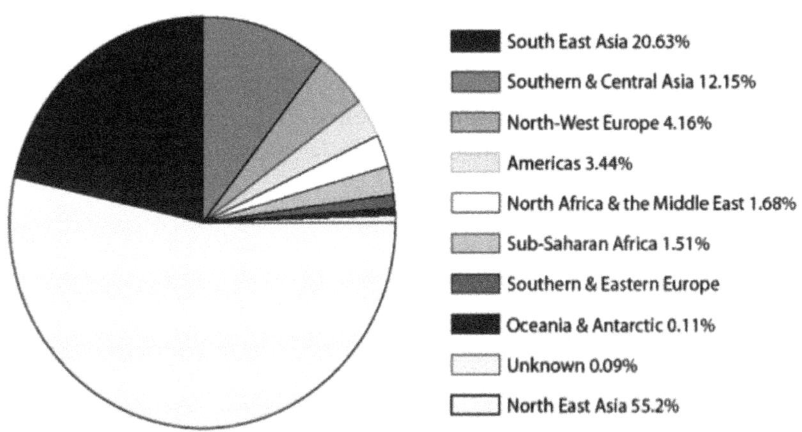

Source: Education Adelaide

dents staying in 'regional areas', which as discussed earlier includes Adelaide, could gain 5 extra points in the assessment for permanent residence. This advantage, however, has been reduced by recent changes to the requirements for permanent residence.

Overseas students are an important part of South Australia's export economy. In 2010 South Australia's export earnings from services were A$2.113 billion, up $95 million on the previous year. Education accounted for nearly half of this total ($1.028 billion) and is continuing to grow while most other export services are declining (Russell 2010, 64). These earnings had grown from only $196 million in 2000.

The Working Holiday Maker (WHM) program also has increased in significance in recent years, increasing nationally from 76,576 in 2000–01 to 187,696 in 2008–09 (DIAC 2009). This program allows young people aged 18–30 to come to Australia to work for a period of up to a year. They have been shown to make significant contributions to some labour markets, especially agriculture, tourism and some services (Harding and Webster 2002; Tan et al. 2009). They also have a significant rate of change to permanent residence. However, it is difficult to assess the extent to which each state or territory gains from WHM since one of the requirements of the visa is that holders are required to spend no more than 3 months in a single job. Since they are holiday makers they travel from state to state. However, one study (Rizvi 2007) showed that less than 2 per cent of WHMs indicate on their arrival cards that they intend for South Australia to be their main state while in Australia. A similar proportion indicated this in their departure cards. Moreover, while a national survey of 956 'back packers' found that 35 per cent had visited South Australia (*Advertiser*, 11 March 2003), a survey in 2000 of 1,774 WHMs found that only 2 per cent had worked in South Australia (Harding and Webster 2002, 25). A more recent survey of 29,178 WHMs found that 3.1 per cent had worked in South Australia (Tan et al. 2009). Moreover, Asians (mainly South Koreans and Japanese) make up only a very small proportion of WHMs.

SHORT TERM MIGRATION

The third category of international migration recognised by DIAC is short term movement involving arrivals and departures when the mover intends to spend less than twelve months at the destination. Figure 12 shows the increase in short term South Australian arrivals from, and departures to, Asia which has occurred over the last decade. South Australia does not receive a proportionate share of overseas visitors to Australia with its 100,500 arrivals in 2009–10 being only 2.8 per cent of the Australian total. The proportion of visitors to South Australia that were of Asian origin was around a quarter in the early 90s but reached a high of 37.6 per cent in 2008–09 and a steady increase in the proportion has been recorded in recent years.

Table 8 shows the main countries of origin of short term visitors to South Australia in 200910 and it will be noticed that only half are Asian countries. This compares with 7 of the top 10 permanent arrival countries and 8 of the top 10 long term arrival origins. Nevertheless, the amount of short term visiting from Asia is increasing.

Figure 12: South Australia: Short term arrivals and departures to and from Asia, 1993–94 to 2009–10

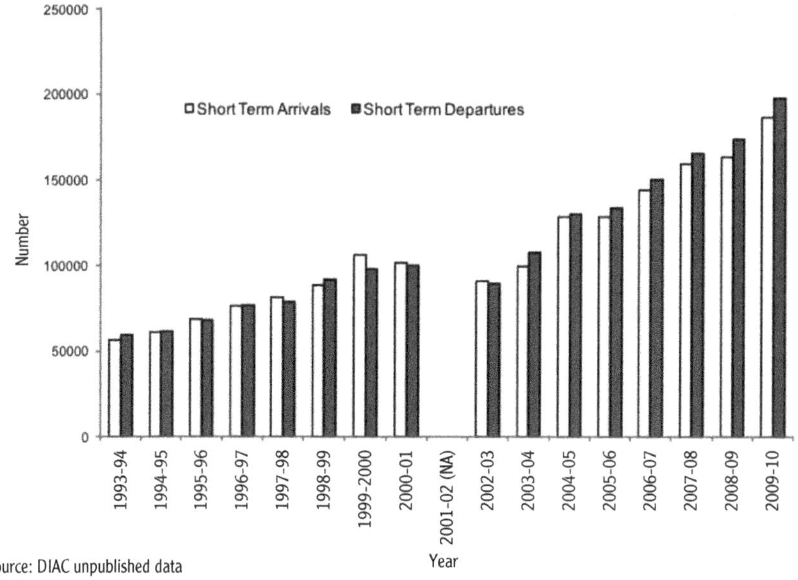

Source: DIAC unpublished data

Table 8: South Australia: Short term visitor arrivals and short term resident departures, main origin/destination countries 2009–10

Origin/Destination	Short Term Visitor Arrival	Origin/Destination	Short Term Resident Departure
United Kingdom	26229	New Zealand	38558
New Zealand	25165	United Kingdom	29712
China	13644	USA	28040
USA	12772	Indonesia	27063
Singapore	9623	Thailand	20437
Malaysia	8275	China	12752
Hong Kong	6271	Malaysia	12374
Japan	6047	Singapore	10945
Germany	5608	Fiji	10618
India	5320	Hong Kong	9155

Source: DIAC unpublished data

The economic impact of short term visiting is often overlooked with the focus being squarely upon the economic effects of permanent and long term migration. However, it is apparent that short term visiting from Asia makes a significant contribution to the state's economy. Table 9 shows the reasons given by short term arrivals from Asia for visiting South Australia and this provides some indication of their economic impact. Clearly, tourism is an important component with more than a half indicating they were coming to South Australia for a holiday. However, the significance of having a substantial Asian population in South Australia for the tourism industry is evident in the fact that a fifth of visitors came to South Australia to visit friends or relatives. It is especially interesting that over a tenth of visitors come to the state to conduct business. Education is also significant.

Table 9: South Australia: Short term visitor arrivals and resident departures to/from Asia by reasons for travel, 2002–03 to 2009–10

Purpose of journey	Short term vis arrive	Short term res depart	Percent Short term vis arrive	Short term res depart
Transit/ student vac	258	140	0.0	0.0
Exhibition	1764	2974	0.2	0.2
Convention/ conference	46518	74768	4.1	4.1
Business	136320	215606	12.0	11.9
Visiting friends/relatives	345263	421394	30.5	23.2
Holiday	388963	944574	34.3	52.0
Employment	30939	43996	2.7	2.4
Education	101296	24974	8.9	1.4
Not stated	32028	54288	2.8	3.0
Other	50192	35519	4.4	2.0
Grand total	1133540	1818233	100.0	100.0

Source: DIAC unpublished data

Table 8 also shows the destination of Australian residents who travel overseas and six Asian destinations are in the top 10. This indicates partly that there is a significant amount of travel to the homeland among immigrants from Asia who have settled in South Australia (Hugo 2008). These visits provide the opportunity to strengthen social and economic linkages between the state and Asian countries.

CHARACTERISTICS OF ASIANS IN SOUTH AUSTRALIA

One of the most universal features of migration is its selectivity by age. Except in special circumstances (as for example in retirement migration) immigration propensity is always greatest in the young adult years and declines with age thereafter. This selectivity is enhanced in the Australian case by deliberate policies to select young adults and families into the settler and temporary migrant streams. This is done by some visa categories being excluded to older people (aged 45+) and a significant element of the points assessment test being age.

The youthful nature of the permanent and long term intakes of immigrants into South Australia are evident in Figure 13 and Figure 14 which show the age-sex composition of recent arrivals. The concentration in the 20's age group is especially marked in the long term arrivals due to students dominating this category. The significance of the increasing numbers in this group is evident in Figure 15 which overlays the total South Australian population at the 2001 (shaded) and 2006 censuses. The blank areas indicate the ages in which there was growth between the censuses. It will be noted that almost all net growth occurred in the older age groups as larger baby boomer cohorts

Figure 13: South Australia: Age-sex structure of permanent arrivals Asia-born, 2001–10

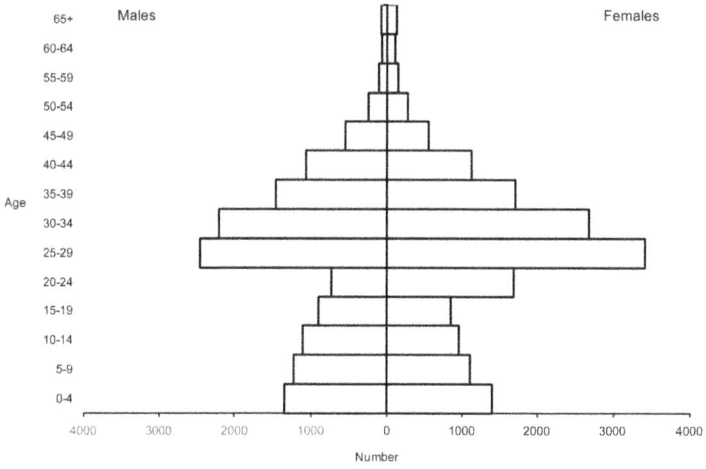

Males
Females
Age
65+
60-64
55-59
50-54
45-49
40-44
35-39
30-34
25-29
20-24
15-19
10-14
5-9
0-4
4000
3000
2000
1000
0
1000
2000
3000
4000
Number

Source: DIAC unpublished data

Figure 14: South Australia: Age-sex structure of long term visitor arrivals from Asia, 2001–10

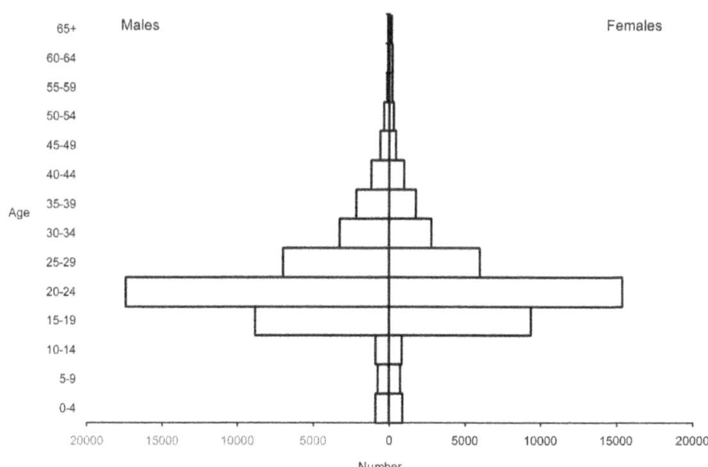

Males
Females
Age
65+
60-64
55-59
50-54
45-49
40-44
35-39
30-34
25-29
20-24
15-19
10-14
5-9
0-4
20000
15000
10000
5000
0
5000
10000
15000
20000
Number

Source: DIAC unpublished data

replaced smaller numbers. However, a major exception is in the 20s age group where there was significant intercensal growth due to the very striking impact of the influx of students in their 20s. This has more than counterbalanced the net migration loss of young South Australians in this age group leaving for interstate and overseas (Hugo 2010).

Figure 15: South Australia: Age-sex structure of the population, 2001 and 2006

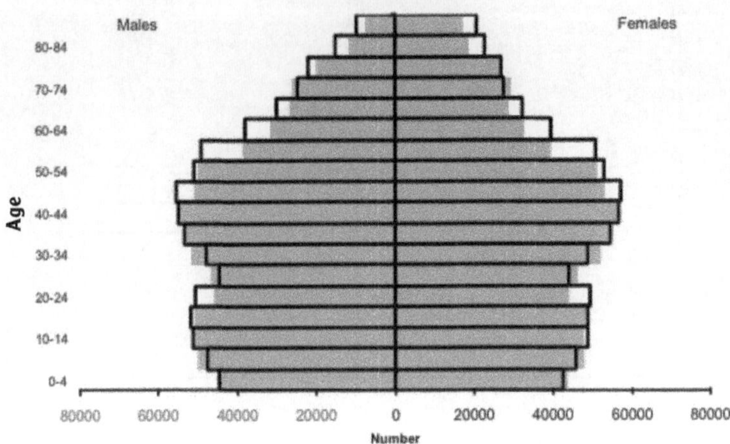

Source: ABS 2001 and 2006 Censuses

The youthfulness of the Asian migration intake has meant that the Asian population has become an increasingly important part of South Australia's working age population. Figure 16 shows how the Asia-born in 2006 made up around 8 per cent of Australia's working age population, three times the proportion in 1981. However, for South Australia the representation has been only half of the national level, reflecting the lower levels of immigration. Nevertheless, Figure 16 shows there was a significant increase between 2001 and 2006 and there will have been an even bigger increase between 2006 and 2011.

It is important to point out that the Asian population of South Australia is more highly educated on average than is the case for the Australia-born. This is evident in Table 10 which compares their education profile at the 2006 census with that of the Australia-born. This is to be expected both because the Asia-born is a relatively young group but also because of the strong focus on skill and qualifications in the Australian migrant selection process. Nevertheless, it is striking that 57.9 per cent of Indians have a qualification of at least a degree (and 33.9 per cent of Chinese) compared with 13.8 per cent of the Australia-born.

Figure 16: Australia and South Australia: Asia-born working age population as a share of the total working age population, 1981–2006

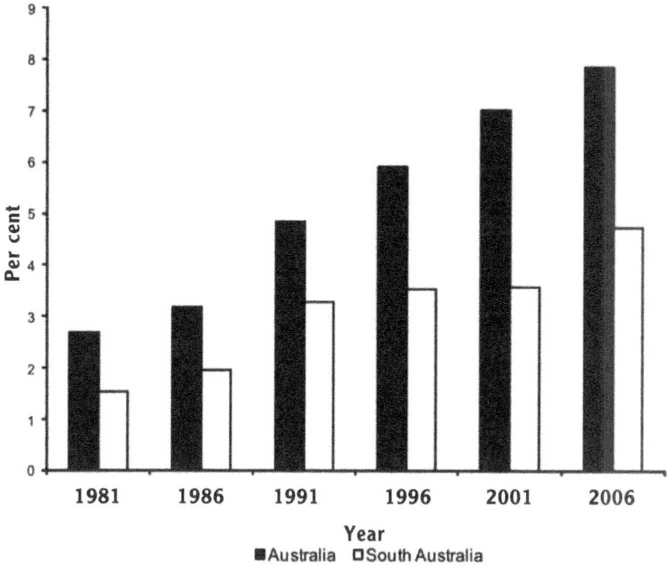

Source: ABS 1981, 1986, 2001 and 2006 Censuses; ABS 1991 and 1996 Census One Per Cent Sample

Table 10: South Australia: Level of post school education of population aged 15 years and over by birthplace, 2006

Source: ABS 2006 Census

	Birthplace (per cent)			
Non-School Qualification: Level of Education	**Australia**	**Asia**	**China**	**India**
Postgraduate Degree Level	1.6	7.4	9.8	20.6
Graduate Diploma and Graduate Certificate Level	1.5	1.1	1.2	2.0
Bachelor Degree Level	10.7	24.4	22.9	35.3
Advanced Diploma and Diploma Level	7.1	8.0	9.6	8.3
Certificate Level	19.8	7.9	6.3	9.5
No Post School Qualification	59.3	51.1	50.2	24.2
Total	100.0	100.0	100.0	100.0
N	800,644	46,781	7,031	5,554

However, the question rises as to the extent to which the skills and qualifications of the Asia-born population are being fully utilised in the South Australian economy. There is evidence elsewhere in Australia of significant 'brain wasting' among some immigrant communities. This refers to the situation where some migrant groups are unable to get a job which is commensurate with their qualifications, experience and skill. This can be through language problems, failure to have qualifications obtained overseas recognised in South Australia or through discrimination in the labour market. To test the degree to which this is occurring with the Asia-born, Table 11 compares the percentage of Asia- and Australia-born in low skill occupations according to their level of education. It will be noted that the proportion of Asians with high level qualifications who are in low skill, low status and low income jobs is strikingly higher than for the Australians and for the UK-born. This represents a loss not only for the individuals involved but also for South Australian productivity. Obtaining a better match between the skills of Asian immigrants, the recognition of these skills and the skills in shortage in the labour market is an important priority for the state's population policy.

Table 11: South Australia: Per centage of employed persons employed as labourers, operators or drivers by level of education and birthplace, 2006

Birthplace	Bachelor Degree or Higher	Other Post-School	No Post-School
Total	3.0	26.3	75.8
Australia	1.8	20.8	77.6
Asia	21.1	17.8	63.0
China	27.6	24.9	47.5
India	57.9	18.7	23.4
UK	1.6	26.3	72.1

Source:ABS 2006 Census

CONCLUSION

Asians are a growing part of South Australia's population and workforce. Without migration the South Australian workforce age population would begin to decline within the next decade. Asia has become the major region of origin of immigrants, especially skilled immigrants, so they will play an increasingly important role in the state's future. As Asian communities grow in South Australia the networks they maintain with their home communities will proliferate and strengthen. These networks are not only important for facilitating further migration but are important potential channels for goods, finance, ideas and other flows which tie South Australia more tightly into Asian economies and societies. It is important to conceptualise South Australia's migration relationship with Asia as a complex interacting one and part of a wider relationship of economic, social and cultural flows.

Asian migration to and from South Australia is here to stay. It is almost certain to increase in complexity, scale and significance. It is important that South Australians adjust to this migration in ways that they have with earlier waves of migrants. There is evidence of discrimination in labour markets and the state has not yet taken full advantage of the potential links which the migrants provide with growing Asian markets. There is considerable potential to better use the skills of Asian migrants and to develop the opportunities they offer to link better with their origin countries.

NOTES

1 National net international migration gain fell from a peak of 315,686 in calendar 2008, the highest ever recorded, to 171,094 in 2010 (ABS 2011, 12).

2 The number of Australia-born persons leaving South Australia for Asia on a permanent basis increased from 142 in 1995–96 to 995 in 2009–10.

3 i.e. foreigners arriving on temporary residence visas who intend to stay in Australia more than one year but don't intend to settle permanently.

REFERENCES

Australian Bureau of Statistics (ABS). *Australian Demographic Statistics*, Catalogue No. 3101.0, ABS, Canberra, various issues.

Australian Bureau of Statistics (ABS). 1986, *Australian Demographic Trends 1986*, Catalogue No. 3102.0, ABS, Canberra.

Australian Bureau of Statistics (ABS). 2011, *Australian Demographic Statistics, December Quarter 2010*, Catalogue No. 3101.0, ABS, Canberra.

Department of Immigration and Citizenship (DIAC). *Immigration Update,* various issues, AGPS, Canberra.

Department of Immigration and Citizenship (DIAC). *Population Flows: Immigration Aspects*, various issues, AGPS, Canberra.

Department of Immigration and Citizenship (DIAC). *Settler Arrivals,* various issues, AGPS, Canberra.

Department of Immigration and Citizenship (DIAC). 2009, *Annual Report 2008–09,* AGPS, Canberra.

Department of Immigration and Citizenship (DIAC). 2011a, *2010–11 Migration Program Report – Program Year to 30 June 2011,* AGPS, Canberra.

Department of Immigration and Citizenship (DIAC). 2011b, *Population Flows: Immigration Aspects 2009–10 Edition,* AGPS, Canberra.

Government of South Australia. 2004, *Prosperity Through People: A Population Policy for South Australia*, Government of South Australia, Adelaide.

Government of South Australia. 2007, *South Australia's Strategic Plan 2007*, Government of South Australia, Adelaide.

Harding, G. and Webster, E. 2002, The Working Holiday Maker Scheme and the Australian Labour Market. Melbourne Institute of Applied Economic and Social Research, University of Melbourne.

Hugo, G.J. 1989, *Atlas of the Australian People Volume V: South Australia*, Australian Government Publishing Service, Canberra.

Hugo, G.J. 1999, A New Paradigm of International Migration in Australia, *New Zealand Population Review*, 25, 1–2, pp. 1–39.

Hugo, G.J. 2006, Temporary Migration and the Labour Market in Australia, *Australian Geographer*, 37, 2, pp. 211–231.

Hugo, G.J. 2008, Quantifying Transnationalism: Asian Migration to Australia, in R. Stojanov and J. Novosak (eds.), *Migration, Development and Environment: Migration Processes from the Perspective of Environmental Change and Development*

Approach at the Beginning of the 21st Century, Cambridge Scholars Publishing, Newcastle Upon Tyne, pp. 172–208.

Hugo, G.J. 2009, Returning Youthful Nationals to Australia: Brain Gain or Brain Circulation?, in D. Conway and R.B. Potter (eds.), *Return Migration of the Next Generations: 21st Century Transnational Mobility*, Ashgate, pp. 185–219.

Hugo, G.J. 2010, Recent and Likely Future Trends in International Migration in South Australia. Draft paper prepared for Planning SA.

Hugo, G.J. 2011, An Overview of Migration Trends and Developments for South Australia, Australia and Globally. Presentation to 2011 Migration Update Conference, Adelaide, 23 June 2011.

Hugo, G., Rudd, D. and Harris, K. 2001, *Emigration from Australia: Economic Implications,* Second Report on an ARC SPIRT Grant, CEDA Information Paper No. 77.

Rizvi, A. 2007, Presentation to Population Advisory Group, 3 April.

Russell, C. 2010, Service Exports Rise on Back of Students, *The Advertiser*, 20 May.

Stevens, C.,1984, The Occupational Adjustment of Kampuchean Refugees in Adelaide. Unpublished BA (Hons) Thesis, University of Adelaide, November.

Tan, G. 2011, The Transnational Migration Strategies of International Students in Australia. Unpublished PhD Thesis, Department of Geographical and Environmental Studies, University of Adelaide.

Tan, Y., Richardson, S., Lester, L., Bai, T. and Sun, L. 2009, *Evaluation of Australia's Working Holiday Maker (WHM) Program*, 27 February, National Institute of Labour Studies, Flinders University, Adelaide, Australia.

CHAPTER 3

Regional South Australia's Engagement with the Asia Pacific Region: Primary Industries

JULIAN MORISON

INTRODUCTION

Australia and indeed South Australia has had a long and prosperous engagement with the Asia Pacific region, particularly with regard to primary industries' exports. Australia has well-established links with the major markets of North Asia and trade with India is growing. Australia also has active and long-standing ties with Indonesia and the other member nations of ASEAN in South-East Asia.

Australia's efforts to boost trade and development in the region is evident by its active membership of the Asia-Pacific Economic Cooperation (APEC) forum, the East Asia Summit (EAS), the ASEAN Regional Forum (ARF) and the Pacific Islands Forum (PIF). As well, Australia works closely with New Zealand and Pacific island states to promote sustainable development, good governance and regional stability in the South Pacific, including through Australia's long-term Pacific Development Partnerships.

In this chapter, the trend in South Australia's primary industry exports to the Asia Pacific region is examined and the implications this trade has for economic prosperity in the State's non-metropolitan regions is considered. The chapter concludes with a brief look at recent opportunities and successful examples of the growing links between South Australia's primary industries and markets in the Asia Pacific region.

MECHANISMS TO ENHANCE EXPORTS GROWTH IN THE ASIA-PACIFIC REGION

Australia has a strong interest in maintaining a rules-based multilateral trading system and is, therefore, a strong supporter of the World Trade Organization (WTO), the only global body overseeing the rules for trade between countries. Australia's top trade priority remains the successful conclusion of the current round of WTO trade negotiations, the Doha Round, which was launched in November 2001. A successful Round would stimulate global economic growth and create substantial new trade opportunities for Australian businesses through global market openings (DFAT 2011).

As leader of the Cairns Group, Australia has been a strong voice for reform in the Round, particularly addressing agricultural trade which is highly distorted by barriers and subsidies. The Cairns Group is a coalition of 19 agricultural exporting countries from the Americas, Africa, Asia and the Pacific.

APEC has evolved to become the leading economic forum in the region, bringing together the leaders of 21 Asia-Pacific economies, including many of Australia's major trading partners. APEC economies account for 68.1 per cent of Australia's two-way trade in goods and services. APEC is an important catalyst in promoting open trade and investment and sustainable economic development in the region.

An important part of Australia's trade policy is reform through free trade agreements (FTAs) (DFAT 2011). FTAs can promote trade and commercial ties between participating countries, and have the potential to open up opportunities for Australian exporters and investors to expand their business into key markets. Australia has bilateral FTAs with New Zealand, the USA, Singapore, Thailand and Chile, and a regional FTA with ASEAN and New Zealand.

The Australia New Zealand Closer Economic Relations Trade Agreement (ANZCERTA), Australia's longest-standing FTA, entered into force in 1983. ANZCERTA provides for free trade on all goods and almost all services. It has underpinned growth in trade between the two countries, with average annual increases of nine per cent during the life of the agreement.

The Australia-United States FTA, entered into force on 1 January 2005. It has led to improved access for Australian industrial and agricultural goods in the USA and has further harmonised the services and investment relationship between the two countries.

The Singapore-Australia FTA (SAFTA), which entered into force on 28 July 2003, eliminated and bound all tariffs at zero. Australia's principal market access gains from SAFTA are through liberalisation of the services sector. The Thailand-Australia FTA (TAFTA), which entered into force on 1 January 2005, eliminated tariffs on around half of Thailand's tariff items, accounting for roughly 80 per cent of Thai imports from Australia. A further 41 per cent of Thai tariffs were reduced to zero in 2010.

The agreement establishing the Association of Southeast Asian Nations (ASEAN)-Australia-New Zealand Free Trade Area (AANZFTA) was signed in February 2009 and entered into force on 1 January 2010. AANZFTA contains regional rules of origin and substantial tariff reduction and elimination commitments, as well as World Trade Organization (WTO)-plus commitments in other areas such as services, which provide commercial benefits to Australian business and thereby strengthen Australia's commercial ties with ASEAN.

Australia is currently negotiating seven FTAs – bilateral FTAs with China, Japan, Korea and Malaysia, and regional FTAs with the Gulf

Cooperation Council, the Trans-Pacific Partnership (TPP) and a new Pacific trade and economic agreement (PACER Plus).

TRENDS IN COMMODITY TRADE

Figure 1 illustrates the sharp increase in the value of trade between South Australia and the Asia Pacific region over the past decade, the result, in part at least, due to Australia's on-going commitment to trade reform and the development of free trade agreements. Imports grew from $2.0 billion in 1999 to $3.3 billion in 2009, a rise of 65 per cent in nominal terms or 20 per cent in real terms. As Figure 1 illustrates, this disguises the longer term trend as imports were impacted significantly by the global financial crisis (GFC) in 2009, falling from a record high of $4.0 million in 2008.

Exports followed a similar trajectory to imports over the decade, increasing from $2.8 billion in 1999 to $4.9 billion in 2009, a rise of 72 per cent in nominal terms or 25 per cent in real terms. SA has a trade surplus with the region ($1.6 billion in 2009) and this has increased over the past decade. As with imports, the GFC sent the value of SA exports to the Asia Pacific region plummeting in 2009, down 21 per cent from the $6.2 billion recorded for 2008.

Figure 1: South Australian commodity imports and exports to Asia Pacific countries ($m)

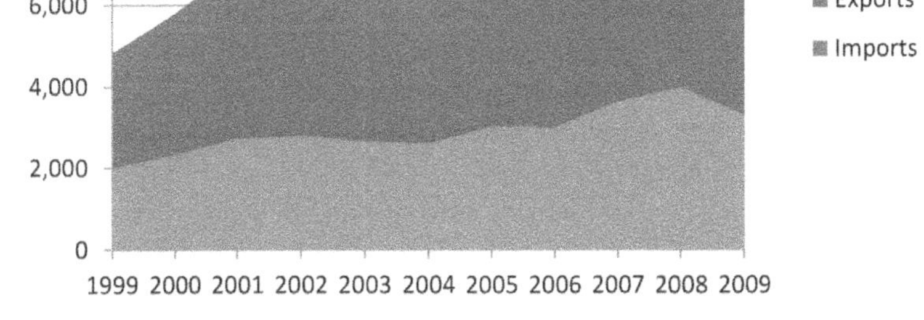

Source: ABS

Closer examination of SA exports to the Asia pacific region (Figure 2) reveals the growth in trade has largely been the result of mining industry expansion, particularly exports of metal ores and metal products (particularly copper, copper ores and iron ore). Other sectors contributing to growth have been wine and food products whilst the value of fishing and agriculture exports fell by almost 50 per cent across the decade.

Figure 2: Selected exports of SA raw and processed primary products to Asia Pacific countries ($m)

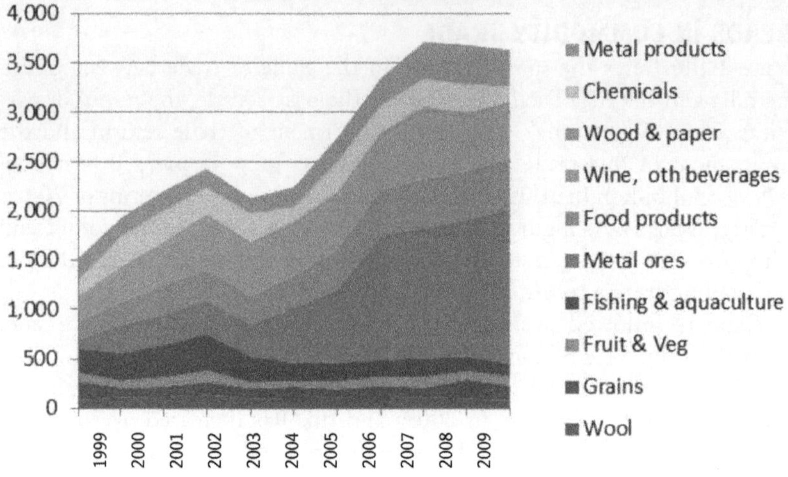

Source: ABS

INDICATORS TO ESTIMATE THE REGIONAL IMPACT OF TRADE IN THE ASIA PACIFIC REGION

Given the importance of the Asia Pacific region's export market to the state economy, an analysis was undertaken to ascertain the implications for the state's regional economies. The South Australian Government divides the state into 12 administrative areas as shown in Figure 3. Metropolitan Adelaide accounts for four of the regions and the remaining eight comprise the non-metropolitan areas of the state.

The input-output method was used to estimate the impact on the state's non-metropolitan regional economies of exports to the Asia Pacific region. A set of regional input-output tables for the State Government regions were available for the analysis (EconSearch 2009a).

The models were originally constructed for Department of Trade and Economic Development, using the GRIT (Generation of Regional Input-Output Tables) method, a 'hybrid' method which utilises local data and computer methods to generate I-O tables (Jensen and West (1986) and West (2009)). Sources of data for the regional I-O models are detailed in EconSearch (2009b).

Estimates of economic impact or economic contribution in this report are presented in terms of the following indicators:

- gross regional product; and
- employment.

Figure 3: South Australian Government Regions

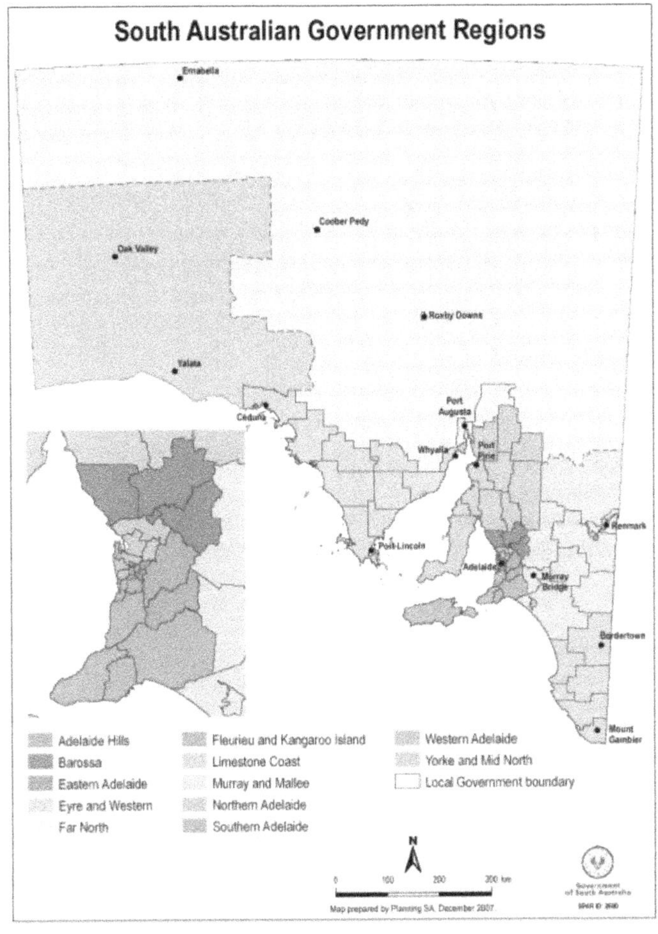

Gross regional product (GRP) is a measure of the net contribution of an activity to the state economy. GRP is measured as value of output less the cost of goods and services (including imports) used in producing the output. In other words, it can be measured as household income plus other value added (gross operating surplus and all taxes, less subsidies). It represents payments to the primary inputs of production (labour, capital and land). Using GRP as a measure of economic impact avoids the problem of double counting that may arise from using value of output for this purpose.

Employment is a measure of the number of working proprietors, managers, directors and other employees, in terms of the number of full-time equivalent (fte) jobs.

EXPORTS TO ASIA PACIFIC COUNTRIES BY SA REGIONS

Based on detailed commodity export by destination data (ABS 2010), estimates were made of the exports of raw and processed primary products to Asia Pacific countries on a South Australian region by region basis. Tables 1 to 3 show the relative importance and diversity of these trade linkages, for three South Australian regional economies, namely the Eyre and Western, South East and Far North regions.

Almost two-thirds of the Eyre and Western region's exports are destined for countries in the Asia Pacific region. While the region's exports are dominated by grains ($164m), fishing and aquaculture products ($232m) and iron and steel products ($205m), it is the latter two that are the most prominent in the Asia Pacific market. Seventy eight per cent of fishing and aquaculture exports (largely farmed tuna) and 82 per cent of iron and steel products (the region includes the City of Whyalla) are exported to the Asia Pacific region, with well over half a billion dollars in exports ($541m in 2006/07) finding their way from Eyre and Western to countries in the Asia Pacific region.

Table 1: Estimated Eyre and Western region exports of raw and processed primary products to Asia Pacific countries, 2006/07

Commodity	All Countries	Asia Pacific	
	$m	$m	Share
Wool	61	38	63%
Grains	164	47	29%
Fishing and aquaculture	232	182	78%
Metal ores	94	61	65%
Food products	66	33	49%
Iron and steel	205	167	82%
Other	20	13	65%
Total raw & processed primary products	840	541	64%

The South East is a slightly more diverse exporter than the Eyre and Western region, with wool ($159m), food products ($225m) and wine ($236m) comprising almost 70 per cent of regional exports, but with vegetables ($64m), fishing and aquaculture ($80m) and wood and paper products ($74m) also significant contributors to regional exports (Table 2). It should be noted that wood and paper products are largely exported through the Port of Portland and are not counted as South Australian exports by the ABS. Because most of the exports of wood and paper products are shipped to countries in the Asia Pacific region, particularly Japan, the figures in Table 2 understate the strength of the direct trade linkage with the region.

Nevertheless, the aggregate value of exports from the South East to the Asia Pacific region, $534m in 2006/07, is similar to that of the Eyre and Western region and represents 59 per cent of the South East region's total exports.

Table 2: Estimated South East region exports of raw and processed primary products to Asia Pacific countries, 2006/07

Commodities	All Countries	Asia Pacific	
	$m	$m	Share
Wool	159	101	63%
Vegetables	64	59	92%
Fishing and aquaculture	80	63	78%
Food products	225	111	49%
Wine and other beverages	236	79	33%
Wood and paper products	74	74	100%
Other	68	48	70%
Total raw & processed primary products	907	534	59%

In the Far North region exports are dominated by metal ores (almost $1.7b in 2006/07) of which approximately two-thirds are exported to the Asia Pacific region (Table 3). Clearly, the region is highly dependent on the mining industry and, in turn, has a significant dependence on the Asia Pacific region. As shown in Table 4, the Far North has the highest valued exports to the Asia Pacific region but also has the highest concentration of exports within a single commodity group, with an estimated 94 per cent of total exports to the Asia Pacific region in the metal ores commodity group.

Table 3: Estimated Far North region exports of raw and processed primary products to Asia Pacific countries, 2006/07

Commodities	All Countries	Asia Pacific	
	$m	$m	Share
Wool	44	28	63%
Metal ores	1,689	1,095	65%
Basic metals and metal products	36	36	100%
Other	29	20	71%
Total raw & processed primary products	1,798	1,180	66%

Table 4: Estimated SA regional exports of raw and processed primary products to Asia Pacific countries, 2006/07

Commodity	South East	Eyre & Western	Far North	Adelaide Hills	Barossa	Fleurieu & KI	Murray & Mallee	York & Mid North	Total
Wool	101	38	28	3	12	25	35	65	307
Grains	4	47	0	0	2	1	19	62	135
Vegetables	59	0	0	27	17	5	59	0	167
Fruit and nuts	1	0	0	39	0	3	39	0	82
Fishing and aquaculture	63	182	0	1	0	13	1	14	274
Metal ores	2	61	1,095	6	5	11	0	5	1,185
Food products	111	33	0	50	18	0	225	32	468
Wine and other beverages	79	0	0	35	333	28	92	32	599
Wood and paper products	74	1	1	0	7	0	5	4	93
Petrochemical and other chemical products	2	5	1	8	8	1	2	17	45
Non-metallic mineral products	0	0	0	0	5	0	1	1	7
Iron and steel	16	167	17	6	10	3	7	19	245
Basic metals and metal products	23	6	36	3	80	2	23	143	316
Total raw & processed primary products	534	541	1,180	178	495	92	508	393	3,922

REGIONAL IMPACT OF TRADE IN THE ASIA PACIFIC REGION

The regional export data presented in Tables 1 to 4 indicate the extent to which exports to Asia Pacific countries are a driver of regional economic activity. Each commodity export group generates direct economic activity in the export industry itself, as well as flow-on economic activity in other sectors of the regional economy through purchases of inputs and the employment of labour. As noted earlier these direct and flow-on effects, measured in terms of gross regional product and employment, have been estimated using regional input-output (I-O) analysis.

Estimates of the economic impact generated in 2006/07 by the SA regional export industries are shown in Table 5. The top row of the table shows the value of primary exports to Asia Pacific countries, data that are consistent with the bottom row in Table 4. In aggregate, across all regions, exports to Asia Pacific countries were estimated to be valued at around $3.9 billion in 2006/07.

These exports generate significant gross regional product (GRP) in all regions, ranging from $70 million in the Fleurieu and Kangaroo Island region (from exports of $92m) to $709 million in the Far North (from exports of $1.18b). In absolute terms, the impact on the Far North economy is more than twice that of any other region. In relative terms, across all regions, the contribution of Asia Pacific exports to GRP averages 15 per cent, ranging from 6 per cent in the Fleurieu and Kangaroo Island region, 7 per cent in the Adelaide Hills and up to 28 per cent in the Far North.

The impact on employment is also an interesting one and in some respects quite different to the GRP effect. Although the relative impact of employment is similar to that of GRP in most regions (averaged 14 per cent across all regions), it is notably lower at 21 per cent for the Far North region. This difference can be attributed to the relatively high capital and low labour intensity of the mining industry.

The low labour intensity of the mining industry is reflected in the fifth place ranking of the Far North region in terms of total jobs generated (3,368 fte jobs), behind the South East (4,709 fte jobs and 15 per cent of the regional total), Murray and Mallee (4,664 and 15 per cent), Eyre and Western (4,622 and 19 per cent) and York and Mid North (3,675 and 13 per cent).

Across all eight non-metropolitan regions in South Australia, the export of raw and processed primary products to Asia Pacific countries generates an estimated 14 per cent of jobs (26,475 fte jobs in 2006/07) and 15 per cent of gross regional product ($2.61b in 2006/07). For South Australia these estimates exclude the processing, transport, handling, storage and other ancillary services that to the export industries that are located in metropolitan Adelaide and interstate.

Table 5: Estimated economic impact in SA regions from the export of raw and processed primary products to Asia Pacific countries, 2006/07

Economic Indicator	South East	Eyre & Western	Far North	Adelaide Hills	Barossa	Fleurieu & KI	Murray & Mallee	York & Mid North	Total
Primary Exports to Asia Pacific ($m)	534	541	1,180	178	495	92	508	393	3,922
Gross Regional Product:									
GRP Impact ($m)	392	398	709	134	306	70	352	253	2,614
Total GRP ($m)	2,681	2,297	2,495	1,842	2,155	1,143	2,444	2,201	17,259
Share of Region Total	15%	17%	28%	7%	14%	6%	14%	11%	15%
Employment:									
Employment Impact (fte)	4,709	4,622	3,368	1,249	3,184	1,004	4,664	3,675	26,475
Total Regional Employment (fte)	32,441	24,619	16,328	17,525	22,218	13,884	30,574	27,453	185,042
Share of Region Total	15%	19%	21%	7%	14%	7%	15%	13%	14%

LINKS BETWEEN SA'S PRIMARY INDUSTRIES AND ASIA PACIFIC MARKETS

The story of exports dependence and regional impact is a somewhat abstract narrative when dealing at the macro, or even regional level. In this final section of the chapter, a closer look is taken at three examples of South Australian regional export linkages with Asia Pacific countries.

ISLAND BEEHIVE HONEY EXPORTS TO JAPAN

The South Australian honey producer, Island Beehive Pty Ltd, is in a unique position amongst other primary producers on Kangaroo Island (KI). For the company and its eight contract producers the island location provides a natural quarantine, protecting it from a range of adverse influences that would otherwise be experienced on the mainland. KI is the only source of pure Ligurian honey bees in the world, giving producers like Island Beehive a niche market. The isolation of Kangaroo Island also means there is a very low probability of contamination from genetically modified (GM) plants. GM free honey is highly sought after by health conscious and environmentally aware Japanese consumers.

Japanese demand for GM free canola, which includes canola grown on KI, has also boosted demand for Kangaroo Island canola honey. This poses mutual gains for the two industries as the production of canola honey increases pollination and hence crop yields, while providing a product suited to tastes and preferences in foreign markets.

There is existing annual Japanese demand for 60 tonnes of canola honey and 40 tonnes of organic eucalypt value at over $500,000 for Island Beehive, with potential to double over the next two years (Davis 2011). Concurrent efforts to establish tourism links with Japan suggests that trade with East Asia, in particular Japan, is a vital and growing opportunity for small and niche market primary producers such as those on KI.

WINE EXPORTS TO CHINA

The wine and grape industry is a key component to the South Australia economy, particularly for several of its regional economies. For the financial year 2009/10 the industry contributed $1.9 billion to state GRP and comprised 19 per cent of state merchandise trade. However in recent years the SA wine industry has not been without its challenges, directly affecting the Barossa, Yorke and Mid North, Murray and Mallee, South East and Adelaide Hills regional economies.

Despite having increased the volume of wine exports by 1 per cent to 453 million litres (for the 2009/10 financial year), the value of these exports fell by 19 per cent to $1.3b. The decline in export value is consistent with the 20 per cent decrease in wine prices to $2.93/litre (FOB). A global oversupply of wine and grapes, and the sudden appreciation of the Australian dollar are the likely contributing factors to the difficulties faced by exporters. The Australian dollar's appreciation illustrates this, rising 72 per cent in value between financial years 2001/02 – 2009/20 to 88 cents (USD/AUD). We can comfortably assume the industries difficulties have been exacerbated by the Australia dollar currently being at parity with the US dollar (November 2011).

That being said, opportunities lie ahead, especially with regards to shifting SA's export market focus. Wine exports to the USA and UK declined in value by 26 per cent and 36 per cent respectively in 2009/10, despite these being the main foreign consumers for SA wine (making up 51 per cent of the market). This is in contrast to China, a growing export market, which has seen the value of exports increase by 25 per cent to $101m over the same time period. The opportunities in China also extend to higher returns for SA exporters, as the average price of exported wine has increased from $1.53/Litre (2008/09) to $3.67/Litre (2009/10). It is suggested that China's growing middle class is the source of this price and volume growth, which now accounts for 8 per cent of SA's wine exports and has become its fourth biggest market.

Recognising this growing opportunity, at the start of 2011 the SA Government contributed $1 million through Primary Industries and Regions South Australia to boost demand for SA wine internationally and domestically. The program is aimed at assisting current and potential exporters: '… through workshops, mentoring, and collaboration with existing wine export trade initiatives' (the then Agriculture Minister Michael O'Brien).

SEIKATSU CLUB CONSUMER CO-OPERATIVE AND DEMAND FOR NON-GMOS

The estimated total of 22 million consumer cooperative members in Japan suggest that such organisations make up a significant share of the Japanese market, and thus pose opportunities and challenges for SA exporters. Illustrating this is Seikatsu Club Consumers' Co-operative with approximately 307,000 members. Consumer co-operatives often have a charter with objectives beyond profits, one of which often relates to the social and environmental impacts of the products they sell. Seikatsu Club Co-operative has a policy of avoiding genetically modified organisms (GMO), as they believe GMOs pose significant health and environmental risks. The following quote from the Co-operative's website states its policy position:

'Seikatsu Club Consumers' Cooperative Union stated firmly in 1997 that principally the genetically engineered foods and crops should be banned and that all foods item were reviewed taking the necessary precautions' (Seikatsu Club Co-operative 2011).

Currently the Co-operative's target is to eliminate all products from their product lines which were derived from more than 10 per cent GMO. As a result of the current ban on GM crops, non-GMO products from South Australia, or at least products which have a relatively low risk of GMO contamination, are potentially an attractive alternative for consumer co-operatives similar to Seikatsu Club.

Since 1998 Seikatsu Club has been importing non-GMO canola from WA, however a number of concerns have arisen following the state's lifting of its ban on GM canola crops in 2008. Prime among these has been the risk of cross contamination of GM canola with its non-GM counterparts. In August 2011 an accident in the township of Williams (WA) involving a truck transporting GM canola emphasised the potential contamination risks to Seikatsu Club's non-GM supply line. The Williams district includes non-GM canola farms which have supply contracts with the Seikatsu Club Co-operative.

Accidents such as this (referenced in a letter from Seikatsu Club and the Green Co-op Consumers' Co-operative Union to the Western Australia (WA) Premier, Colin Barnett, 1st of September 2011 (Seikatsu Club Co-operative 2011), demonstrate the risk of contamination and highlight the difficulty in segregating GM and non-GM products to ensure an acceptably low probability of contamination. As a result, South Australia's ban on GM canola crops may offer additional security to concerned buyers such as the Seikatsu Club Co-operative, placing the State's regions in a good position to meet increasingly specialised demands in markets of the Asia Pacific region.

CONCLUSIONS

Access to export markets is fundamental to the health and prosperity of regional South Australia. The analysis provided in this chapter demonstrates how important international trade is to regional economies with exports to countries in the Asia Pacific region accounting for between 6 and 28 per cent regional economic activity, averaging around 15 per cent of GRP and 14 per cent of regional jobs.

The regional impacts can be expected to continue to grow as the current mining industry expansion continues, particularly in the Far North and Eyre and Western regions. An interesting observation from the analysis is that the employment impacts per million dollars of exports are significantly lower for mining industry commodities when compared with the impacts of exports in the fishing, forestry, food products and wine industries which suggests that regional jobs growth from the current mining boom is likely to be much lower than the rate of growth in export volumes and values.

Data limitations mean that the estimated impacts of exports on the economies of regional South Australia are likely to be underestimated, particularly in the South East region where a large proportion of forestry products are exported through Victoria and therefore not included in South Australia's export statistics.

For South Australia as a whole the reported impacts do not tell the full story as the estimates exclude the processing, transport, handling, storage and other ancillary services to the export industries that are located in metropolitan Adelaide.

REFERENCES

Australian Bureau of Statistics (ABS) 2009, *Australian National Accounts: Input-Output Tables – Electronic Publication 2005–06*, ABS Cat. No. 5209.0.55.001, Canberra.

Australian Bureau of Statistics (ABS) 2010, *International Trade Customised Report*, from a special data request from the Australian Institute for Social Research, The University of Adelaide, May.

Davis, P 2011, quoted at www.island-beehive.com.au/news/news.php, viewed on 17/11/2011.

Department of Foreign Affairs and Trade (DFAT) 2011, *Australian trade policy and news*, viewed on 15/11/2011 at www.dfat.gov.au/trade.

EconSearch 2009a, *Economic and Environmental Indicators for South Australia and its Regions, 2008/09*, report prepared for the Department of Trade and Economic Development, May.

EconSearch 2009b, *Input-Output Tables for South Australia and its Regions, 2008/09: Technical Report*, report prepared for the Department of Trade and Economic Development, May.

Government of South Australia 2010, *Budget Statement 2010/11*, Budget Paper 3, Adelaide.

Jensen, R.C. and West, G.R. 1986, *Input-Output for Practitioners, Vol. 1, Theory and Applications*, Office of Local Government, Department of Local Government and Administrative Services, AGPS, Canberra.

Mangan, J. and Phibbs, P. 1989, *Demo-Economic Input-Output Modelling with Special Reference to the Wollongong Economy*, Australian Regional Developments 20, AGPS, Canberra.

Seikatsu Club Co-operative 2011, Website viewed on 17/11/11 at www.seikatsuclub.coop/english/.

West, G.R. 2009, *IO9 Users' Guide and Reference, Part B (DRAFT)*, Department of Economics, University of Queensland, St Lucia.

Other websites viewed:

www.southaustralia.biz/News/2010/06/23/Wine-mission-to-China.aspx

www.southaustralia.biz/News/2011/02/15/Program-to-boost-wine-sales.aspx

www.island-beehive.com.au/news/news.php

www.seikatsuclub.coop/english/stop_gmo_e.html

CHAPTER 4

International Education – Deepening Engagement

BARRY BURGAN and JOHN SPOEHR

INTRODUCTION

South Australian educational institutions, educators and researchers have a long history of engagement with the Asia Pacific region. More recently however this engagement has been transformed and accelerated through the growth of International education. International education has been one of the fastest growing sectors of the South Australian (and Australian) economy. Between the 2001 and 2006 Census, employment in education in South Australia grew at 15%, over double the rate for the economy as a whole. At the Australian level, this contribution has been recognised in studies by Access Economics, commissioned by the Australian Council for Private Education and Training (ACPET).[1] These studies examined the economic benefits of international education as an export industry and the flow-on impacts from international student expenditure as well as their visiting friends and relatives. They concluded that the 28,000 international students who studied in South Australia in 2008 and their visiting friends and relatives, supported an estimated 6,800 jobs and generated a total value-add of $680 million.

It is no surprise that in the context of global economic instability that Australian universities have sought to better understand what the likely impact of a decline in international student enrolments might be. A recent report for Universities Australia by Deloitte Access Economics modelled the impact of a decline in international student numbers, both for the higher education sector and the broader Australian economy. They estimate that a downturn in international student enrolments over time of 30% would result in an annual decline in GDP of $6.2 billion and the loss of 57,000 jobs. If this impact were experienced proportionately in South Australia, it would result in a reduction in GSP (Gross State Product) of $350 million and 3,200 jobs.

In this chapter we examine the contribution of international education to South Australia. We suggest that despite recent volatility in enrolments flowing from the impact of global economic instability and a high Australian dollar, international education is likely to remain a very significant vehicle for economic, social, political and cultural engagement between South Australia and the Asia-Pacific region. Focusing on ways to improve the engagement in the short term will produce benefits for students that will help to underpin the sector for many years to come.

INTERNATIONAL STUDENTS AND SOUTH AUSTRALIA

In 2010 there were around 32,000 international students in the SA education sector. Nearly 50% of these were enrolled in higher education and 25% in Vocational Education (see Table 1 and Figure 1).

Table 1: International enrolments by sector in SA, 2010

Higher Education	15,820
VET	8,575
ELICOS	5,445
Schools	2,481
Other	1,971
Student Enrolments	34,292

Source: www.aei.gov.au/research/International-Student-Data/

Figure 1: International enrolments – SA, 2010

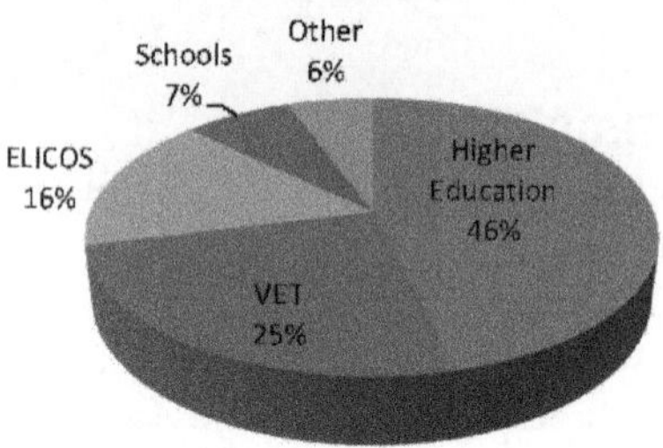

Source: www.aei.gov.au/research/International-Student-Data/

Over the period 2002–2010, enrolments in South Australia grew at an average 15.2% per year. Figure 2 shows that the growth has primarily been in the VET (Vocational Education and Training) and higher education sectors. This growth was substantially greater than for Australia as a whole, where growth averaged 10.7%. South Australia's share of the international education market increased from 4.0% in 2002 to 5.6% in 2010. This growth was distributed across all sectors, but particularly in the VET sector where the SA share increased from 2.6% to 4.2%, and in higher education where the share increased from 4.2% to 6.5%.

There has been a substantial shift in the make-up of the international student population over recent years. Figure 3 illustrates trends by country of origin. A high proportion of students from South East Asia (Singapore, Malaysia etc) reflects historical linkages stretching back to the Colombo plan, the dominant market in the early 2000's – representing 55% of the enrolment base, with China 17%, and India 2%. By 2010 enrolments of Chinese students had risen to 39% of the total, India to 19% and the Middle East to 5%. The absolute number from South East Asia remained relatively constant (with enrolments from Vietnam replacing declines from markets such as Malaysia and Singapore) but the growth came from these other markets.

A significant slowing of growth rates was evident in 2010 – particularly in the VET and ELICOS (English Language Intensive Courses for Overseas Students) sectors and in the number of students from India – and most significantly in the ELICOS sector. Arguably the strong growth in enrolments

Figure 2: International student enrolments – SA, by education sector

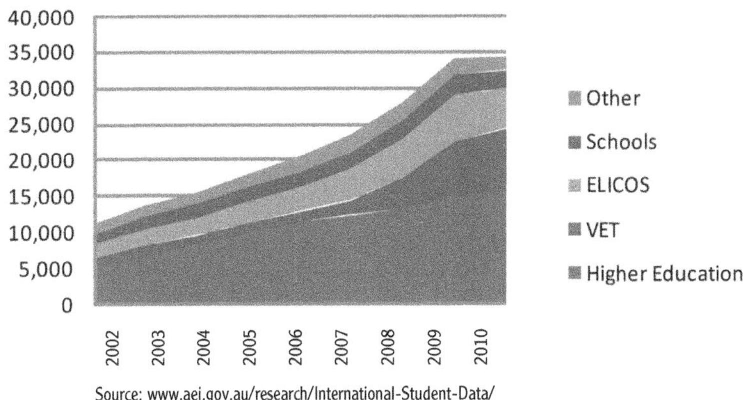

Source: www.aei.gov.au/research/International-Student-Data/

Figure 3: International student enrolments – SA, by country of origin

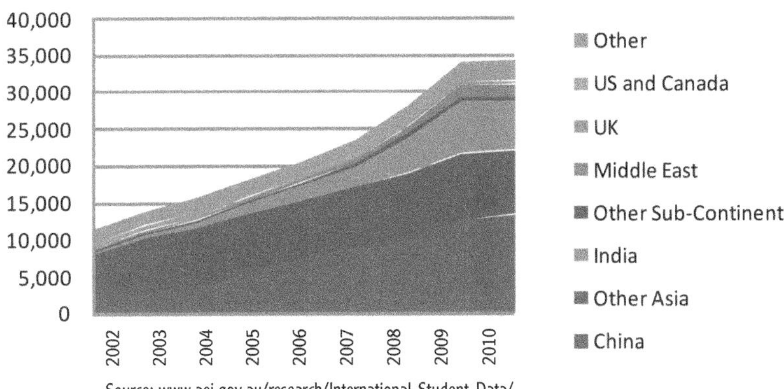

Source: www.aei.gov.au/research/International-Student-Data/

experienced during the latter half of the last decade was always going to be difficult to sustain given the value of the Australian dollar and harm done to the Australian international education brand by concerns about educational quality and racism experienced by Indian students.

The dilemma facing Australian education institutions become clearer in 2011. As of August 2011 enrolments were down 12.5% in South Australia, and 7.9% in Australia. While all sectors were affected, ELICOS was hardest hit (a continuation of the trends from 2010). The main causes of this decline area summarised below.

The longer term benefits of international education depend on the quality and reputation of education, and ensuring that immigration policies are responsive to employer needs for suitably qualified graduate international students. This strategy is likely to be more widely adopted when labour market conditions begin to tighten internationally (Hawthorn 2010).

While the decline in the Australian dollar in response to the GFC provided a temporary competitive advantage, relative to the Euro and China's RMB, this advantage was eroded by a resurgent $A. Moreover the weakening of the US dollar internationally is likely to increase the competitive advantage of the US as a destination for international students. Upward pressure on the living costs of students living in Australia is also likely to be an inhibiting factor along with an increase in the level of fees charged by institutions. An ongoing barrier has been a lack of affordable and appropriate accommodation for international students in Australia.

The short-term outlook for international education enrolments in Australia is not positive. Deloitte Access Economics (Deloitte Access Economics 2011, iv) have forecast a decline in international commencements of around 30% across Australian Universities over what was previously expected the next few years based on the confluence of factors discussed above. They do however forecast some recovery over the medium term.

Figure 4: Difference in enrolments between projections for universities and counterfactual scenario

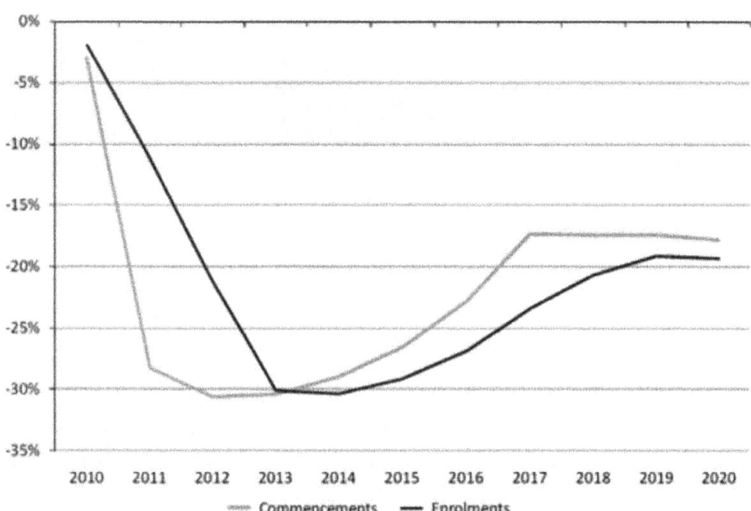

Source: Deloitte Access Economics, Broader implications from a downturn in international Students, Report for Universities Australia, 30 June 2011

MEASURING THE ECONOMIC VALUE OF INTERNATIONAL EDUCATION

Typically economic value has been estimated in terms of contribution to Gross Domestic or Gross State Product and employment, and this is the focus of the recent Access Economics reports in this area. In the following section we apply a similar methodology, focusing particularly on the underlying factors that generate the economic impact, to enable understanding the breadth and context of the impact.

CONTRIBUTION TO INTERNATIONAL EXPORTS

International students, and the expenditure they create, can be considered a contribution to international exports – even though that spend occurs in South Australia, and on items such as accommodation and in retail stores.

STUDENT EXPENDITURE

There are a number of estimates with respect to the export spend of international students in South Australia. ABS estimates of student expenditure in the state of $741 million for 2007/08 is the base of the initial Access work. Australian Education International have since updated the numbers of 2010 – and the total SA based education overseas export income is estimated at $1,028 million.[2]

For a more detailed perspective, there are two sources of expenditure estimates. Education Adelaide provided estimates of average student fees per education sector in 2009, as follows:

Higher Education	$ 19,972.12
VET	$ 13,149.63
Schools	$ 13,413.21
ELICOS	$ 4,121.83
Other	$ 18,050.00
Total	$ 15,232.56

Source: Education Adelaide, except for ELICOS, which has been independently estimated from English Australia[3]

The second source of data is for expenditure on other goods and services, and is taken from a survey undertaken by Education Adelaide for SA students in 2005–06. This identified $333.1 million spend on goods and services (including items such as accommodation and food), as illustrated in Figure 5.

This survey, while a little dated, represents the best available consumption or expenditure allocation, and the survey base is directly relevant to the SA situation.

For the purpose of the modelling undertaken here it is assumed that in 2010, the average spend on fees is as described above, with a 3% increase. It is then assumed that students from each sector spend similar amounts on general living per week and this is calibrated using the estimated spend on fees above and the numbers of students to produce the AEI estimate for education travel services of $741 million) of $14,960 per student in all sectors but ELICOS, and $5,210 for ELICOS (based on and average length of study of 14.6 weeks), and assuming the average student stays an additional two weeks on top of their study period. The assumed proportional distribution of this spend, based on the estimates above is detailed in Table 2.

Figure 5: Estimated overseas student expenditure by item in South Australia, 2005/06

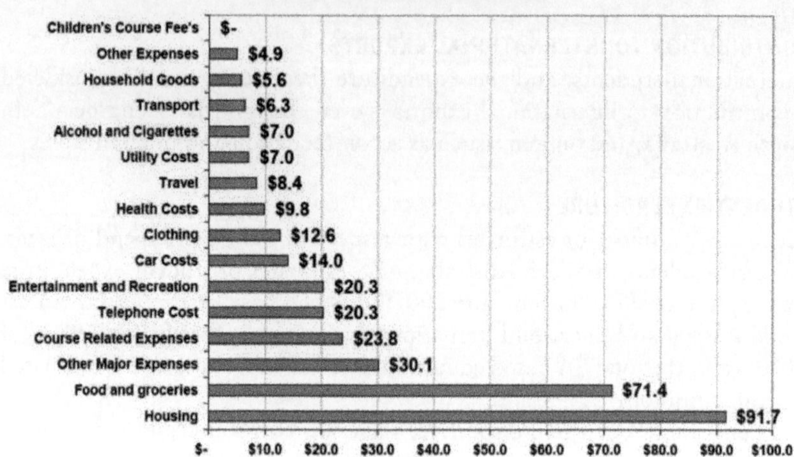

Source: Education Adelaide modelling, based on AEI Cost of Living Report, (August 2005)

Table 2: Estimated student spend by category of spend[4]

	Proportion inc Education	Proportion excl Education	Spend in 2010 ($m)
Education Services	53.7%		551.7
Housing	12.8%	27.5%	131.2
Food and Groceries	9.9%	21.4%	102.1
Course related expenses	3.3%	7.1%	34.0
Telephone Cost	2.8%	6.1%	29.0
Entertainment and Recreation	2.8%	6.1%	29.0
Car Costs	1.9%	4.2%	20.0
Clothing	1.8%	3.8%	18.0
Health Costs	1.4%	2.9%	14.0
Travel	1.2%	2.5%	12.0
Utility Costs	1.0%	2.1%	10.0
Alcohol and Cigarettes	1.0%	2.1%	10.0
Transport	0.9%	1.9%	9.0
Households Goods	0.8%	1.7%	8.0
Other	4.9%	10.5%	49.9
	46.3%	100.0%	476.5
	100.0%		1028.2

Source: Modelled amounts based on assumptions as above

Table 3 provides a summary of the expenditure estimates for 2010.

Table 3: Estimated export contribution of the spend of international students to the SA economy – 2010

Estimated Spend	1027.2
Education Services	551.7
Housing	131.1
Food and Groceries	102.1
Other	234.3

Source: Modelled outcomes

OTHER INTERNATIONAL EDUCATION EXPORT SPEND

It is recognised that there is an additional impact from the visits of friends and relatives to students studying in South Australia, and that there are other international education expenditures by the sector (e.g., consulting income, correspondence courses etc – under ABS definitions this excludes operations of off-shore campuses).

It is assumed that every international student attracts the average of ½ a visit per year from friends and relatives, that they spend the average of an international tourist visiting Australia as per the Access Economics report, and using the industry allocations as per the Access report. With SA multipliers the result is for a slightly lower value added impact, and a slightly higher employment impact.

For other activity, as noted above it is assumed that the SA education sector earns its proportional (relative to student base) share of other income as estimated in the Access Economics report. Table 4 illustrates the estimated spend on this basis, and these other aspects add a further $50 million of annual impact.

Table 4: Estimated spend associated with visits of friends and family and other international education in South Australia – 2010

Friends and Family Spend ($m)	31.5
Other Activity Spend ($ m)	32.8

Source: Modelled outcomes

RELATIVE EXPORT CONTRIBUTION

Table 5 provides a list of relative overseas export value by category of spend for the top ten merchandise exports – measured on the SITC 3 digit industry classification (combining copper and copper concentrates. In 2010, education was the third largest international export earner for the state.

Table 5: Overseas exports by category from South Australia, 2009–10

Commodity/Service	$ million
Alcoholic beverages	1,344
Copper and copper concentrates	1179
Education-related travel	1028
Iron ore and concentrates (b)	624
Meat	565
Wheat	452
Lead	410
Silver and Platinum	207
Motor vehicles	190
Refined Petroleum	155
Vegetables	143

Source: Table 38: Australia's Trade by State And Territory, 2009–10, DFAT

CONTRIBUTION TO ECONOMIC ACTIVITY

The system of national accounts recognises that the level of economic activity is measured by Gross Domestic Product (GDP) or Gross State Product (GSP) at the state level. Therefore while the export contribution is one measure of level of activity, an alternative is the contribution to GSP, and employment. In order to estimate this contribution the spend above is allocated to industry sectors within an economic model (input–output) framework,[5] and then transformed through this model to provide estimates of impact on economic activity. The impacts are measured in two ways which are:

- A narrower measure which includes the incomes and employment created through the direct spend effect (i.e. in education, and in retail sector) plus the impact induced through the production linkages (i.e. the education sector buys inputs from elsewhere in the economy).[6]
- A broader measure, which includes the above, but also includes the flow through impact induced by consumption linkages (i.e. the employment created with the education sector involves increased consumption which also creates an economic impact.

In terms of allocation to industry sectors, the following assumptions have been adopted:

- Education services are allocated fully to the education sector.
- Housing is allocated one third to ownership of dwellings (implying increased values), one third to construction activity annually, and one third to property services (tenancy management).
- Food and Groceries is allocated one third to retail (the margin), one third to food products, and one third to imports.
- Other is allocated proportionally to general household spend across the sector (including imports).

Table 6 provides the estimated results of the assessment for 2010 using the narrower definition of impact (direct and production induced). The total contribution to GSP is estimated at $844 million in 2010, and the total FTE's at 7,540.[7]

Table 7 illustrates the estimated contribution from these additional components of international student activity. The modelling suggests that 850 jobs (FTE's) were created in the state in 2010 as a consequence of international education, in addition to that from student spend.

Tables 8 and 9 provide the modelled results of the impact of SA based international education on the SA economy including the consumption induced impacts, as discussed above.

The impact of the estimated student spend in 2010 represents around a $1.4 billion contribution to GSP, with the creation of 10,400 jobs, of which 4,750 are in education and the remaining, 5,100 in other areas of the economy.

The additional impact of the expenditure of friends and families, and

Table 6: Estimated export contribution of the spend of international students to the SA economy excluding consumption induced impacts

Estimated Spend ($2010 m)	**1028.2**
Education Services	551.7
Housing	131.1
Food and Groceries	102.1
Other	243.3
Value Added ($ m)	
Wages and Salaries	648.3
GOS	195.3
Total	**843.6**
Employment (FTE's)	
Education	4,759
Real Estate and Housing	122
Food and Groceries	340
Other	2,322
Total	**7,544**

Source: Modelled outcomes

Table 7: Estimated economic contribution of the additional international education spend excluding consumption induced impacts

Friends and Family Spend	
Spend ($m, 2010)	31.5
Value Added ($m, 2010)	20.8
Employment (FTE's)	**379**
Other International Education Activity Spend	
Income/Spend ($m, 2010)	32.8
Value Added ($m, 2010)	31.0
Employment (FTE's)	**470**

Source: Modelled outcomes

Table 8: Estimated economic contribution of the spend of international students to the SA Economy including consumption induced impacts

Estimated Spend ($m, 2010)	**1028.2**
Value Added ($ m, 2010)	
Wages and Salaries	918.2
GOS	455.0
Total	**1373.2**
Employment (FTE's)	
Education	4,759
Real Estate	122
Food and Groceries	340
Other	5,202
Total	**10,424**

Source: Modelled outcomes

other activity adds a further $90 million contributed to GSP and a further 1,200 jobs.

Table 9: Estimated economic contribution of the additional international education spend including consumption induced impacts

Friends and Family Spend	
Spend ($m, 2010)	31.5
Value Added ($m, 2010)	37.4
Employment (FTE's)	**508**
Other International Education Activity Spend	
Income/Spend ($m, 2010)	32.8
Value Added ($m, 2010)	51.8
Employment (FTE's)	**691**

Source: Modelled outcomes

CONTRIBUTION RELATIVE TO OTHER ECONOMIC SECTORS

Based on the estimates above, the total quantified impact of international education in 2010 for South Australia can be summarised as:

- An export spend of $1.092 billion ($1.028 million directly, and $64 million through visiting friends and relatives and other international education activity) which represents approximately 1.3% of GSP
- A contribution to GSP (i.e. incomes being created) of $1.5 billion, or 1.8% of GSP
- Around 11,600 jobs (FTE's) created, which represents around 1.6% of employment. The estimates include 4,200 of these jobs being created in education, which represents an estimated 7% of the employment in the sector.

CGE MODELLING OF IMPACT

The estimated spend of international students, and their visiting friends and relatives was modelled above using an input output framework, similar to that applied in other studies like that undertaken by Access Economics. However a superior modelling option (particularly at the national level) is a CGE modelling framework. A CGE model allows for supply side constraints, and also predicts outcomes from a broader range of financial variables including inflation, impact on Government finances etc. For these reasons the estimated spend in 2007/08 is applied as a demand shock to the Monash Multi-Regional Forecasting Model.[8]

An earlier study by the Centre of Policy Studies on the economic contribution of international students to the Australian economy[9] concluded, that in 2000, international students in Australia contributed $3.7 billion in export revenue (which represented 0.55% of GDP). This represented:

- a 0.23% increase in real GDP, and a 0.39% increase in real consumption
- a 0.37% increase in employment.

Therefore the contribution to GDP is less than half the estimated spend. This result is a consequence of the crowding out discussed above, with educational exports pushing the exchange rate up by 1.95%, and increasing inflation by 0.38%. Moreover the modelling also suggests that over time, the impact declines as economic adjustments mean that exports in other areas decline, and the final impact is for an increase in real GDP of only 0.03%. The study of regional impacts concludes that South Australia would actually benefit from not having international students, due to crowding out effects. It should be noted that South Australia had a relatively small share of international students at that time.

This analysis adopts a different line of inquiry, examining what would happen to the state economy if international students were not attracted to South Australia, regardless of the situation for Australia as a whole. At the outset we note that since the above studies were undertaken, not only have the number of international students and their spend increased as a proportion of exports/GDP for Australia as a whole, South Australia's share of the number of students has increased.

The starting point for this analysis is to supplement earlier use of the RISE input–output model with an application of CGE modelling, where the SA economy has an international education spend of $1.092 million (or 1.3% of GSP). For this purpose it is assumed that students are additional to the Australian economy (i.e. not attracted from interstate).

The results of the consumption spend associated with international education in South Australia are shown in Table 10.

These results suggest that international education in 2010 added around $780 million in GSP, over $1,300 million in Real Consumption and 15,000 jobs. These results are very similar to the broader level of analysis using the input–output tables (as would be expected), but it also tells us that:

- Prices are 1.08% higher as a consequence, with a significant impact on house prices (in excess of 3%)
- The benefits of student spend will be somewhat offset by the fact that servicing of that spend will compete with other industries for resources, creating cost pressures and as such interstate exports in other industries would fall.

ADDITIONAL ASPECTS OF IMPACT

The growth in international education has impacts beyond the education sector. This section examines some of these impacts.

DEMAND FOR ACCOMMODATION

The estimates above indicate that there is an estimated spend in South Australia by international students of $130 million.[10] A significant component of this is expenditure is in the accommodation sector.

Table 10: Estimated economic contribution of the additional international education spend CGE modelling

Demand Shock Modelled ($ million, 10 values)	
South Australia	1092
Other Australia	0
National	1092
% Change in National Macro Variables	
Real GDP	-0.14
Consumption	-0.03
Investment	0.00
State govt	0.00
Fed govt	0.00
Exports	-0.610
Imports	0.070
CPI	0.000
Employment	-0.030
% Change in SA Macro Variables	
Real GDP	0.970
Real consumption	1.740
Investment	1.400
State government	0.000
Federal government	0.000
Interstate exports	-1.470
International exports	4.260
Interstate imports	1.440
International imports	0.950
CPI	1.080
State direct taxes	3.530
Employment	2.250

Source: Modelled outcomes

A South Australian Centre for Economic Studies (SACES) study commissioned by Education Adelaide is reported in an Education Adelaide accommodation fact sheet as estimating that 18,035 international students in 2005 used:

- 3,889 private rental dwellings (most by more than one student);
- 2,189 homestay places (living with local families); and
- 2,533 institutional places.

These ratios are roughly confirmed by Harrison's Student Accommodation Survey 2008, also presented in the Education Adelaide fact sheet, which indicates that, 'Around half of international students live in shared private rental accommodation, followed by 23% in purpose built student accommodation'.

These estimates imply an average of a little over 3 students per private rental dwelling, 1.4 students per home stay and 1 student per institutional place. Again it is noted this does not allow for students whose parents buy houses in which they can live. This is not picked up by the survey, but from qualitative evidence it does happen to some degree.

Table 11 indicates these estimates in terms of demand in proportion to 2010 student numbers. It is noted that supply constraints on institutional places are likely to constrain accommodation growth in that sector, and that demand is more likely to be met by the private rental sector. It is assumed that the growth in institutional places has been limited by 80%, and further than home-stay has also been constrained (90% of proportional growth).

Table 11: Estimated demand for student accommodation

Private rental dwellings	9,001
Homestay	3,642
Institutional (rooms)	3,727

Source: Modelled outcomes

The calculations suggest that private rental dwelling demand in 2010 represents 1.4% of the dwelling stock in metropolitan Adelaide, and 5.7% of the rental stock, and 7.8% of the private rental stock (based on 2006 ABS Census data). This is a large explanatory factor for the very low vacancy rates in private sector rental vacancy rates in Adelaide. The Housing Industry Prospects Forum (March 2010) describes the private rental market in Adelaide as 'very tight'. Figure 6 illustrates vacancy rates in private rental stock over the last 40 years. It is apparent that the decline in vacancy rates and tightening of the market is closely allied with growth in international student numbers.

Figure 6: Vacancy rates in private rental accommodation – Adelaide

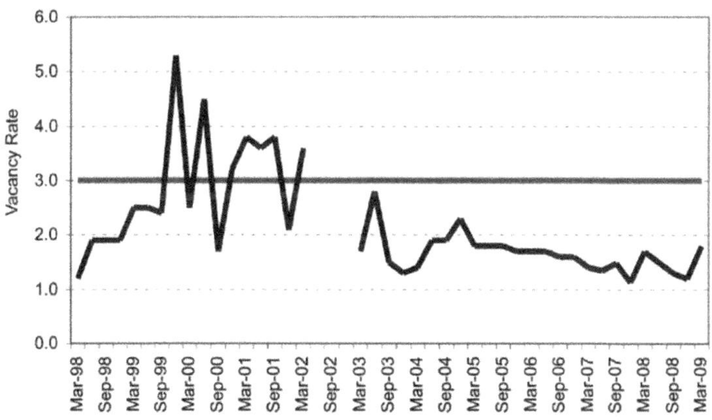

Note: Data for period June 2002 to December 2002 not available.

Source: Housing Industry Prospects Forum Report, March 2010

INVESTMENT IN EDUCATIONAL INFRASTRUCTURE

The growth of international students has required or enabled some significant improvements in education infrastructure in South Australia. New and expanding private education providers have leased and invested in facilities. Existing institutions in higher education and schools have similarly invested in new property (University of Adelaide investment program, Flinders University leasing city premises etc). While in part this would be captured in the student fees paid (which fund the improvements), it would not be fully captured given the modelling framework. However it is not really possible to 'isolate' the expenditure on infrastructure linked to international students per se, and as such the economic contribution of this component has not been quantified.

Based on the information and the assumptions, the enrolment numbers are concentrated in the CBD – accounting for 65% of total enrolments. However, the accommodation presence is much more broadly distributed, with the regional distribution being quite even. However this must be carefully interpreted as it is evident from the Harrisons survey that the greatest demand is for students to live within the vicinity of where they are studying – specifically within walking distance.[11] The current distribution may be limited by supply constraints rather than reflect actual demand. This issue is discussed further in the constraints section, but the suggestion is that while presence is evenly spread, there is unmet demand in the CBD. As noted above 65% of students are enrolled in institutions based in the CBD (22,000) but only 24% live there. While there are competing pressures in relation to cost and access, it could be reasonably assumed that this represents a significant shortfall. Of the 14,000 students who study in the CBD, but live outside – it would probably be conservative to suggest that more than a third would 'prefer' to live in the CBD if affordable accommodation was available. This would imply (again conservatively) that there is an existing shortfall of around 5,000 bed spaces in the CBD.

AIRPORT DEMAND

The growth in international students has a significant impact on the demand for airport services. It is noted that this is largely excluded from the estimates of economic impact above, as bookings etc are largely seen as external. Table 12 illustrates the demand for airport services at Adelaide airport derived from international students. This estimate is based on assumptions that international students take an average of 1.2 flights per year home (return) of which half are international flights, and half are international flights connected through another domestic airport (e.g. Adelaide – Sydney – Shanghai). It is further assumed that international students will be engaged is some tourism activities and visit other areas within Australia, and so it is assumed there will be an average 0.3 trips (departure and return) per student to other Australian localities through Adelaide Airport. International students therefore account for an estimated 100,000 trips (1750 per week) through Adelaide airport, or 1.3% of total airport demand.

Table 12: Estimated demand for international student airport services

Commencing flights (int)	17,146
Commencing flights (dom)	34,292
Returning flight (int)	17,146
Returning flight (dom)	34,292
Total	102,876

Source: Modelled outcomes

Based on the country of origin parameters as illustrated in the charts above, Table 13 provides estimates of demand for airport services by international students. It is noted that large number of these services are provided indirectly (i.e. through other Australian ports or through links to other international destinations). The modelling indicates for example, that international students underpin demand for 240 seats a week on average to and 240 seats from China, and friends and relatives travel would add a further 100 seats per week.

Table 13: Estimated demand for international student airport services – final destination by country

China	19,146
India	9,812
Malaysia	4,827
South Korea	3,899
Hong Kong	3,640
Viet Nam	2,058
Japan	1,706
Singapore	1,117
Taiwan	913
Thailand	720
Other	9,315
Total	57,153

Source: Modelled outcomes

WIDER BENEFITS OF INTERNATIONAL EDUCATION

There are a wide range of social, strategic and cultural benefits that flow from the presence of international students in SA. Many of these were highlighted in a recent Universities Australia report (2009) undertaken by Strategic Policy and Research in Education. The media release linked to the report concludes that 'The benefits of international education go far beyond the immediate economic contributions made by students who come to Australian universities to undertake their studies' (1).

Among the key findings of this report are that the benefits of international education can be categorised as follows (the report provides supporting argument for the existence of each of the benefits:

- *Broad Internationalisation: Impacts on Universities* –an increased international focus of Universities supporting internationalisation of research and curriculum, transnational education and pathways to higher education.

- *Impacts on Students in Australian Universities* – benefits of cultural exchange, for international students studying in Australia, but also for local students who interact with them and learn more about the culture of other countries, and also through the increased participation of local students in exchange and overseas components of their courses.
- *Outcomes for International Graduates and Alumni* – the study experience of international students is generally positive ('85% were either very satisfied or satisfied with studying in Australia, 98% would recommend studying in Australia to friends and family, 83% were either very satisfied or satisfied with the course they were completing and 67% would recommend their course to friends or family' (p 5)) and further that many stayed in Australia for work giving benefits to them and to the community. The Universities Australia report suggests that 'Australia's universities have provided the backbone of Australia's modern migration system. Overseas students or former overseas students have provided over half of the increase in skilled migration over the last decade' (p. 5).
- Impacts on Public Diplomacy – creating a positive image for Australia and opening doors and exerting influence.
- Impacts on Conventional Diplomacy and Trade Links – networks established through international education have a demonstrated impact on business and trade development.

CONCLUSION

South Australia's engagement with the Asia Pacific region has been deepened over the last decade by the strong growth of international education – engagement that has significant economic and social impacts on South Australia.

The immediate impacts can be modelled using a range of assumption and indicates that international education represented in 2009–10 the third largest overseas export from the state ($1.03 billion), and supports up to $1.5 billion of real income generation in the state, and 12,000 jobs. While much of the economic activity is in education itself, a great deal of it is more broadly spread.

A broader perspective of the implications is presented in terms of creating critical mass for enhanced airport services (which provides better access for South Australian residents), and in terms of the impact residential property markets and student accommodation.

But the longer term implications, while harder to demonstrate, can in many ways be considered the most beneficial aspect of the recent patterns of growth in students – particularly the links being established with China.

The challenge for the future is to create even greater economic and social benefits from the level of student demand that presents itself, and to support actions to encourage balanced levels of demand.

In some ways the boom in international student demand can be regarded as significant as the forthcoming mining boom, or the rapid growth in the wine industry. It presents an amazing short and long term opportunity for the state to become more engaged with South East Asia into the future. To build on this foundation South Australia must focus on ensuring that international students have high quality educational and social experiences.

NOTES

1 Access Economics, *The Australian education sector and the economic contribution of international students*, April 2009, and Access Economics, *The economic contribution of international students and economic outlook in South Australia*, June 2009.

2 Source: AEI, Research Snapshot, *Export Income to Australia from Education Services in 2010. May 2010.*

3 ELICOS Australia Cost of Study ELICOS.com notes that 'The cost of English Language tuition in general ELICOS courses varies depending on the city you go to and the language centre you choose. Tuition Fees range from AUD$250 per week to AUD$350 per week for regular ELICOS courses, involving 25 hours of tuition per week' Other ELICOS data suggests that the average length of stay for students is 14.7 weeks. If it is assumed that tuition fees in South Australia are slightly below the national average (at $280 per week) this suggests the average cost per course/student is $4,122.

4 For comparison purposes, the report Brisbane, *City of Education: Economic Impact of International Students*, July 2007, identifies that 'The economic impact of international students for Brisbane is based on a variety of variables. In total, direct economic impacts were estimated to be $1.3b'. From their survey, they suggest education fees accounted for 40% of the expenditure, and other 60%. Accommodation was estimated at 27%.

5 The latest input output tables for the state of SA are for the year 2006/07 and have been prepared by Econsearch, and are presented with the report *Economic and Environmental Indicators for South Australia and its Regions, 2006/07* for the SA Department of Economic.

6 This is the methodology adopted in the Access Study. This is occasionally done in multiplier based studies, based on arguments that wages spend is less directly linked to immediate activity, and so this is a conservative adjustment. However, in sectors such as education where the cost structure is heavily labour oriented, it could also be considered that this results can be quite a significant understatement.

6 These are slightly lower results over all for 2007/08 than the Access study – primarily because of the different treatment of accommodation spend (with a proportion allocated to ownership of dwellings), treatment of retail trade as a margin industry and the fact that regional multipliers tend to be a little lower than national multipliers.

8 Modelling undertaken using Gempak Software – supplied by The Centre of Policy Studies, Monash University.

9 Giesecke, J., *The Domestic Economic Effects of Foreign Students, A CGE Analysis for Australia,* Centre of Policy Studies, and Giesecke, J., *Foreign Students and Regional Economies: A Multiregional General Equilibrium Analysis,* Centre of Policy Studies.

10 This implies an average of $3,800 per student enrolment on accommodation. As per previous assumptions, if it is assumed that the average student pays for accommodation for 48 weeks of a year (and of ELICOS students for 14.6 + 2 weeks), then the average accommodation spend implied is around $90 per week. This is somewhat lower than what students are advised as average accommodation costs, and also direct surveys. For example Harrison's Student Accommodation Survey 2008, undertaken for Education Adelaide indicates an average of $150 per week. The median rent in Adelaide is of the order of $245 for a two bedroom unit, and $299 for a three bedroom house. The lower level modelled here can be partly explained by the multiple tenancy, in the context that the average length of stay/rental costs is less than 48 weeks, and also by the qualitative evidence that there is some housing investment on behalf of international students (where the student would not pay any rent).

11 Harrison's survey concluded that the 'most important attributes for international students when selecting accommodation are:

- Cost (76%)
- Availability of public transport (67%)
- Safety / security (59%)
- Distance from institution (58%) – specifically, the ideal travelling time is between 5 to 15 minutes, walking or by transport.
- Furnished (48%)'.

REFERENCES

Access Economics. 2009, The Australian education sector and the economic contribution of international students, April.

Access Economics. 2009, The economic contribution of international students and economic outlook in South Australia, June.

Centre for the Study of Higher Education. 2009, The University of Melbourne, The impact of English language proficiency and workplace readiness on the employment outcomes of tertiary international students, August.

Deloitte Access Economics. 2011, Broader implications from a downturn in international Students, Report for Universities Australia, June.

Education Adelaide Fact Sheet. 2008, Harrison's Student Accommodation Survey.

Government of South Australia. 2010, Key Findings and State Government Response to the Taskforce on Enhancing the Overseas Student Experience in Adelaide.

Neri, F. and Ville, S. 2006, The Social Capital Experience of International Students in Australia: The Wollongong Experience, Faculty of Commerce – Economics Working Papers, University of Wollongong.

Strategy Policy and Research in Education Limited. 2009, The Nature of International Education in Australian Universities and its Benefits, September 2009, Report for Universities Australia.

South Australian Centre for Economic Studies. 2005, Economic Impact of International Education on SA.

Universities Australia media release. 2009, Thursday 15 October, Study highlights diverse, long-term benefits of international education.

CHAPTER 5

Asian Ambivalence and South Australian Parliamentary Travel

GREG McCARTHY and JENNIFER BAIN

INTRODUCTION

This chapter is divided into two parts, part one explores the theory of ambivalence toward Asia, which is the product of Australia's settler-colonial past, and this being framed by national ideological debates. The second part relates this ambivalence to the parliamentary travel of members of both the House of Assembly and the Legislative Council in South Australia. We argue that this travel is predominantly within a European logic, but that there is a tentative engagement with Asia by South Australian parliamentarians. In contrast, Premier Mike Rann and his ministers have concentrated their portfolio travel to Asian countries but there seems to be no clear overall pattern or strategic focus.

NATIONAL AMBIVALENCE TOWARDS ASIA

This opening section contends that there is ambivalence towards Asia within Australia that affects our contacts with Asian countries. This ambivalence is due to our settler-colonial history, where European culture is the touchstone of both the familiar and the superior. In this construction, Asia is the exotic other, which historically was essential to the imperial discourse but lingers on today in the form of a linear path to (Western) civilisation, where Asia is considered inferior to the West (Said 1978; Wang 2007; Ahluwalia 2010). This sense of superiority is an effect of both the remnants of colonialism, along with the imperial arm of US, which reinforces the notion of the West versus the rest dichotomy. Today, however, confronted by the economic decline of Europe and the over-extended reach of the US, Asia is seen as leading the world economically yet not culturally. The rise of the Asian giants; China, Japan and India has led to the notion of an Asian century to match the American century thus highlighting the urgent need to redress s the negative character of the ambivalent binary, where Western civilisation remains the highest order of development and social organisation.

Like their constituents, parliamentarians are shaped by this cultural sense of superiority towards Asia. For parliamentarians this cultural superiority is overlaid by the ideological contests between the political parties, principally played-out at the national level, where the political leaders seek to construct a political consensus that not only matches their world view but, by coinciding with the views of the voters, reinforces their electoral strategy. In recent times this electoral contest has been conducted over the notion of 'Australian values', which privileged Anglo-Saxon cultural, political and language norms over those of Asia (Johnson, Ahluwalia and McCarthy 2010). It was John Howard in campaigning for the prime ministership, who articulated this position most stridently when he said there was no need for Australia to start 'disavowing our history, or disowning our values, or changing our institutions' in order to improve relations with 'Asia' (Howard 1995).

Despite a tentative foreign policy approach to Asia, the Howard government developed relatively successful diplomatic and trading relations with Asian countries. Notwithstanding this success, "Asia" remained an ambivalent category for Howard. Indeed, part of his acceptance of the need to increase 'Asian' immigration, was his belief that Asians could fully integrate into Australian society by conforming to the norms and practices of Western civilisation. In general, Howard was consistent in the privileging of Western values over Asian values, and, in particular, those values which he believed Australia shares with other English-speaking countries such as Britain and the US (Howard 2006).

These dynamics changed with the election of the Mandarin speaking Kevin Rudd as Prime Minister in 2007. Like his Labor predecessors, Paul Keating and Bob Hawke, Rudd believed that the growth of the economies of China and India would transform the world's economic order, and he contended that to meet this challenge Australian children would need to be 'Asia literate' (Rudd 2007; see Keating,1992). His reflections on the place of Australia in Asia was founded on the belief that Australia could no longer rely on being the 'lucky country', where natural resources were the major basis for the maintaining a high standard of living. Instead, Australia would have to invest in productivity and human capital if it was/were to be competitive with Asia.

In short, Rudd and Howard had distinctly different ambivalences towards Asia. Howard was shaped by his strongly held view of the linear growth of civilisation, with the West as the pinnacle of human kind, though certain Asians, with guidance, could integrate into Western civilisation. In contrast, Rudd approached Asia from a position of concern, in which he argued that Australia was ill-equipped for the Asian century, and as such its status would decline as a middle-power. Both versions of this ambivalence required different engagements with Asia. Howard assumed a business as usual approach trading with Asian countries but remaining culturally separate. For his part, Rudd called for an urgent strategic approach to embrace Asia in a more calculated and culturally aware manner, to enable Australia to survive in this heightened competitive environment.

This study shows that South Australian parliamentarians were caught between these two positions. For the most part when travelling as parliamentarians the destinations were overwhelmingly Western countries, whereas in contrast, State Ministers orientation increasingly turned towards Asia for their ministerial travel. In general the politicians' approach, from both major parties, has been to follow that of John Howard, and engage with Western countries. There is a growing awareness however, by several parliamentarians, of the urgency to turn towards Asia in a far more strategic and culturally embracing manner. The following data reveals that more South Australian parliamentarians and ministers will need to shift their orientation to a more calculating approach toward Asia if the State is to benefit from the Asian century.

PARLIAMENTARY MEMBER'S TRAVEL AND OVERCOMING AMBIVALENCE

This section examines the travel by South Australian parliamentarians in the period 2002–2010, which coincide with the debates concerning the rise of Asia and the change in national leadership. Equally, it coincides with a fundamental shift in the South Australian exports and imports, with Asia replacing Europe and US as the number one source of export income for the State. The study shows that South Australian parliamentarians tend to follow traditional Western cultural (roots and) routes overseas rather than explore the diverse cultural and political nature of Asian countries. They do so out of personal familiarity with the West, but also with the rational of serving their constituents' European historical origins and pursuing their citizenship rights, particularly in Greece and Italy

In legislative terms, it is important to note that it is only since 1983 that South Australian parliamentarians have had the right to travel overseas at taxpayers' expense. The parliamentary travel allowances are set by the South Australian Remuneration Tribunal, which also sets the allowances for the judiciary and senior public servants (*Parliamentary Remuneration Act 1990*). While the Remuneration Tribunal sets the rules and allowances, it is the Cabinet that approves any member's overseas travel. Once the overseas travel has been taken, the member is required to present a written report, which is then tabled in the parliament. It is from these reports that we draw upon to determine both the overall pattern of travel and the reasons offered for that travel.

MEMBER'S TRAVEL BY DESTINATION

Between 2002 and 2010 there were 180 destinations visited by parliamentarians as part of their travel entitlement distinct from Ministerial trips when travelling overseas. Of these, there were 78 trips to the United Kingdom and Europe (43%), 27 trips to the United States and Canada(15%), 47 to the Asian region (27%), 15 to the Pacific region(8%), 5 to Africa (3%), 4 to Israel

(2%), 3 to the Middle East (1.6%)and 1 (0.5%) to South America (Figure 1 and Chart 1).

Figure 1: Parliamentary travel by destination 2002–2010

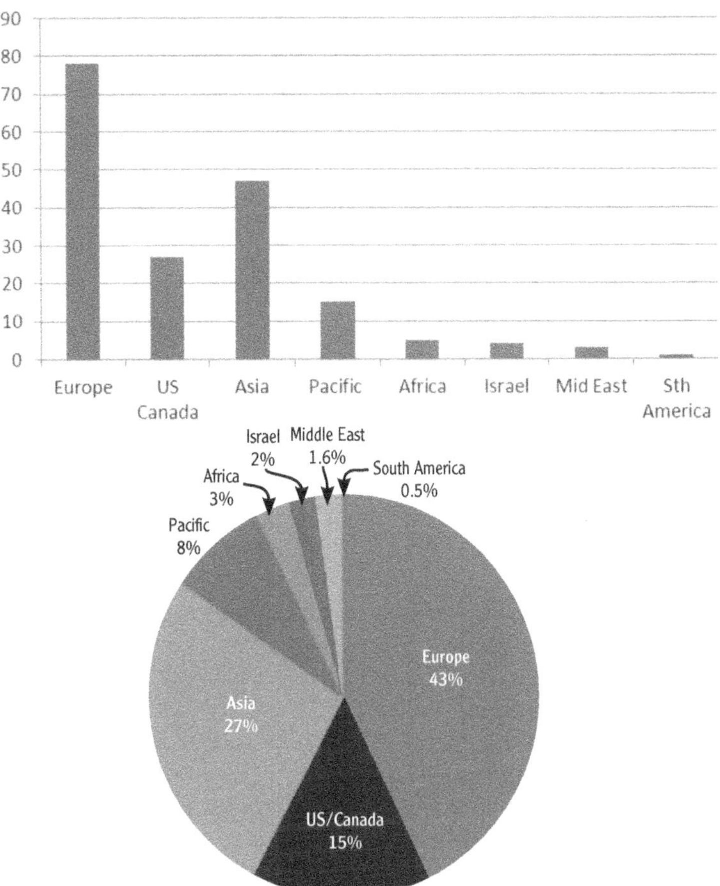

The general pattern of travel is related to the South Australian election cycle with elections held in 2002, 2006 and 2010. Parliamentarians tend to be busy on electoral politics in the twelve to eighteen months preceding State elections, then use the non-critical election periods for overseas study trips. As well, there is usually a lag time for reports to be tabled in parliament and this explains the relatively low result for 2010. In addition to the listed data in the tables, the pattern in 2011 remains consistent with the trend of privileging the West over Asia: there were 20 parliamentary trips; 3 to the US, 10 to Europe (including the UK), 6 to Asia (2 to Vietnam, 2 to China (one by Premier Rann), 1 to Singapore 1 to India by Minister Foley and one to the Galapagos Islands of South America.

Figure 2: Members' parliamentary travel by year asia versus non-Asia

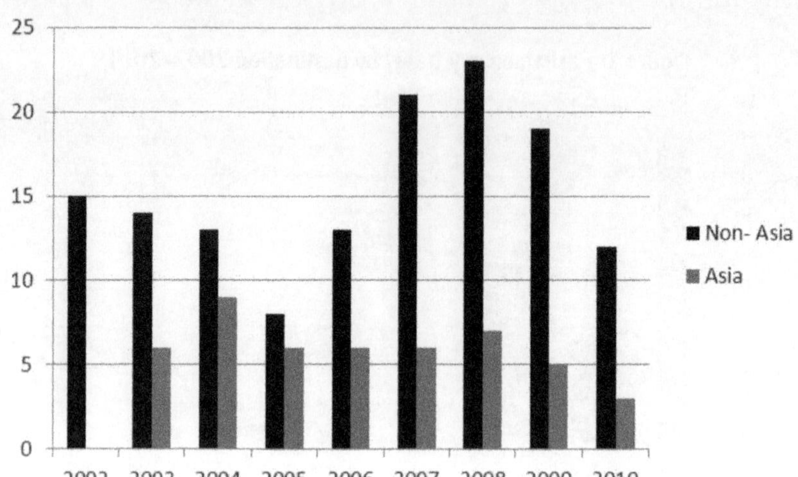

MEMBER'S TRAVEL BY CATEGORY

When the parliamentary travel by destination is broken down by category, economic justifications is the most common explanation for parliamentarian's trips. This justification is closely followed by parliamentary and governmental studies, then environmental policy, followed by exploring countries of their constituents' heritage. As well, parliamentarians investigated a wide range of social policy issues and women's policy areas.

In analysing theses parliamentary travel reports we have divided them into the following categories: Economic policy (EC), Parliament and government (PG), Environmental policy (EV), Social policy (SP), Women's policy (W) and Constituent – Diaspora reasons (C). There were usually multiple reasons for travel and categories blur (see Figures 3, 4 and Appendix A).

As the breakdown of parliamentary travel reports reveals, the most common reason given is that of furthering the State's economic development including pursuing economic opportunities for their electorates. However, there are also widespread reasons given for overseas travel, which are founded on policy issues pertaining to South Australia. These include transport, health systems, education, crime, water security and drought relief. As noted, parliamentarians also travel to develop their parliamentary skills via legislative conferences, investigating other Western parliaments and pursuing constituent issues.

In contrast, when travel to Asia is disaggregated from the general pattern, the reasons offered for travelling are weighted heavily towards the State's economic benefits rather than broad social and cultural policies or governance (see Table 4). In no small part this is because the political structures, policy processes, and the histories of Asian countries are little understood

Figure 3: Overall parliamentary members' travel by category

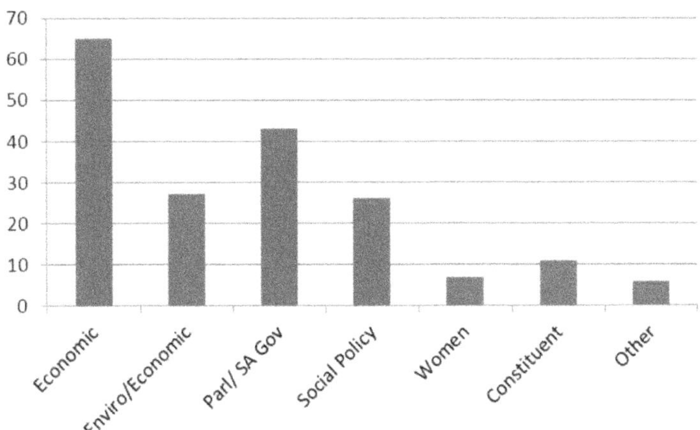

by the parliamentarians and the general public alike. Moreover, the language barriers and cultural specificities are genuine hurdles for political exchanges. Nevertheless, it seems to be a significant lost opportunity as many Asian countries are experiencing policy dilemmas akin to those of South Australia, including, for example, the implications of ageing populations, health expenditure and environmental concerns, notably in both Japan and China. Finally, what is evident in the travel reports by parliamentarians to Asia is the failure to showcase how South Australia could share its positive experiences of good governance, sound public administration and policies with Asian countries.

Figure 4: Parliamentary travel to Asia by category

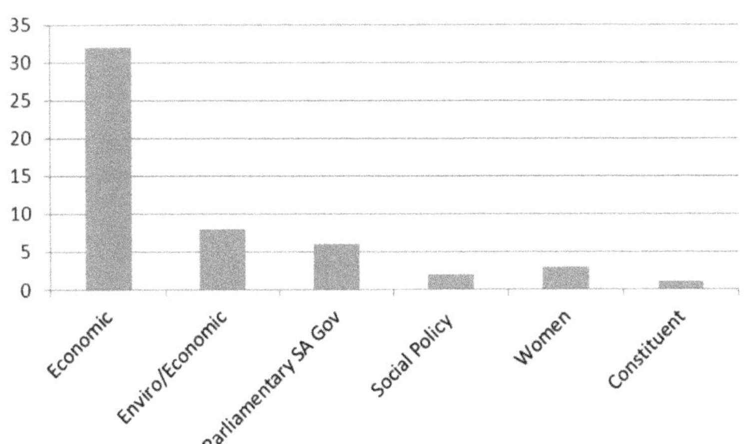

TRAVEL REPORTS BY MEMBERS

The development of the taxonomy on overseas travel reports shows that there are two notable trends. The first is the exploration of policies and governmental ties with liberal democratic countries, across a wide spectrum of concerns, is generally in keeping with John Howard's approach. The second trend, which is more in a developmental stage, is the engagement with Asia that follows Rudd's call for an urgent and strategic turn towards Asian countries and their cultures so as to sustain Australia's standard of living and its strategic role in the region. As the comments below indicate John Rau, Tom Koutsantonis and Martin Hamilton-Smith are advocates of a more holistic engagement with Asian countries (see Appendix A). This bipartisanship currently centres on China but there is also attention given to Malaysia and Vietnam, whilst Premier Rann has held had a sustained interest in India. What is striking in the parliamentary trips to Asia is the lack of parliamentary and ministerial travel to Japan given the long-term economic ties in the motor vehicle industry and overall limited engagement with India.

MINISTERIAL TRAVEL OVERSEAS

In comparison to trips taken by parliamentarians, where Europe and US-Canada predominated, overseas travel taken by ministers on ministerial business is heavily focused on Asia in no small part reflecting the shifting character of the State's export market from Europe to Asia. From the table below (Appendix B) there is clear evidence of ministerial engagement with Asia across a range of countries. The ministerial trip data was obtained via the Leader of the Opposition, Isobel Redmond, using a Freedom of Information request. The data shows that there were 57 overseas destinations, 46 being to Asia, 7 to the Middle East, 3 to Europe and 1 to the US. In effect, 80% of the ministerial trips were to Asia, compared to 26% for the parliamentarians. The implications of this disparity is that the ministers are following the tide of economic activity with Asia as opposed to the parliamentarians who explored a wider range of issues and interests not tied to portfolio imperatives. However, what is surprising about the ministerial travel, which accords/compares with that of the parliamentarians, is the lack of engagement with Japan with the exception of Treasurer Foley. India likewise, with the exception of Premier Rann has taken a strong interest in developing trade and cultural links. It seems he has not fully recognised the strategic potential of China only visiting the country on the odd occasion and has also neglected totally Japan. In general, there seems to be no coherent strategic or systematic approach by the ministers or the parliamentarians towards building, economic, cultural and personal ties with specific Asian countries.

CONCLUSION

The chapter commenced with Australia's ambivalent engagement with Asia, which can be traced back to at least the nineteenth century. This was highlighted since the 1990s by the different manner with which Prime Ministers Howard and Rudd dealt with Asia. Having set the context of the national ambivalence towards Asia we then turned to South Australia and explored how this was duplicated within State politics as represented in parliamentary travel overseas. The data collected shows a clear bias towards travel to Europe that matches the dominant cultural values of Australia and South Australia. The findings raise questions as to whether parliamentarians need to develop a wider perspective on the State's future direction in Asia rather than its European past, when they plan their taxpayer funded study trips.

Our analysis of South Australian parliamentary reports conforms to the contextual theory that there is a clear personal preference for overseas study tours to concentrate on European or U.S –Canada destinations, even though there has been a fundamental shift in South Australia's economic relations towards Asia. The overseas travel reports show that parliamentarians pursue issues relating to the South Australian economy in regions of the world where there is no language barriers and a common understanding of liberal-democratic traditions. South Australian parliamentarians also took advantage of the Westminster tradition, attending Commonwealth parliamentary conference engaging in debates on the functioning of Western democracies. There is also a keen interest in exploring environmental concerns such as wind-power and desalination in a variety of countries, from Israel to the United Kingdom and India. There were also numerous trips where parliamentarians sought to connect with the background of their constituents in Europe, especially in Italy and Greece. Finally, parliamentarians went to Europe and America to explore a wide range of social policy issues and to maintain South Australia's proud history of supporting women's rights.

When it came to Asia, South Australian parliamentarians were somewhat selective, concentrating on Singapore, Hong Kong, Malaysia, Vietnam and of late China. The trips to Singapore and Hong Kong are understandable as they are both stopping-over destinations and where the English language is readily spoken. The turn towards China is a natural flow on from it becoming the State's major trading partner. The reports indicate that there is bipartisan support for more constructive engagement with Asia in general, and China in particular, (e.g. Lea Stevens, Paul Holloway, Tom Koutsantonis, Martin Hamilton-Smith and Jing Lee)but that this will have to be built on a deeper cultural understanding of Asian societies, if the ambivalence is to be overcome.

When comparing parliamentarian travel overseas, based on their study trip entitlement with that of the Rann ministry, there was found a clear disjunction between the two groups. The ministers overwhelmingly travelled to Asia to pursue their portfolios, whereas parliamentarians predominantly went to Europe. In both cases, there is no systematic approach by either the parliamentarians or the ministers towards Asia and this is particularly clear in respect of Japan, China and India. A case in point, while Premier Rann has taken a keen interest in India other ministers have only travelled to India on two occasions; and parliamentarians have only visited a similar number in total. This example confirms our argument an ambivalence remains towards dealing with Asia, with both parliamentarians and ministers still have not recognising the need for a strategic engagement with specific Asian countries, in order to build respect and a deeper understanding between different cultures and historic backgrounds to be in a position to substantively engage with the shift in geopolitical power towards Asia. This strategic engagement needs to be shaped in terms of longitudinal cultural links that build on the economic and personal ties, importantly building on the potential that is created by the large influx of students who come from Asia to study in South Australia. However, this strategic turn is more likely to be slow in coming with the majority of parliamentarians remaining rooted in Western values for their overseas study trips at the expense of gaining a deeper understanding of Asian culture. Moreover, they are ignoring the economic opportunities currently existing in Asia that the potential to build South Australia's long-term prosperity.

Appendix A: Travel by date and Parliamentary members

Year	Member; Party;Chamber	Destination(s) on Members Report	1	2	Cat	Key reasons given/justifications
2002	J. Rankine ALP HA	USA Canada	Am		SP	Early intervention in Childhood health, Youth volunteering program
2002	K. Hanna ALP HA	UK	E		PG	Legal Aid, Crime Prevention, UK Parl., Biotech
2002	M.Williams & I. Venning LIB HA	SouthAfrica	Af		EC	Agriculture wine Industry, culture, gain political links
2002	R.Geraghty ALP HA	USA, Canada	Am		EV	Mass Rapid Transit System, ways to increase Public Transport patronage
2002	T. Koutsantonis ALP HA	Greece	E		CD	Links with Greek constituents, World Hellenic Assembly; Dual Citizenship, pensions
2002	R. Kerin LIB HA	Hong Kong London Italy	A	E	EC	Fisheries in HK, food & wine in UK & Italy
2002	J. Snelling ALP HA	UK	E		PG	Mental Capacity Bill, Policing H. of Public Accounts Comm., Parl System
2002	J. Rankine ALP HA	Can & USA	Am		SP	Early childhood health intervention
2002	J. Hall LIB HA	London, Madrid, Bilbao, Paris Reims	E		EC	Food, wine tourism, nuclear waste storage, World Conf. for Rural women; A Bilbao-Guggenheim for Adelaide?
2002	J. Scalzi LIB HA	Switz,Italy, Neth, Belg, Sweden, Russia, France	E		SP	Drug & alcohol Policy, Law & Order, Juvenile crime, Drug Summit
2002	J. Meier LIB HA	Scandinavia	E		PG	Parl systems, Renewable Energy, Nuclear & other Waste, Glass making
2002	L. Penfold LIB HA	Spain	E		W	World Conf for Rural Women
2002	D. Kotz LIB HA	Canada	Am		PG	CPA Conf
2002	V.Ciccarello ALP HA	Ottawa Rome London			PG	CPA Conf, Film Industry reps, SA expats
2003	L. Penfold LIB HA	India	A		W	Rural Womens Congress
2003	L. Penfold LIB HA	India	A		EV	Windpower & Desal, opps for SA food produce
2003	J. Hill ALP HA	USA	Am		PG	Health policies, Environment & conservation
2003	M.Brindall LIB HA	Fiji	P		SP	Multiculturalism in the Fijian context, relations to equity, economy & education
2003	M.Buckby LIB HA	USA	Am		SP	Chicago Children's Museum & Conf
2003	M. Brindall LIB HA	Thailand	A		EC	Mekong River Management policies, Education
2003	J. Rau ALP HA	Berlin, Germany	E		PG	Constitution & Parl system, drug policy & therapy centre
2003	D. McFetridge LIB HA	UK, Europe	E		EC	UK Public Dental, policing, Parliament, Voluntary Euthanasia Netherlands; Light Rail, Nuclear Waste France
2003	I. Gilfillin DEM LC	UK	E		EV	GM Crops & Foods
2003	I. Redmond LIB HA	North Dakota USA	Am		SP	Aged Care system in North Dakota, Hostels & Nursing Homes,GM foods
2003	J. Hall LIB HA	UK, Germany & USA	E	Am	EV	Water (Rhine River), nuclear waste disposal, immigration policy, tourism, problem gambling, women in politics

2003	P. Lewis IND HA	Indonesia	A		PG	Comm Parl Assoc Conf
2003	G. Gunn LIB HA	USA	Am	NZ	EC	GM crops & Citizen Initiated Ref
2003	W. Matthew LIB HA	UK	E		EC	World symposium on Nuclear Industries
2003	P. Lewis IND HA	Bangladesh	A		PG	Comm Parl Assoc Conf
2003	T. Cameron SA FIRST LC	Indonesia	A		EC	Foreign aid, Trade & investment
2003	L. Stevens ALP HA	NZ	P		PG	Aus & NZ Food Regulation
2003	M.Atkinson,ALP HA C. Zollo ALP LC& V. Cicarello ALP: HA,	Cyprus Greece Malta Italy	E		CD	Constituent links to Mediterranean countries.
2003	V. Chapman LIB HA	USA	Am		PG	Law & Order & Education
2003	V. Ciccarello ALP HA	Cyprus Greece Malta Italy	E		CD	Visiting countries of constituents, interpreter in Italy
2003	G.Thompson ALP HA	UK	E		SP	Youth Crime, Law & Order, Mental health care
2004	L. Breuer ALP HA	UK France Switzerland Germany	E		CD	European born constituents; alternative energy & aquaculture
2004	M. Hamilton Smith LIB HA	US	Am		EC	G'day LA, Silicon Valley, wine, tourism -direct flights to Adelaide, Caltech model for SA, 'We totally under appreciate the potential within our universities for economic growth generation' (12)
2004	R. Kerin LIB HA	Hong Kong	A		EC	Promoting SA farmed kingfish
2004	J. Rankine ALP HA	Singapore Hong Kong	A		EC	Food Industry contacts
2004	M. Brindall LIB HA	NZ	P		EV	NZ Natural Resource Management
2004	V. Chapman LIB HA	Japan	A		CD	Open art exhibition of constituent
2004	D. Brown LIB HA	UK & France	E		SP	British Health System, French biotech, wine Industry, Aus troops in WWI & II
2004	J. Meier LIB HA	UK	E		EV	Windfarms, visit Cornwall as 'Little Cornwall' in his electorate
2004	F. Bedford ALP HA	NZ	P		SP	Academic Conf communications & politics
2004	M. Hamilton Smith LIB HA	Singapore, UK & Cyprus	A	E	EC	Links Uni of Adelaide in Singapore, issues on behalf of SA Greek community, UK police system
2004	A. Redford LIB LC	Taiwan	A		EC	Economic & cultural delegation hosted by Taiwan Chamber of Comm
2004	M. Wright ALP HA	England, Spain, Switz, France	E		EC	Government\ processes & education
2004	A. Redford LIB LC	Singapore	A		PG	Racing Industry, Changi Prison- Correctional services
2004	J. Rankine ALP HA	UK & Spain	E		SP	Early childhood development, increase volunteering,- youth
2004	M. Brindall LIB HA	Thailand & Cambodia	A		EC	Economic Opp's, Australia/ Thai FTA
2004	M. Atkinson, V.Ciccarello ALP HA	Balkans, Slov, Croat, Bos & H, Serb & Mont	E		O	Yugoslavia post- Tito people, politics economy; relationship to SA,
2004	P. Lewis IND HA	Korea	A		EC	Education market, cultural exchange & trade development
2004	T.Cameron SA FIRST LC	Malaysia	A		EC	Trade & investment opportunities

2004	T. White ALP HA	Spain & Malaysia	E	A	PG	Tconf. post Madrid Bombing, urban development,Urban development Conf in Malaysia
2004	P. Lewis IND HA	Philippines	A		PG	Comm Parl Assoc Conf
2004	R.Lucas LIB LC	USA	Am		EC	Trade & Investment, economic development
2005	J. Hall LIB HA	Vietnam, Cambodia, Thailand, Malaysia	A		W	Trafficking of women & children in sex industry
2005	K. Reynolds DEM LC	Papua NG	P		O	Traditional law & culture in PNG compare to Aus Indigenous, Ausaid
2005	R. Kerin LIB HA	China	A		EC	
2005	D. Ridgway LIB LC	Portugal & Hong Kong	A		EV	Transport & Env Conf, Austrade in HK re closure of SA office
2005	T.Cameron SA FIRST LC	Thailand	A		EC	Trade & investment opportunities
2005	C.Schaefer LIB LC	UK	E		EC	Food & Wine Industry, biosecurity
2005	I. Gilfillin DEM LC	UK & Europe	E		EV	GM Crops & Foods
2005	I. Venning LIB HA	France, UK & California	E	Am	EC	Wine Expo in Bordeaux, Public Transport, met with conservative Party reps in UK, US- wine market, nuclear energy
2005	S.Kanck DEM LC	Tanzania	Af		W	Investigate rape & gendered Violence, HIV law & women's groups in Tanzania
2005	G.Thompson ALP HA	Canada & Boston	Am		SP	Foetal Alcohol Syndrome Domestic/ Family Violence initiatives, American Political Science Conf
2005	J.Dawkins LIB LC	Italy, France, UK, Ireland	E		EC	Trade & culture exchange in Italy & France, water management UK, utilising charity orgs, local gov in Ireland
2005	J. Rau ALP HA	China	A		EC	Experience first-hand changes taking place Chinese economy,speak to Chinese businessmen & gov officials 'There is a risk to Australia generally in too much focus on Business Migrants'.
2005	T.Cameron SA FIRST LC	Philippines & Hong Kong	A		EC	Trade & investment opportunities for SA, investment climate & laws,
2005	G. Gunn LIB HA	USA	Am		EC	GM crops,tattoo & body piercing Industry
2005	M. Hamilton Smith LIB HA	Thailand & Brunei	A		EC	Trade & Tourism, Karen refugees from Nth Thailand
2006	B.Such IND HA	Singapore	A		PG	Parliamentary System, Mass Transit Light Rail, Museums & SA Alumni
2006	T.Koutsantonis ALP HA	Singapore, China & Hong Kong	A		EC	China; said; 'I feel the need to explore the market which is set to benefit South Australians most', gain Chinese view of Australia, developing our markets
2006	B. Such IND HA	UK, Isle of Man, Canada	E	Am	PG	Comm Parl Assoc; Parliaments, Museums & Light Rail
2006	D.Ridgway LIB LC	France	E		PG	90th Anniversary ANZAC ceremony
2006	S. Key ALP HA	UK & Netherlands	E		SP	Voluntary Euthanasia & Palliative Care
2006	D.McFetridge LIB HA	Paris, London & NY	E	Am	EC	Nuclear Power France/ UK, Tourism,Arts centres & museums
2006	G.Thompson ALP HA	USA	Am		SP	Youth Crime, domestic violence & sexual assault, lower socio-economic areas
2006	J. Lomax Smith ALP HA	UK & France	E		PG	90th Anniversary ANZAC ceremony

2006	J. Rau ALP HA	China	A	EC Trade & commercial opportunities, visit Shanghai & Shangyu, recommends SA Parliam't set up a Parliam'tary Group focusing on China
2006	M.O'Brien ALP HA	UK	E	SP Studied Specialist High Schools in Eng & for lower social economic groups in SA
2006	D. McFetridge LIB HA	NZ	P	PG Comm Parl Assoc Conf
2006	L. Stevens ALP HA	NZ	P	PG Comm Parl Assoc Conf
2006	M. Atkinson, L.Simmons & V. Ciccarello ALP HA	Singapore & Vietnam	A	EC Economic policies, defence & police ties in Singapore, parliam'tary system & Human rights in Vietnam
2006	R. Kerin LIB HA	UK	E	EC Biotech & Food Industry, Aquaculture
2006	S. Key ALP HA	China	A	W Asian Media & Communications Forum & World Women Presidents Forum
2006	T. White ALP HA	France & Italy	E	EC Lobbying for International Engineering Conf for Adelaide in 2011, international student Industry in OECD
2006	V.Chapman LIB HA	England, France	E	PG UK historical ties with Australia, the similarity of our legislative & legal systems & our conventions overlapping.
2006	L. Stevens ALP HA with P. Holloway ALP LC	Hong Kong, Shanghai, Jinan, Qingdao, Beijing, Xian	A	EC With delegation 20th anniversary of sister state relationship with Shandong province, promote SA as the educational capital of Australia
2006	M. Lensink LIB LC	UK	E	W Attends Conservative Women's Conf, Mental Health
2007	K. Hanna IND HA	Egypt, Israel & Occupied Territories	ME	O Egypt Interested in religion, history & culture, poverty, Israel & Occ'p territories historical overview
2007	S. Kanck DEM LC	Palestine, Israel	I	SP Human Rights Abuse, Apartheid
2007	D. Ridgway LIB LC	UAE	ME	EV Biosaline, growing crops with saline water
2007	L. Stevens ALP HA	USA & Canada	Am	O Confucius Institutes (CI) in Vancouver & San Francisco as CI Ambassador, CIs, Port& Transport System
2007	M. Hamilton Smith LIB HA	Greece	E	CD Relationship between Greek villages & constituents, local origin of families & how this has contributed to SA life of Greek community
2007	V. Ciccarello ALP HA	Italy	E	EC Building ties with Puglia region, Education, Business
2007	M. Parnell Greens SA LC	UK	E	EV IPCC Conf, Comm. Parl Assoc Conf.
2007	S. Wade LIB LC	Singapore	A	EV Water Conf & tour of water infrastructure
2007	A. Evan FF-LCs	Indonesia	A	PG Christian Democrat political groups
Jul-07	J. Snelling ALP HA	Cook Islands	P	PG Comm Parl Assoc Conf
2007	M. O'Brien ALP HA	UK	E	PG Assess programs of Blair Governm't
2007	P. Caica ALP HA	China, Hong Kong Macau	A	EC Trade Mission
2007	T.Koutsantonis ALP HA	Greece	E	CD Invited by Greek Parliam't, this trip focus on pension rights
2007	G. Gago ALP LC	Germany, Sweden, Scotland, Ireland, Italy	E	EV Waste Managem't & Recycling (Env &min'g), Drug & alcohol policies, visit national parks in Scot/Ire
2007	I. Redmond LIB HA	NZ	P	PG Scrutiny of Legislation Conf
2007	I. Venning LIB HA	Chile, Argentina, Brazil, Peru, Bolivia	SA	EC Chile Chamber of Commerce potential sister relationship between Barossa Valley & Wine area in Chile, beef Industry; Iindigenous cultural tourism in Peru,potential for Australian Aboriginal tourism
2007	L.Simmons ALP HA	Italy	E	CD Visits region in Italy of Morialta constituents

2007	G. Gunn LIB HA	USA & Canada	Am		EC	Visits Nebraska- GM crops & rodeo regulation -
2007	I. Evans LIB HA	Singapore, India, Thailand	A		EV	Desal Plant Sing Trade, Com Parl conf in India
2007	L. Penfold LIB HA	Hong Kong, Mynanmar, Taiwan	A		EV	Business opps for Eyre Peninsula; trade,ports,fishing, aquaculture, agriculture techs
2007	L. Bignell ALP HA	Israel, Europe, Washington	I	E	O	Hebrew University & Israel education
2007	M. Lensink LIB LC	Israel	I		EV	SA water issues & Israel water policy
2007	V. Chapman LIB HA	Switzerland& Italy	E		SP	Health Systems in Switzerland & Rome, visited WHO.
2007	D. Pisoni LIB HA	USA	Am		PG	Gov services & delivery went to NY/ Wash, Mid West & California
2007	P. Holloway ALP LC	NZ	P		PG	Food Regulation Ministerial Council
2007	R. Lucas LIB LC	USA	Am		EC	Trade & investm't, eco developm't, contacts functions in NYC
2008	M. Hamilton Smith	Dubai	ME		EC	Desal Plant, tour of Jebel Ali man- made harbour port
2008	R. Kerin LIB HA	Dubai, India, Thailand, China	A		EC	Met with Aus, English & Scottish expats in Dubai on doing business in Dubai
2008	T. Kenyon ALP HA	Canada	Am		EC	Went as rep to largest mining conf. in the World to attract more mining
2008	L. Bignell ALP HA	Russia	E		EC	Building business ties & exports to Russia, wine & food
2008	M.Williams LIB HA	Singapore & Spain	E	A	EV	Studying desal'n Industry in Spain, water policy in Singapore
2008	M. Atkinson, ALP HA D.Hood, FF LC V. Ciccarello, C.Fox ALP HA,	UK, Poland Turkey	E		PG	Antisocial behaviour in UK,2006 SA election policy, Counterterrorism, surveillance CCTV, Pol& Economic Ops, Turkey Anzac & Aus ties
2008	M. O'Brien ALP HA	USA & Canada	E		EV	Study Transit Orientated Developm't- Portl&, San Francisco, San Diego, Sacram'to, Washington D.C & Vancouver
2008	R. Wortley ALP LC	Japan	A		EV	Underground system, Transport Union reps, Transport infrastructure, Education, Healt & various
2008	J. Rankine ALP HA	NZ	P		PG	Meeting with Aus Federal/ State & NZ reps Consumer Affairs Council
2008	J. Dawkins LIB LC	France, UK, Czech & UAE	E	ME	EC	Trade with SA agriculture, seafood, wine in each location
2008	R. Geraghty & L.Simmons ALP HA	Hong Kong	A		SP	Education, hospital 'cluster' system of hospitals & institutions
2008	S. Kanck DEM LC	Spain	E		SP	Alcohol & Harm Reduction Conf
2008	D. Ridgway LIB LC	UK	E		PG	Comm Parl Assoc Conf
2008	R. Lawson LIB LC	Sth Africa	Af		PG	Comm Parl Assoc Conf
2008	S. Key ALP HA	Greece	E		PG	ALP Delegate to Socialist International Congress
2008	S. Wade LIB LC	Canada & UK	Am	E	PG	Correctional Services, Disability & Road Safety
2008	T. White ALP HA	UK & France	E		W	Attends Women Engineers Conf lobbying for Adelaide conf 2011
2008	D. McFetridge LIB HA	Singapore, London, Netherlands, USA	E	Am	EV	Singapore – water & renewable, Portl& USA public transport/ light rail
2008	A. Pederick LIB HA	NZ	P		EE	Climate Change & Business Conf
2008	I. Venning LIB HA	Hong Kong & Canada	A	Am	EC	Opportunities for Barossa Boutique wineries in HK, in Canada agricultural/ trade issues GM crops, Wheat exp.

2008	J. Snelling & L. Simmons ALP HA	Singapore & Vietnam	A		EC	Trade Opportunities with both, Parliam'tary systems,human rights in Vietnam
2008	L. Stevens LIB HA	UK, Europe & Canada	E	Am	EV	Solar & renewables, rehab of the Rhine River in relation to River Torrens, Early Childhood Developm't
2008	A. Bressington IND LC	Sweden	E		SP	Attended World Forum against Drugs
2008	I. Evans LIB HA	NZ	P		EC	Study policy areas: Gambling, Building Reg, Tourism & Rugby
2008	G. Gunn LIB HA	France UK	E		EC	Anzac Day 90th Ann, GM crops
2008	T. Stephens LIB LC	Germany	E		EC	Looking at stadia used in German World Cup Soccer
2009	J. Gazzola ALP LC	UK, Ireland & USA	E	Am	SP	Child Protection Initiatives, Housing for Homeless, Disability funding
2009	L. Breuer ALP HA	UK	E		SP	Child abuse, sexual violence, gendered violence & Brit welfare.
2009	M. Hamilton Smith ALP HA	USA	Am		EC	G'day USA, met with business reps
2009	R. Wortley ALP LC	Vietnam	A		SP	Education, Employm't systems in Vietnam, plus Acquaculture
2009	I. Redmond LIB HA	UK & France	E		SP	Crime Reduction, Obesity in Elderly & ANZAC Service France
2009	M. Williams LIB HA	NZ	P		PG	Australian Public Accounts Committee Conf
2009	G. Thompson ALP HA	Canada	Am		EC	Wine Mission, urban design & Public Transport
2009	M.Atkinson & R. Geraghty ALP HA	Greece & Ukraine	E		CD	Issue of genocides- Greece& Ukraine
2009	J. Snelling ALP HA	UK, France & Czech Rep	E		PG	Parliam'tary systems, meetings with Dept Heads re structures & committees, Agent General, Nuclear Energy in UK
2009	S. Wade LIB HA	Singapore	A		EV	Singapore Internat'l Water Conference, water & waste infrastructure
2009	L. Bignell ALP HA	UK	E		EC	G'Day UK, SA wine, sustainablity concerns for SA, suburban sprawl, water
2009	G. Brock IND HA		A		EV	Investigate range of alternative energy technologies & acquaculture.
2009	R. Geraghty & L.Simmons ALP HA	Italy, France & UK	E		CD	Meet with Rep for Italians living overseas, 27 % of Morialta residents Italian, Hospitals in UK, school based nutrition system, UK parliam'ts
2009	T. Koutsantonis ALP HA	Greece	E		CD	Met with political leaders as rep of Hellenic Diaspora citizenship issues, Elgin Marbles, Pontian genocide
2009	G. Portolesi ALP HA	Calabria, Italy	E		EC	Educn higher research between SA & Calabria, 85,000 Italian heritage in SA, 30,000 CaALPrese
2009	I. Venning LIB HA	Tanzania	Af		PG	Comm Parl Assoc Conf
2009	B. Such IND HA	NZ	P		PG	Policing: Speed, Laser guns, domestic violence, Christchurch City Council structure & processes
2009	M. Lensink LIB LC	USA	Am		PG	Aus delegate to Conservative Conf 'International Democratic Union Youth Leaders Forum'
2009	T.Stephens LIB LC	Hong Kong	A		EC	International Wine & Spirits Fair, Attends Races
2009	T. White ALP HA	UK & Brussels	E		PG	Comm Parl Assoc Conf
2009	C. Fox ALP HA	Denmark	E		EV	Represented Premier Copenhagen Climate Summit

2010	D.Hood FF LC	Israel	I		EV	Water infrastructure, desal, water harvesting, 'religious harmony' invited by Chamber of Commerce, Uni Vice Chancellors delegation
2010	M. Rann ALP HA ALP HA	UK & USA	E	Am	EV	Economic, Climate Change, Social Policy, Crime, Urban Design, & Education
2010	S. Key	Netherlands	E		SP	Voluntary Euthanasia & success or failure of regulated sex Industry
2010	M. O'Brien ALP HA	China	A		EC	Problem of wine glut aim to lift SA markets in China, World Expo.
2010	F. Bedford ALP HA	UK	E		PG	Animal Management; Corruption commission, History Museum, natural childbirth, service clubs, SA suffragist Murial Matters
2010	G.Thompson ALP HA	Germany, England & Scotland	E		EV	Visits medium & High Density 'redevelopm't'/ Transit Oriented Developm't in Germany & then UK.
2010	M.Hamilton Smith; D.McFetridge, LIB HA C. Zollo, ALP LC	China	A		EC	Deepen understanding of China – 'a country which will play an increasingly important role in the lives of South Australians in coming years
2010	T. Stephens LIB LC	London, Croatia	E		EC	Tourism sector, links to SA Croatian Sporting Clubs
2010	B. Sneath ALP LC	Italy	E		SP	Joint Union Rally in Rome & Italian Consul re closure of consulate in Adelaide
2010	L. Breuer & R. Geraghty ALP HA	UK	E		SP	Gender issues, Community based welfare programs inc disabled into employm't, Welsh & Scottish Parliam'ts
2010	M. Atkinson ALP HA	Ethiopia	Af		O	Minister for multicultural affairs, description of Ethiopia
2010	I. Hunter ALP LC	Canada	Am		PG	Com Parl Assoc Conf
2010	R.Anderson LIB HA	Canada	Am		PG	Comm Parl Assoc Conf, Canadian political system
2010	A. Pederick LIB HA	Brussels & France	E		PG	Comm Parl Conf, International Governm't Institutions & European, WWI French Battlefields
2010	G. Brock IND HA	China	A		EC	Mining Conf, seeking companies to set up in Port Pirie

Party Code: ALP=Australian Labor Party; LIB= Liberal Party of Australia; IND=Independents; DEM=Australian Democrats; FF=Family First: SAFirst=South Australia First Party; Greens =Australian Greens Party

Chamber Code: HA= House of Assembly; LC =Legislative Council

Appendix B: Ministerial travel

Minister	Year	Country	Duration	Persons travelling (if known)
Premier Mike Rann	2002	Hong Kong	November	M Rann, C Hannon, S Halliday
	2003	South Korea, China	31/10 – 7/11	M Rann, Unknown
	2004	Spain, Germany, UK, United Arab Emirates	8/05 – 19/05	M Rann, A Duigan,
	2004	India	16/10 – 23/10	M Rann, Unknown
	2005	India	28/09 – 5/10	M Rann, Unknown
	2006	India	28/10 – 5/11	M Rann, Unknown
	2008	India	12/03 – 22/03	M Rann, L Parker, E Lange
	2008	China	6/10 – 13/10	M Rann, (B Cunningham), N Alexandrides, L Stevens (N Bolkus, C Schacht)
Treasurer Kevin Foley	2002	Singapore, Hong Kong, China	3/08 – 12/08	K Foley, B Tufnell, C Wall
	2004	Japan, France, Germany, UK	6/02 – 12/02	K Foley, M Brown, K McGloin
	2004	Japan	11/04 – 13/04	K Foley, K Ellis
	2004	Japan	15/05 – 18/05	K Foley, J Kent
	2005	China, USA	19/04 – 4/05	K Foley, E Lawson
	2006	Malaysia	22/04 – 26/04	K Foley, P Summerton, N Chapman
	2006	Japan	14/11 – 16/11	K Foley, DTED representative
	2006	Spain, Bahrain, United Arab Emirates	18/11 – 4/12	K Foley, S Leahy, N Chapman
	2007	Singapore	25/03 – 28/03	K Foley, S Sproule
	2007	China, Kuala Lumpur	14/04 – 24/04	K Foley, P Summerton, E Roberts
	2008	Malaysia, Philippines	5/07 – 14/07	K Foley, P McAvaney, S Swalling
	2009	Malaysia, Vietnam	16/04 – 24/04	K Foley, D Romeo, A McCormick
Paul Holloway Minister Mineral and Resources	2002	Korea, Japan, Hong Kong	21/04 – 28/04	P Holloway, K Gent
	2004	Hong Kong, China	20/04 – 30/04	P Holloway, spouse and staff
Minister Industry and Trade	2004	Malaysia, Thailand, Singapore	11/08 – 20/08	P Holloway and staff
	2004	Malaysia	9/09 – 13/09	P Holloway and staff
	2005	Japan, Hong Kong, China, Vietnam	3/06 – 17/06	P Holloway, K Gent, Ministerial Adviser
	2005	India, United Arab Emirates	24/09 – 5/10	P Holloway, K Gent, Media Adviser
	2006	China	4/11 – 14/11	P Holloway, spouse (at own cost), K Gent, Ministerial Adviser
	2008	China	April	P Holloway, K Gent
	2008	Laos	June	P Holloway
	2009	China	17/10 – 23/10	P Holloway, O Brown
Pat Conlon Minister for Energy	2007	United Arab Emirates	14/01 – 19/01	P Conlon, Unknown

REFERENCES

Ahluwalia, P. 2010, *Out of Africa: Post-structuralism's colonial roots.* London: Routledge.

Howard, The Australian, 4–5 May 2002, p. 1. Full text of interview at www.theaustralian.news.com.au/printpage/0.5942.4264645.00.html.

Howard, J. 1995, *The Role of Government: A Modern Liberal Approach.* The Menzies Research Centre, 1995 National Lecture Series. Parliament House, Canberra.

Howard, J. 2006, 'A Sense of Balance: the Australian Achievement in 2006', Address to the National Press Club 25 January 2006. PM's News Room: Speeches. Canberra: Department of Prime Minister and Cabinet. www.pm.gov.au/news/speeches/speech1754.html. Consulted 15 Feburary 2006.

Johnson. C. Ahluwalia, P. and McCarthy, G.2010, 'Australia's Ambivalence Re-Imagining ASIA', Australian Journal of Political Science, Volume, 45, 1, 2010, pp. 59–74.

Keating, P. 1992, 'Australia and "Asia" ', Asia-Australia Institute Address, Sydney, 7 April 1992, as cited in M. Ryan (ed.) *Advancing Australia: The Speeches of Paul Keating, Prime Minister*, pp. 187–196. Sydney: Big Picture Publications.

Rudd, K. 2007, Parliamentary Debates, House of Representatives, 10 May 2007, p. 134.

Rudd, K. 2008, A Conversation with China's Youth on the Future, Peking University, 9 April 2008. www.pm.gov.au/media/Speech/2008/speech_0176.cfm. Consulted 8/4/2011.

Rudd, K. 2008a, Press Conference Sanya. 12 April 2008. www.pm.gov.au/media/Interview/2008/interview_0192.cfm. Consulted 8/04/2011.

Said, E. 1978, *Orientalism.* New York:Vintage.

Sheridan, Greg ' "Asia" fears Rudd's China fixation', *Weekend Australian*, 3–4 May 2008, p. 3.

Wang H. 2007, 'The politics of imagining Asia: a genealogical analysis', *Inter-Asia Cultural Studies*, 8, 1, March 2007, 1–33.

Wesley, M. 2007, *The Howard Paradox: Australian Diplomacy in 'Asia' 1996–2006.* ABC, Sydney.

CHAPTER 6

South Australia and China

GERRY GROOT and GLEN STAFFORD[1]

INTRODUCTION

South Australia's engagement with China today is in many ways similar to what it was over one hundred and fifty years ago; marked by occasional outbursts of hyperbole and fear but surprisingly low key in light of China's dramatic rapid rise to become the state's largest trading partner, a key source of migrants and temporary home to thousands of Chinese students. Despite this growing importance, politically, culturally, socially and even commercially, levels of South Australian engagement and interaction with China are rather low-key. In this second decade of the 21st century when China has already become the world's second largest economy, other aspects, such as interest in learning Chinese, active interest in deepening political understanding, increasing cultural exchanges and the like, are only marginally more obvious than our interactions with any other Asian nation, or are even in decline. For example, when in April 2010, then Premier Mike Rann went to China on a rare official visit, it received minimal media coverage at home and no major announcements in mainstream media resulted. These low levels of interest fail to reflect China's rise or the opportunities this might present.

A remarkable aspect of Sino-South Australian interactions is that at least at first glance, the length, the scale and variety of interactions, particularly economic ones, have not resulted in any significant popular or even political consciousness except, perhaps, wariness. This situation is despite the obvious increases in the numbers of ethnic Chinese on South Australian streets, the rise of a substantial Chinatown around Adelaide's Central Market area, the post-1980s Chinese student boom, the ubiquity of the 'Made in China' label, the movement of local manufacturing to China and constant talk of the promise of the ever growing Chinese market. Recent fears of possible Chinese takeovers of local resources merely serve to highlight the impression that the more our relations with China change, the more some things seem to stay the same.

This chapter traces the development of Sino-South Australian relations by firstly describing our historical links and then the different stages of Chinese migrations to South Australia. This examination will illustrate the growth and changing nature of Chinese involvement in the state since formal settlement in1836. The current composition of the Chinese communities will be be outlined to highlight its complexity. As a result, it will become clear that any discussion of '*the*' or simply 'a' single Chinese community are misleading oversimplifications. A brief overview of the organisational make-up of these communities and their newspapers serves to emphasise these differences. Such an understanding will also help explain aspects of the subdued nature of their presence despite the increasing visibility and some prominent success stories. At a more institutional level, cultural exchanges are briefly outlined before the growing commercial and trade links are quantified. This is followed by a discussion of institutional and political links from the local to the state-to-province level which emphasises the growing power disparities between the two, in favour of China. The conclusion will stress recent state government initiatives which may help redress this growing imbalance and highlight the desirability of a broader approach to encourage China literacy and help South Australians benefit from relations with China, not only in economic terms but also much more broadly.

HISTORY

If those in England thinking about how to colonise South Australia at the beginning of the nineteenth century had done things perhaps only a little differently, the history of our relations with China, and even key aspects of Australian history would have been very different. Robert Gouger (1802–1846) for example, proposed supplying labour for the then yet to be established colony by drawing on Chinese sources (Rendell, 23). Little could he know that the street named after him would become synonymous with Chinese restaurants and China town. Somewhat later, Edward Gibbon Wakefield (1796–1862), apparently impressed by the accounts of Chinese workers in Penang and Singapore as sober hard working and obedient workers, also spoke very approvingly of them as potential labour in the new colony (Wakefield 1833, 272). After settlement in 1836 and the formalisation of government, the South Australian Legislative Council in 1847 also discussed schemes to import Chinese labour. It revisited the idea in 1852 when the new colony was struggling with the defection of many of its workers to the Victorian goldfields. However, these suggestions were rejected by the Colonial Secretary as a potential health burden (*South Australian Register*, September 4 1852). Nevertheless, a few Chinese did begin finding their way to the colony of their own accord (Rendell, 23). In 1842 for example, there was already a Chinese carpenter working in Port Adelaide (SACAS.com.au).

By 1845 there were fewer than three hundred Chinese across the whole of Australia, mostly brought in as agricultural labour (ABS, *Year Book Australia* 1928). By the 1850s, though, with the discovery of gold in Victoria, some of these workers moved to join in the rush and were soon joined by many more coming direct from China. Numbers soon reached around 50,000 and resentment from the white immigrants competing with them was almost immediate. The first attempts to restrict Chinese access came with Victoria's ten pound poll tax of 1855. Ships began sailing to Robe in South Australia from where the Chinese miners could walk overland to the goldfields and avoid the tax levied in Victoria's ports. In total perhaps more than 16,000 passed through Robe on their way towards Ballarat between 1857 and 1863 (Cawthorne 1974, np). Although a few found work on stations along the way or established market gardens en-route, as a whole, these men left little trace in South Australia except some landmarks, such as Chinamen's Well, named after them (Bell and Marsden, nd, 13).

Politically though, South Australian authorities soon came under pressure. Initially, the shock of the large numbers of arrivals aroused alarm in Adelaide and led to the dispatch of troopers from Adelaide to ensure matters did not get out of hand. However, as the Chinese moved eastwards as soon as practicable and were very orderly and disciplined, the troopers were soon recalled State Library of South Australia, South Australia's first Chinese panic had quietly evaporated. The second response required mollifying Victorian anger at the avoidance of their poll tax. South Australia too, began trying to first restrict and then prevent the arrival of more Chinese. In 1856, the colony passed its first anti-Chinese legislation. Domestically, political pressure also mounted quickly. By 1886, Adelaide trade unions were calling for the abolition of 'Chinese and coolie' migration on the grounds of unfair competition for local labour and claims that '... the presence of Chinese in largeness in any community has a very bad moral tendency' (*SA Register,* Sept 7 1886). In part because of this local hostility but also because the Chinese who came to Australia were overwhelmingly sojourners rather than migrants, men seeking to earn a good living, save money and return home. The numbers of Chinese in South Australia (excluding the Northern Territory which was also then governed from Adelaide), totalled a mere 347 in 1881 and dwindled to 251 plus 116 'half castes' in 1925 (ABS, Census 1925).

Despite the considerable obstacles, some of the few Chinese who remained, nevertheless managed to become successful. The cases of YSW Way Lee who came to Australia in 1874 and the Sym Choon family are reasonably well known. An entrepreneur and successful businessman Way Lee was naturalised in 1882 and became politically active as a critic of the mistreatment of fellow Chinese. He is commemorated with a building named in his honour at the University of South Australia (Burrit et al. 2009). John Sym Choon came to South Australia in 1890 and was unusual in managing to bring his wife. His subsequent business success, however, did not prevent him being assaulted on Adelaide streets. (*SA Register,* January 23 1903). Sym Choon's daughter, Gladys, is likewise notable for being a well-educated and successful entrepreneur. Gladys also inadvertently gave rise to what at the end of the twentieth century became a well-known Adelaide fashion brand, Miss Gladys Symchoon.

For perhaps the majority of the few nineteenth century arrivals, widely dispersed as market gardeners and in lowly occupations such as laundrymen and furniture makers, life was largely solitary and likely very lonely. They were severely limited by a lack of education in either Chinese or English. After Australian federation in 1901 they were also prevented from bringing brides from China as a deliberate consequence of the new White Australian Policy (WAP) aimed at excluding Asians from Australia and encouraging those present to leave. One of the few consolations for those in Adelaide was likely to have been participation in the religious rituals and probably the freemasonry-equivalent Hongmen 'joss' house celebrations at Town Acre 55 in Adelaide's West End (Eagle, Jose and Kean 2006, 9). Demolished in 1985, this tin temple to the god *Guandi* was the local centre for Chinese cultural celebrations which, presumably because many are conducted with dramatic costumes, drums, cymbals and fireworks, often attracted unwelcome attention from larrikins (SACAS). Some Chinese also attended the nearby Adelaide City Mission Chinese School in Light Square which operated for forty years from 1883 (SACAS). As a result the Chinese immigrants gradually assimilated as Christians but for decades there was effectively a Chinatown between Light Square, Morphett Street and Hindley Street with eighteen Chinese shops and other establishments around the temple (in Eagle Jose and Kean 2006, 11).

At the government level, South Australian politicians supported both the close scrutiny of Chinese labour and the WAP. Yet the action which had the most potential for long-term influence over relations with China was the colony's little-known enthusiastic participation in Australia's contribution to the suppression of the Boxer Uprising of 1899–1901. Protesting the activities of foreign missionaries and the expansion of railways and believing themselves impervious to bullets, the Boxers slaughtered thousands of Chinese Christians, killed European missionaries and eventually besieged Peking. Keen to support Britain, the Australian states sent troops and vessels in March 1900. South Australia sent *The Protector*, its only ship, but by the time it reached China, the naval action was over. *The Protector* eventually sailed home after having undergone extensive maintenance in Hong Kong at the expense of the British Admiralty (Nicholls 1986). More positively, a decade before in 1889, Adelaide had receive a special proclamation from the governors of Jiangsu and Anhui Provinces thanking South Australia's Chinese residents and the general citizenry for raising more than a thousand pounds to help relieve their terrible famine (History Trust of South Australia)

South Australia also provided missionaries to convert Chinese to Christianity. The most well-known of these was perhaps the Scot, William Fleming, who after failed attempts at being educated in Chinese at the Adelaide City Mission, was eventually sent to China where he was murdered in Guizhou in 1898 (Peterson, no date).

By 1940, the few remaining Chinese in South Australia were well established and their children had largely merged into the general population through intermarriage. It was the Second World War which led to a new influx of Chinese after 1945. Japan's defeat saw the effective end of European colonialism and the eventual rise of many newly independent Asian nations, changes which meant that more and more exceptions to the WAP had to be made to allow Asian visitors, including Chinese.

Relations with China itself were complicated by the Chinese Communist Party's civil war (1946–1949) with the Nationalist (Guomindang) government of the Republic of China. When the communists eventually defeated the Nationalists in 1949, the Australian government recognised the Nationalists, now isolated on the island of Taiwan (AKA Formosa) as China's legitimate government. As a result, there was very little direct interaction with the communist People's Republic of China (PRC) until after 1972 and Australia's switch of diplomatic recognition. There was, however, some interaction. Left-wing activist groups like the Australia China Friendship Society, at both national and state level, were active in demonstrating public support for the PRC from the mid-1960s onwards. The South Australian branch sold PRC publications from its East Bookshop in Rundle Street, collected English language books to be sent to China, organised tours and lobbied for Australia to switch diplomatic recognition to the People's Republic and away from Taiwan. One significant supporter of such recognition was Sir Walter Crocker, a distinguished former ambassador and later Governor of South Australia who both advocated such recognition and supported the Society's efforts (Crocker 1972, 204; *Australia-China Review*, August 1983).

The general Australia-PRC hiatus notwithstanding, the gradual easing of the WAP soon saw small but important new groups of Chinese visitors to South Australia. Key among these were students arriving under the Colombo Plan, established in 1949–1950 to promote interaction and understanding of particularly South and South East Asia, through student scholarships and academic exchanges. This initiative was very successful. By 1957, the *Adelaide News* could report: '… obviously it isn't easy for Asians to settle into life here. But it is probably easier than it was, say six or seven years ago. Instances of abysmal ignorance and intolerance have grown less' (Oakman 2010, 201). Partially as a result of exposure to these high profile, high achieving students, support for the full WAP had by the 1960s, declined to only 16% (Oakman 2010 211). A new problem had instead become how to overcome an increasing reluctance of such students to return home (Ibid. 97). These Colombo Plan students, especially those of Chinese descent, marked a key breach of the WAP. In 1950, the University of Adelaide enrolled 94 such students, including 50 from Malaysia, many of whom were ethnic Chinese, and a number of these eventually married local women (the father of Senator Penny Wong, the Federal Minister for Finance and Deregulation in 2011, being a notable example).

As immigration restrictions on Asians eased, a slow trickle of newcomers began. In the 1960s and 1970s migrants started coming via Hong Kong and from former British colonies such as Singapore and particularly Malaysia where anti-Chinese policies were hardening as Australia's were relaxing. No longer sojourners, these migrants were mostly professionals arriving together with wives and families. The manner of arrival of many other Chinese changed dramatically in 1975.

The end of the Indo-Chinese wars in South East Asia, beginning with the fall of South Vietnam to the communist Socialist Republic of (North) Vietnam in April 1975 and later Cambodia to the *Khmer Rouge*, was followed by Australia's first wave of Indo-Chinese 'boat people' refugees arriving in Darwin. About 33% of these arrivals were of Chinese descent (Price 1999, 16 fn 19) mainly Chaozhou (Teochow) and Cantonese speaking. However, in contrast to the situation of ethnic Vietnamese, many of these Chinese were able to readily take advantage of existing Chinese associations and adapt quickly (Viviani 1996, 122). The obvious manifestation of these new arrivals was a dramatic increase of Asian faces on Adelaide streets and a proliferation of Chinese/Vietnamese restaurants and shops. Many of the few existing such businesses owned by Cantonese speaking Hong Kong Chinese, gave way to the new arrivals.

At the same time, these Hong Kong migrants were boosted in the lead up to the Colony of Hong Kong's official return to Chinese sovereignty in 1997. Many emigrated to avoid any potential problems after the PRC regained control and because they had little faith in the PRC's policy of 'one country – two systems'. In the late 1980s and early 1990s, Hong Kong residents were the largest single group of Chinese migrants to Australia (Ip 2000).

This sudden influx of Asian settlers did not necessarily meet with approval from all quarters of South Australian society and there were recurrent outbreaks of anti-Asian racism and xenophobia, most notably from groups like National Action with their 'sink the boats' slogans and posters which attracted up to one hundred and fifty members and supporters to their Adelaide protests (Whitford 2011, 223) although not specifically anti-Chinese, from 1975 into the late-1990s. Writing in the context of 2011 though, this outbreak of fear and panic in some quarters now seems to have been relatively mild and the successful integration of these arrivals eventually allowed most of the fears of another 'Asian Invasion', to gradually dissipate even if racist elements in the general population have not necessarily disappeared.

THE CHINESE IN SOUTH AUSTRALIA TODAY

Australia's switch of diplomatic recognition from the Republic of China on Taiwan to the People's Republic of China in 1972, the abolition of the WAP, the beginnings of the rise of international education as an 'export' industry, together with the continuous loosening and refashioning of immigration rules to encourage skilled migration, had by the 1980s resulted in Australia receiving thousands of Mainland PRC Chinese arrivals. This new shift occurred as a result of dramatic changes within China. With the death of Mao Zedong in 1976 and the gradual economic reform and opening up that followed and accelerated in the 1980s, many took the first opportunity to legally leave China to seek work and better opportunities elsewhere, including as students. Between 1985 and 1990 Australia received over such 40,000 students, many of whom were using the cover of learning English or other vocational skills in order to find work or migrate permanently (Forster 1996, 116).

Most of these ostensible students would likely have been eventually forced to return to China but for the Chinese Government's violent suppression of the Chinese students' movement protesting the rising cost of living, lack of jobs and corruption of April–June 1989. The televised images of students, particularly those in Beijing's Tian'anmen Square, and of the use armed force to suppress them, together with fact that the students had been calling for more democracy and freedom, resonated strongly in Australia. Adelaide saw thousands of people, Chinese students and local supporters, marching along King William Street protesting against the Chinese Government. One consequence was the Hawke Labor Government's subsequent decision to give permanent residency to all Chinese students who arrived before June 30 1989. Later arrivals faced some conditions but these were still less onerous than for other potential migrants (Forster 1996, 117). As permanent residents, this group was able to begin the process of family reunion and bring over their spouses, children and, in many cases, elderly parents. Still, in 1991–92, China-born settler arrival comprised only 1.8% of the total for the state and remained below 200 per annum until beginning to increase in 2003–2004. By 2007–2008, the proportion of China-born arrivals peaked at 10.7%, a disproportionally large share of the national total (Yip 2010, 4). (See Figure 1) The PRC is now the state's third largest source of migrants, after the United Kingdom and the suddenly prominent India (See Figure 2)

Key to these increased numbers were changes to federal immigration policies that gave South Australia a small but important advantage when seeking new settlers. The Commonwealth policy of decentralising migration in the form of the Regional Sponsored Migration Scheme has been of particular importance as the whole state, including Adelaide, is defined as a regional centre. This definition has the effect of making Adelaide an easier entry point than the otherwise more attractive but harder to migrate to Sydney, Melbourne and Brisbane. Under the industry-sponsored 457 visa class, Chinese migrants have also moved to regional areas proper, such as Murray Bridge, where employment rates were very high at 88% (Yip, 2010 122). These forms of sponsored migration have become particularly important, reaching 30% in 2005–06 and continue at high levels (Yip 2010, 32).

Business migration has also contributed to South Australian development. The state government's Business Migration Team, part of Immigration SA, promotes, assesses and helps local business sponsor business migrants. In 2007–2008 there were 296 such business migrants to the state (Yip 2010, 77). The same year this group made up 69% of the state's total business migrant intake (Ibid, 78) Figure 2 also points to another key source of migrants,

Chinese students who stay on after completing their degrees, 525 out of a total 1430 new settlers in 2008–2009 who were overwhelmingly young professionals albeit with a significant number had trouble finding suitable work (Ibid, 120)

The other important group of Chinese in Australia, Taiwan-born or emigrants from Taiwan, is not strongly represented in South Australia with only about 500 arriving between 1982 and 1999 (Ip 2001). Despite being a particular target of business migration recruitment the presence of Taiwanese is perhaps the most low key of all Chinese groups and there were only 620 in the state in 2006 (Dept of Immigration and Citizenship).

Figure 1: Settler arrivals to SA by birthplace – China

Source: DIAC Settler Arrivals

Figure 2: Top 10 Source countries, permanent additions, SA 2008–2009

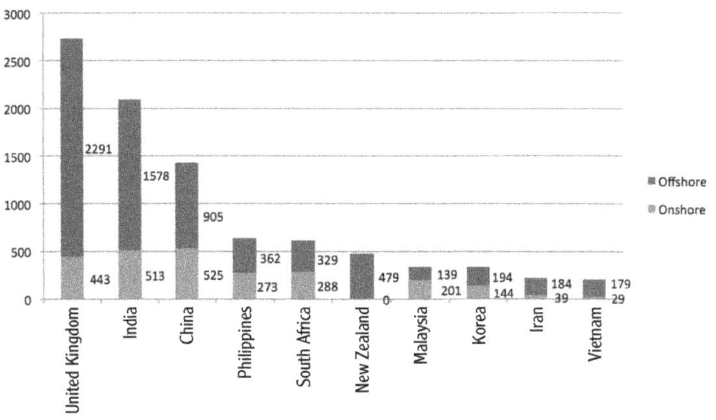

Source: DIAC Settler Arrivals

This analysis of the history and composition of the state's Chinese community helps explain why by the 2006 census, the state had some 25,366 ethnic Chinese of whom only 8,076 were China-born and only 1,185 had both parents born in Australia (Department of Immigration and Citizenship). Since the 2006 Census China-born settlers continued arriving at around 1000 per year to total 14,140 by December 2010 (MulticulturalSA 2010) as clearly reflected in Figure 1. The new Chinese migrants are also boosted substantially by the more than 13,000 Chinese students (in 2010) studying at all levels, from primary school to TAFE and university (Rann 2011). Significantly though, even among the 8,000 Chinese-born in the 2006 census, self-identifying speakers of the official language, Mandarin, only comprised some 5,000. 'Chinese' as a description of ethnicity then, covers groups of many different origins and backgrounds. However, PRC-born Chinese are increasing rapidly and changing the composition of the notional Chinese community in important ways.

On a related note, South Australia is also home to the nation's largest grouping of Uighurs, a Turkic people from the PRC's western region, particularly Xinjiang, it is doubtful, however, if many identify themselves as 'Chinese'. One relatively casual estimate puts the number of Uighurs in Australia at approximately 2,000, with half living in South Australia (Migration Museum of South Australia 2011). Similarly, there are also a small number of ethnic Tibetan immigrants from the PRC. Technically, ethnic Tibetans and Uighurs are also China-born and this may mean that that the figures which can be so readily taken to imply that China born equates with the Han Chinese majority, may be somewhat misleading.

Organisationally, the nominal 'Chinese community' comprises numerous, often relatively small groups which effectively represent different countries of origin, language groups, politics and interests. Of these, the business related organisations are of most interest because even those representing what the Chinese and Taiwanese governments would regard as 'Overseas Chinese', can be useful vehicles for doing trade with China, Taiwan or others in the extensive Chinese Diaspora. The earliest known Chinese group was active more than a century ago. The Chinese Emperor Reform Association was active in Adelaide agitating for support for Chinese political modernisation (*The Advertiser* May 11 1907).

In 1971 the Chinese Association of South Australia was formed and has operated out of clubrooms in Black Forest since 1984 (Personal communication with Dr Yen Chingwang) Today, perhaps the most inclusive organisation is the long established Chinese Welfare Association of South Australia. Special interest groups include the Australian Chinese Medical Association which brings together Chinese doctors while a number of Chinese groups including the Overseas Chinese Association of SA, also run six Saturday language schools teaching Mandarin Chinese. Others include the Mainland Chinese Association helping more recent arrivals while the state's small numbers of Taiwanese are represented by the Taiwanese Association of South Australia.

There is also some considerable effort by PRC students and academics to organise across the many campuses of the three universities with the Chinese Students Association and the Federation of Chinese Scholars in Australia, to mention a few, are very active in supporting their constituencies and often work closely with Chinese embassy officials (Feng 2011).

Much more obvious are the numerous commerce and trade related organisations reflecting the diverse backgrounds of many Chinese migrants, such as the Hong Kong Business Association, The Chinese Chamber of Commerce, The Australian Singapore Business Association, the Australia Brunei Darussalam Business Council, and the Australia Malaysia Business Council and perhaps others. These were recently joined by the China-Australia Entrepreneurs Association Inc. (CAEAI), a more inherently commercial group with provides newly arrived PRC business migrants with services including clubrooms and it has a strong focus on facilitating relationship building such as supporting for example, the Flinders Ports-Xiamen Port city deal and council sister-city links. It also publishes its own glossy magazine, *China Australia Entrepreneurs* notable for its inclusion of letters of congratulations from the premier Mike Rann, the Chinese ambassador and other political notables, on its 2009 launch (*China Australia Entrepreneurs* September 2009).

The other important trade-related organisation is the local branch of the Australian China Business Council (ACBC). With membership overlapping the ethnically-based ones, the ACBC supports businesses trading with China and is actively involved with making representations to government, participating in official trade missions and as part of the Council for International Trade and Commerce of South Australia (CITSA).

Another reflection of the variety within the Chinese communities is the number of Chinese newspapers, each of which tends to target a different audience and which are distributed for free. The oldest, the *South Australian Chinese Weekly* (Nanao shibao) and its readership seems to be mostly Overseas Chinese and Taiwanese although it has become more inclusive with each new wave of migrants. The newest, *Adelaide Chinese News* (Xin bao) is aimed at Mainlanders as is the more recent *I-Age* (I-shidai) which seems to straddle a middle ground. Another publication, the Christian *Sameway* (Tonglu ren) founded in 2005, is also relatively inclusive of a wide variety of Chinese groups reflecting its religious outlook and highlighting the growing influence of Christianity among all such groups. In related vein, another paper with wide distribution but published elsewhere is *Epoch Times* [Dajiyuan shibao], the qigong meditation religious group Falun gong mouth-piece, which runs a strong anti-communist line.

Despite the Chinese population having grown substantially, it is only in recent times that some Chinese South Australians from the post-1970s arrivals became well known. In the 1980s, Malaysian-born Cheong Liew for example, rose to first local and national prominence as a chef and became internationally famous as a proponent of 'fusion' food. His cousin, Khai Liew, has become a famous furniture designer. In just the last few years, the artist Poh-Ling Yeow also became a nationwide celebrity as a chef after appearing on the reality TV series Masterchef, in 2009. Adam Liaw subsequently shot to prominence the same way.

In politics though, influence has been diffuse. This is despite some high profile successes such the election of China-born Alfred Huang to the Adelaide city Council in 1992 and as Lord Mayor of Adelaide in 2000. The mayoral election of 2010 were also notable the vigorous but ultimately unsuccessful attempt by Brunei emigrant Francis Wong to become the second Chinese mayor. Malaysian-born Ms Jing Lee was elected to the South Australian legislative council in 2010 but has been a low-key presence since. At present, the state's Chinese are still effectively a collection of numerous disparate groups, a feature working strongly against the ability to develop political influence. As the numbers of PRC arrivals in particular continue to increase rapidly, this may change although there is a strong tendency to avoid overt involvement in mainstream politics among all groups, perhaps particularly the latter. Feng argues that as result of political indoctrination in China, those who came as a result of the events of 1989 require considerable and painful 'resocialisation' to allow them to embrace liberal democracy (Feng 2011). However, the post-1990s Chinese student, subjected to intensive 'patriotic education' in the wake of the events of 1989, are heavily influenced by PRC state-sponsored transnationalism and hence often inclined to vociferous protests at events seen by them as anti-Chinese in the light of such education. The most telling example of this process was the 'Protect the Torch' rallies and protests against Western media depictions of Chinese government action against Tibetans in the lead up to the 2008 Beijing Olympics (Feng 2011, 126). Thousands of students, including several busloads of students from Adelaide, went to Canberra to participate. This nationalism also encourages many students to work for causes which they see as promoting China, such as Confucius Institutes, language teaching and other cultural initiatives.

CULTURAL EXCHANGES

The switching of diplomatic recognition to the PRC in 1972 and the subsequent establishment of the Shandong-South Australia Sister Province relationship, allowed among other things, the beginnings of cultural exchanges most notable for the impact of Chinese exchanges, particularly blockbuster art exhibitions. One Consequence of diplomatic recognition was *The Chinese Exhibition* national tour triumph of 1977. Nationwide, almost 600,000 people went to see it and it was similarly successful in Adelaide, setting the scene for the follow up Qin Shihuang *Entombed Warriors Exhibition* of 1983 and the 1993 *Imperial China* Exhibition. Crucial to the ability to mount such blockbusters however, was Commonwealth support via the International Cultural Corporation of Australia ltd and substantial commercial sponsorship.

The establishment of the South Australia-Shandong Sister State relation in 1986, also led to numerous smaller exchanges, notably by South Australian musicians touring China and visits by groups such as the Shandong Tradition Music Orchestra but these initiatives are not comparable to the blockbusters of previous decades. There have been some initiatives such as the University of South Australia's *Writing a Painting Project* of 2006, combining Chinese and Aboriginal influences (Eagle, Jose and Kean 2006). However, perhaps the most significant initiative promoting Chinese culture but certainly not limited to China, has been the increasing importance of the OzAsia Festival. Since it began in 2008, OzAsia has promoted Asian artists and culture of all sorts and every year includes contributions from both the PRC and the Chinese Diaspora more generally. Original works with substantial local involvement include Gabriella Smart's work with noted Chinese composer Tan Dun. One of the festival's great successes has been its promotion of the Chinese Lantern Festival which draws in participants from schools across the state as well as many Chinese and Asian community groups to parade their specially made and usually fantastic lanterns. During OzAsia in 2010 it also attracted some 18,000 spectators to the Festival Theatre (ABC 7.30 Statewide, Sept 2 2011)

Panda diplomacy is perhaps the most obvious manifestation of cultural exchange and goodwill building in South Australia. In late October 2009, *China Daily* announced that 'Panda diplomacy helps repair Sino-Australian rift'. As result of intensive diplomatic efforts by then Prime Minister John Howard and Foreign Minister, Alexander Downer starting in 2007, pandas Wang Wang and Funi arrived with great fanfare in Adelaide in December 2009. The pandas are actually on loan at considerable cost, some $10 million over ten years and it was hoped that the resultant boost in visitor numbers would more than compensate costs incurred. Despite a major rise in visitors, this boon had not materialised by 2011 and the zoo was instead facing financial difficulties (*The Australian*, 22 June 2011).

Another important element helping to raise the local public profile of both Chinese culture and particularly, Shandong, has been the establishment of the Confucius Institute at the University of Adelaide (CI) in 2007, then only the third in the nation. The CI, supported by the University and the Chinese Government via the Chinese National Office for Teaching Chinese as a Foreign Language (Hanban), promotes the learning of Chinese and interest in Chinese culture. However, as each Institute has a great deal of flexibility to chart its own course and in addition to liaising with and supporting Chinese community groups, language teachers, the Adelaide CI has been active in trying to broaden its appeal and utility to all parties interested in dealing with China has worked closely with the Australia China Business Council (South Australian branch) from its inception.

ECONOMIC LINKS

Elsewhere in this volume, South Australia's relationship with Japan was described as 'wide ranging and deep rooted' but relations with China are not only similarly deep and wide, in contrast with many other longstanding relationships, they are deepening and growing fast. In 2009–2010 China-bound exports reached $1.251 billion, 2.7% of the national total, surpassing the United States, hitherto the state's major trading partner (DFAT, Aust trade by state and territory 2009–10, 17). If Hong Kong is added, the total reaches $1.528 billion. This contribution amounts to a significant part of the state's 4% share of national exports and 6.3% of GDP (Smith 2011, 4 fn 6)

The composition of these exports in Figure 3 reflects a recent but fundamental shift from agricultural products and copper, towards a growing emphasis on mining more generally, mainly ores and concentrates, together with rapid growth in the export of beverages, principally wine. The latter is high profile and relatively labour intensive while the long awaited mining boom of which the ores are a key part, is not only extremely capital intensive and employing few people directly, it is largely out of sight in the state's deserts where few Adelaideans go. To-date, large investments in mining include Sinosteel Uranium, a joint venture with PepininNini and the China National Offshore Oil Corporation (CNOOC) joint venture with Altona and Arkalinga in coal and oil.

Figure 3: Exports from South Australian to China by commodity – Top 4 1999–2009 ($'000s)

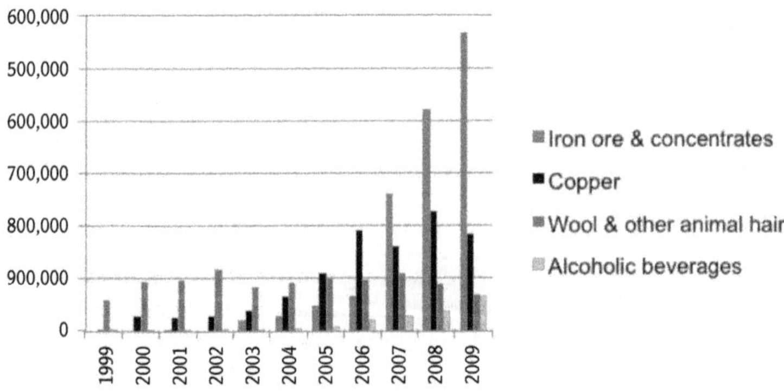

Source: ABS, Catalogue 5368.0 International Trade in Goods and Services

The Chinese use of Australian exports, among others, to produce manufactured products for export is also clearly reflected in South Australia's imports as reflected in Figure 4 which clearly depicts the ever increasing proportion of Chinese imports and indirectly partially reflects the shift of manufacturing to China, including by South Australian companies. Famously

Adelaide manufacturers like Hill's Industries and Gerard Corporation, formerly Gerard Industries, are notable examples of this trend to manufacture offshore to stay competitive, vital for any company but contributing to the steady decline of local manufacturing.

Figure 4: Imports to South Australia from China by commodity – Top 4 1999–2009 ($'000s)

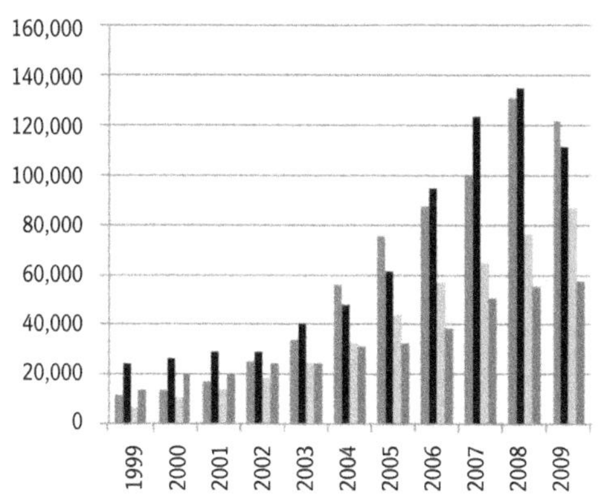

Source: ABS, Catalogue 5368.0 International Trade in Goods and Services

The other key aspects of mutual trade are those of education and tourism. Unfortunately, Figure 5 implies that inbound tourism has declined since the peak of 2006–2007 although anecdotal evidence indicates that numbers have risen since. South Australia's share of the Chinese tourism market is small, accounting for only around 1% of Australia's total.

Figure 5: Visitors to South Australia from China

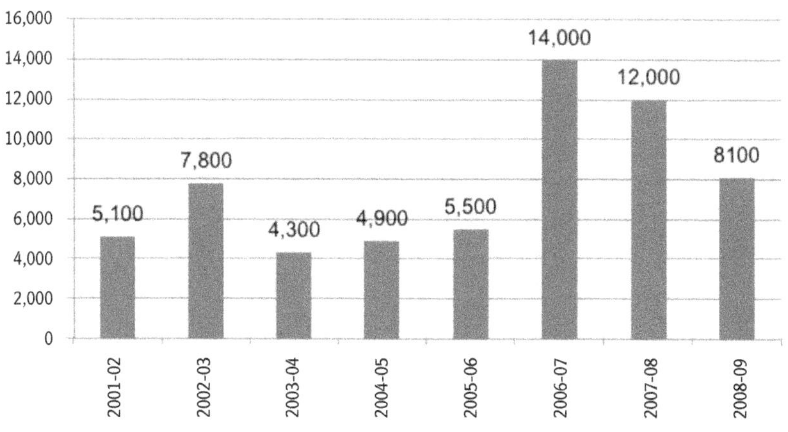

In education though, the story is in many ways much more positive it is not without problems. In 2000, education as an export was worth $196 million. In 2010 education earnings reached $1.05 billion (DFAT Aust trade by state 80), 5.6% of the national total, a success in line with South Australia's population and share of the economy generally. Chinese students make up the bulk of this growth and the dramatic increase in their numbers at all levels of the education system is clear reflected below in Figure 6. The total number of such students in 2010 exceeded 13,000.

Figure 6: International students from China in South Australia (enrolments)

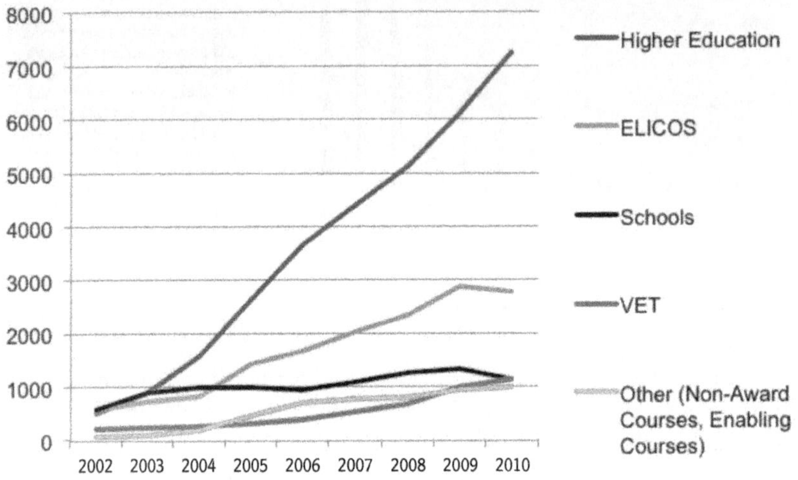

Source: Australian Education International

INSTITUTIONAL AND POLITICAL LINKS

This growth of Sino-South Australian economic relations has been the basis for the development of political link. Current institutional and political links are now much more positive than in the twentieth century. Both the state government and local governments have been actively building relations although it is often difficult to assess how successful these have been even after several decades.

South Australian Local governments have attempted to establish sister-city relationships with numerous cities and regions in China:

- Charles Sturt Council: Qingzhou City, Shandong and Yicheng City, Hubei
- Renmark Paringa: Shishi City, Fujian
- Whyalla: Erzhou, Hubei
- Port Adelaide: Yantai, Shandong

- Port Pirie: Suizhou, Hubei
- Murray Bridge: Sanmenxia, Henan (ceased)

None of these arrangements have been obvious successes and they seem to exist more in name than in substance. While such linkages may have looked attractive to Chinese partners in the 1980s and early 1990s, the growth of the Chinese economy has been such that the attraction of Australian partners is likely to have waned very quickly. The nature of Chinese local governments (politically powerful, centrally controlled often resource rich municipal authorities with no concerns about re-election) – compared to Australian councils (large areas, small population, administratively and financially weak and dependent which also lack much ability to influence or direct foreign investment) meant that any Chinese hopes of substantial Australian investments were unachievable. This problem of power imbalance is implicitly recognised by the Commonwealth (See the 2005 *Commonwealth Report on the Australia China Relationship*, Chapter 16, 330) and, bearing in mind that the total population of South Australia is only 1,650,000 (ABS 2010) when in 2000 China already had 138 cities with more than one million, the power discrepancies become stark.

Although there was keen interest from Chinese local authorities in visiting South Australia, this soon became a financial burden on local councils with the result that the South Australian Local Government Association established a for-profit body to organise such visits. The main motive from the Chinese side had become as excuses to allow travel junkets (Groot, Interview 2009 and Goodman in Mackerras 1996, 175). It seems significant then that there was no South Australian contribution to the 2005 *Commonwealth Report on the Australia China Relationship* which concluded that there was 'Considerable evidence' that sub-national relations between Australia and China had strengthened. In South Australia though, it is not clear, that they have brought about any clear economic or other advantages.

At an even lower level but worth noting, have been a number of sister-school relations such as the Saint Peters College relationship with Shanghai's City West High School. There are also regular trips to China by South Australian students learning Mandarin Chinese or interested in aspects of Chinese culture. These relationships may well bear long-term fruit but are not centrally coordinated or facilitated by the Department of Education and Children Services (DECS) nor records kept. Goodman noted a number of these relationships in the early 1990s but again, there is little evidence of tangible long-term benefits (in Mackerras 1996, 183). In the past, DECS helped send school principals on tours of China but in recent times, the Confucius Institute in conjunction with Shandong University has organised four such tours and one for October 2011.

The state's universities have also had a longstanding interest in developing relations with China at many levels, from academic exchange to recruitment of students and mutual study-abroad agreements and scholarships. Flinders University for example, has a long running and highly successful offshore program with Nankai University in Tianjin dating from 2000 from which more than 1500 people have since graduated.

Perhaps the most obvious example of cooperation has come from the University of Adelaide's sister university agreement with Shandong University in the form of Australia's third Confucius Institute. Shandong provides staff and student volunteers to help the Institutes work in South Australia and helps organise study and travel opportunities to China.

The origins of South Australia's relationship with Shandong Province (population 96 million) reveal a complex mix of political approaches by the Chinese side. Unofficial expressions of interest in such a relationship were passed to the state government by members of the Australia China Friendship Society. The Minister of Agriculture, Frank Blevins visited Shandong in 1985 and Professor Andrew J. Watson of the University of Adelaide's Centre for Asian Studies subsequently carried out preparatory research on behalf of the state government. On April 3, 1986 Labor Premier John Bannon signed the formal Sister-State relationship documents in Ji'nan, Shandong's capital while Governor Li Chang'an signed on behalf of the Shandong Provincial People's Government. The new relationship was intended, according to Bannon, 'to … greatly assist the flow of information, advice and practical support available from the Australian Government on projects of mutual interest' (*Australia China Review*, August 1986). The 25th anniversary was celebrated in 2011 with reciprocal visits: Premier Mike Rann to Shandong in April and a visit to Adelaide by Shandong Vice-Governor Guo Zhaoxin in October 2011.

Sometime after the relationship was established, South Australian offices were established first in Shanghai in 1995 with the appointment of Mr Ken Xu as the South Australian Commercial Representative. An office in Shandong's capital Ji'nan, was opened later. By 2006, the Shanghai office had to expand to larger premises and was reorganised in 2011, presumably to reflect the growing bilateral trade.

Yet, despite South Australian ministerial visits to China being heavily trade-related (See McCarthy and Bain, this volume) and the subsequent considerable investment in trade offices, it could not be said that there was any clear strategy to boost trade relations and develop a comprehensive whole of government approach to support it. Only in early 2011 did the government move towards such an approach. An important catalyst in this move seems to have been the January 2011 white paper released as part of the China Briefing events by the Confucius Institute and the state Australia China Business Council, *Business Engagement with China: a strategy for South Australia's future?* (Wheatley 2011). The ACBC had long advocated a systematic and substantial approach to dealing with China and whitepaper was followed by extensive consultations with DTED to draw up a detailed strategy for dealing with China. Another push in this direction was a detailed discussion paper by opposition MP, Martin Hamilton-Smith, the Shadow Minister for Industry and Trade in June 2011. Whatever the motivators, a comprehensive strategy with involvement across all departments is much more likely to bring significant economic rewards and possibly accompanying cultural and social ones than achieved hitherto.

It's perhaps worth noting that Hamilton-Smith was one of the six parliamentarians who participated in the first Confucius Institute-organised study tour of China for state legislators in 2010. A second followed in August 2011 for another five members. This initiative may go some way towards redressing the problem of limited engagement with Asia in general and China in particular as noted by McCarthy and Bain in this volume but it is likely that in this case Hamilton-Smith's interest was long standing.

CONCLUSION

This chapter has charted some dramatic changes in the Sino-South Australian relationship, from fear and trepidation to substantial engagement on many levels including historic, migration, cultural and economic. Moreover, the latter has increasingly dominated but in ways that are not necessarily obvious to the public. It also sketches some of the strengths, weaknesses, opportunities and threats to our relations.

Among the weaknesses are the very imbalances that have been described; the dominance of economics over other aspects including the dominance of mining and education exports, the relative weakness of political-cultural engagement, and a general lack of interest by South Australians and their representatives in understanding China to any significant extent. The shallowness of current understandings is also an issue. Even at the official level, it would seem that the relationship with Shandong has not been taken seriously enough as even basic information on the nature of the relationship, its extent, when it was commenced and the like, are not yet readily available via sources like the Internet. Nor do reciprocal visits by politicians receive much attention in the local press. Other actions, such as reforms to the South Australian Certificate of Education with its unintended consequence of undermining the study of languages, further weakens the already low incentives for young Australians to study 'hard' character-based languages like Chinese. Without clear incentives to take up study of Chinese at university, the state is likely to have trouble finding local talent to help take maximum benefit from opportunities in China unless these are all publicised in English language media and conform to Anglo-cultural norms.

Neither have all fears of China have disappeared. Even though Chinese FDI in real estate, from homes and farms, totalled $2.4 billion nationally in 2009–2010, about equal to British investment but only two thirds the American total, it has nevertheless aroused some angst, including in South Australia. Member of the Legislative Council, Robert Brokenshire, has worked with a local talkback radio station 5AA to collect signatures for a petition trying to prevent Chinese investors buying up of farmland (5AA 2011). In 2010, South Australian senator Nick Xenophon had warned of the dangers of Chinese food imports undercutting local producers (*Adelaidenow*, 29 April 2010) and the lack of information on who in fact owns Australian land (Senate Economics Committee 2010, 55). Trepidation still exists but issues like ownership of resources by Chinese companies, especially State Owned Enterprises, need to be discussed, debated and sensibly resolved in the state and national interest and not fall victim to the hysteria which has plagued relations in the past.

Nevertheless, the strengths of the relationship also include the growing economic integration and existing but underutilised frameworks of cultural and political engagement such as the sister-state relationship, the work of non-government organisations like ACBC and the network of Chinese community groups, the work of the universities and a significant history of other interactions, all of which can be readily seized on to build stronger engagement in the future. As reflected above, both the Labor Government and the Opposition seem to be realising the benefits of improving relations with and understandings of China and learning how to make more of potential opportunities of which there are many. Rather than fear Chinese imports of food for example, a more productive approach could be to learn how to supply China with the 'clean and green' produce and foods of all sorts that its increasingly urban, wealthy and discerning consumers are now demanding (Rasmussen 2010). While it may not often be economic to manufacture products locally, much more can be done to design and promote innovative products using South Australian talent and to train Chinese to do likewise. Some of these things will happen as a result of market forces but much more would be realised if the state government could work effectively with all the parties involved to develop and support a multi-dimensional economic, political and cultural approach to guide and assist engagement. While state-guided industrial policy is generally out of fashion in the West in favour of more market based, laissez faire approach, state guidance of economic and related development is a key reason behind Chinese economic success. Perhaps this is an area we could learn from.

A focal point for strategy development going forward is the preparation by DMITRE of a China 'Directions Paper' which will is the foundation for the development of a new China strategy by the end of the year.

NOTE

1 The authors would like to acknowledge the help of Sandra Horne and Cynthia Yip in the research for this paper.

REFERENCES

ABS, Australian Bureau of Statistics (1925), 1301.0 *Year Book Australia.*

AdelaideNow www.adelaidenow.com.au/news/national/nick-xenophon-claims-importing-chinese-food-compromises-australias-security/story-e6frea8c-1225860374021.

Australia China Review. 1982, 'Sir Walter Crocker's Address to the Australia China Friendship Society National Conference', August 1982.

Australia China Review. 1982, 'Shandong now a targeted Province', August 1986.

Australian Education International, *International Student Data*, www.aei.gov.au/research/International-Student-Data/Pages/default.aspx 2011.

Bell, Peter and Susan Marsden, *Kingston SE – An Overview History* (no date, post 2006) *www.sahistorians.org.au/175/bm.doc/kingston-se--an-overview-history.doc.*

Burrit, Roger, Dylan Walker and Amanda Walker. 2009, *Way Lee: 100 Years On,* University of South Australia, Adelaide.

Cawthorne, Ellen Mary. 1974, *The Long Journey: The story of the Chinese landings at Robe during the gold rush era 1852–1863* (Self published, no page numbers).

China Daily. 2009, 'Panda Diplomacy helps heal Sino Australian Rift', 31 October 2009. www.chinadaily.com.cn/china/2009–10/31/content_8877063.htm www.immi.gov.au/media/publications/statistics/comm-summ/_pdf/taiwan.pdf.

Crocker, Walter. 1971, *Australian Ambassador: International Relations at first hand,* Melbourne University Press, Melbourne.

Department of Immigration and Citizenship, *Community Information Summary: China-born*, www.immi.gov.au/media/publications/statistics/comm-summ/_pdf/china.pdf.

Eagle, Mary, Nicholas Jose and John Kean. 2006, *Writing a Painting: March 2006,* University of South Australia, Adelaide.

Feng, Chongyi. 2011, 'The Changing Political Identity of the "Overseas Chinese" in Australia', *Cosmopolitan Civil Societies Journal*, Vol. 3, No. 1, pp. 121–138.

FiveAA, China sets sights on Australian farms – Download Petition Here www.fiveaa.com.au/audio_china-sets-sights-on-australian-farms-download-petition-here_98207.

Forster, Keith. 1996, 'Immigration', in Colin Mackerras (Ed.) *Australia and China: Partners in Asia*, Key Centre for Asian Languages an Studies, Griffith University, Macmillan, South Melbourne.

Flinders Nankai Relationship http://blogs.flinders.edu.au/flinders-news/2010/11/08/china-faces-challenges-as-it-becomes-largest-economy/.

Goodman, David. 'China's Provinces and Australia's States: Sister States and International Mates', in Colin Mackerras (Ed) *Australia and China: Partners in Asia* (Key Centre for Asian Languages an Studies, Griffith University, Macmillan, South Melbourne, 1996).

Hamilton-Smith, Martin. 2011, *South Australia's Trade with China*, June 2011.

History Trust of South Australia, www.history.sa.gov.au/migration/collections/historical_relics/chinese_proclamation.htm.

Migration Museum of South Australia, 'East Turkistan Uighur Culture – A history of the Uighur people of South Australia', (Telephone discussion, September 2001). For details of exhibition see www.history.sa.gov.au/migration/exhibitions/east%20 turkistan.html.

MultiCultural SA www.multicultural.sa.gov.au/documents/ ArrivalstoSAsince2006Censusto1Dec2010_alphabetical.pdf (Based on Department of Immigration and Citizenship Settlement Database January 2011).

Nicholls, Bob. 1986, *Blue Jackets and Boxers: Australia's Naval Expedition to the Boxer Uprising*, Sydney, George Allen and Unwin.

Oakman, *Daniel.* 2010, *Facing Asia: A History of the Colombo Plan,* ANU E-Press, Canberra.

Peterson, Bob, *Into Darkest Adelaide*, www.history.sa.gov.au/chu/programs/history .../ BobPetersonPaper.pdf.

Price, Charles. 1999, 'Australian Population: Ethnic Origins' *People and Place*, Vol. 7 No. 4, pp. 12–16.

Rann, Mike. www.theaustralian.com.au/national-affairs/south-australian-premier-mike-rann-woos-indians-to-study-in-safest-state/story-fn59niix-1226030277943.

Rasmussen, Bruce. 2011, 'Finding the Key to China trade Conundrum', *Australian*, 31 August 2011, Business, p. 25.

Rendell, Margaret P. 1952–1953, 'The Chinese in South Australia before 1860', *Proceedings of Royal Geographical Society of Australasia*, SA Branch, Vol. 54, pp. 23–33.

SACAS South Australian Chinese Adoption Support, www.sacas.com.au/ culturesahistory.htm.

Senate Economics Committee, Foreign Acquisitions Amendment (Agricultural Land) Bill 2010 www.aph.gov.au/senate/committee/economics_ctte/foreign_acquisition_ farmland_2011/report/report.pdf.

South Australian Register (Published between 1836 and 1931).

State Library of South Australia, www.slsa.sa.gov.au/manning/sa/immigra/asian.htm.

Wakefield, Edward Gibbon. 1833, *England and America: A comparison of the social and political state of both nations,* Richard Bentley, London.

Viviani, Nancy. 1996, *The Indo Chinese in Australia: From burnt boats to barbecues,* Oxford University Press, Melbourne.

Wheatley, Glen B. 2011, *Business Engagement with China: a strategy for South Australia's Future?* January 2011 Confucius Institute and the Australia China Business Council.

Whitford, Tory. 2011, 'A political history of National Action: Its fears, ideas, tactics and conflicts', *Rural Society*, Vol. 20, No. 2, pp. 216–226.

Yip, Cynthia S.C. 2010, *China Born Migration to South Australia: Population and labour force Implications,* MA Thesis, University of Adelaide.

CHAPTER 7

South Australia and India

PURNENDRA JAIN and PETER MAYER

INTRODUCTION

Despite commonwealth links and many institutional and political similarities, Australia's ties with India remain weak, especially when compared to Australia's deep interest in, and ties with, other parts of Asia (Mayer and Jain 2010). Indeed, India is a latecomer in Australia's contemporary engagement with nations of the Asia Pacific. Even for former Prime Minister Paul Keating, who more than any prime minister before him could be considered a key catalyst in building Australia–Asia ties, India was not part of his Asia vision.[1]

Australian engagement with India at the subnational level has been even weaker. Some state governments began to engage India in the late 1990s as they saw commercial opportunities through commodity exports in an emerging market, and then through education and skilled migration. South Australia was initially not one of these states, instead remaining unconcerned about India's partnership potential (Jain 2004). The government and educational institutions in South Australia remained focused on their traditional markets in Southeast Asia and pursued rising interest in China.[2]

It was not till 2004, Mike Rann's third year as Premier that his government began to consider the potential for South Australia of commercial links with India. Since then India's presence in South Australia has diversified and increased many fold. But while Rann's political leadership and focused approach have certainly played a major part in South Australia's growing engagement with India, there is no strong evidence to suggest that South Australia has taken any particularly innovative approach that would distinguish it from other states of Australia. This state's engagement is in line with the national trend, though it came a decade later than states like Western Australia[3] and is weaker than in other states, such as Victoria.[4] The most distinctive feature of South Australia's relationship with India results from federal government policy – the Regional Sponsored Migration Scheme (RSMS) and Skilled Regional Migration Scheme (SRMS) that designate Adelaide as a 'regional' capital (the only mainland capital in this position). By lowering visa requirements, these schemes have made Adelaide attractive destination for migrants and also led to a steady flow of students enrolling in the vocational education and training sector through a large number of private colleges producing a sudden spike in the number of Indians living in Adelaide.

As we explain in this chapter, after a long period of mutual disinterest, the advent of India's economic strength at the start of the 21st century has awakened interest within the South Australian government to pursue mutual benefits. Today, India along with China seem to be the principal destinations for the state government's engagement in Asia. Political leaders see economic and other opportunities with these countries as similar to that they saw in Japan in the closing decades of the twentieth century. To set the contemporary development in perspective, we start with historical links between South Australia and India.

HISTORICAL LINKS

The British colonial connection with India was over a century old in the 1830s when the ink on Edward Wakefield's manifesto for a possible South Australian colony was still wet.[5] South Australia would be linked to India directly through shared colonial heritage. Indeed, connections with India, initially developed through personal connections via the East India Company, appear to have been embedded in the new colony from its foundation. Barely three years after the arrival of the first British colonists in South Australia, David Crafers established a rude hotel 'a poor place, just a rough bush hut with thatched roof and mud floor' (The Crafers Centenary Committee 1939, 4) in the Adelaide Hills. The 'Tiers' as the region was then known, was notorious as the home of criminal gangs who specialised in cattle duffing and highway robbery. Robert Martin's history of the Stirling District draws a tantalising and lurid connection between these criminal activities and India, since historians believe the 'unscrupulous English company' that sent employees to South Australia was the British East India Company:

> It is said that an unscrupulous English company [the East India Company] sent employees to South Australia to forward enterprises both legal and illegal. Much in the style of present-day criminal organizations, the company ran hotels and other legitimate businesses, whilst engaging secretly in crime. On the payroll was a gang of former sailors who, from a base in the Old Tiers [Adelaide Hills], traded in stolen cattle. They set up a brothel near the Crafers Inn, so that Tiersmen need not make the journey to Adelaide. Germans on their way to market were again victims of extortion.

The gang in the Tiers was supposedly answerable to the English company's chief agent in South Australia, the 'Mr X' of this story, who in later years became one of the colony's wealthiest, most influential and most philanthropic citizens. At various stages of his career (so it is said) he cultivated connections in high places, to both further his nefarious activities and conceal evidence of them (Martin 1987, 37).

Various instances of Indians working in South Australia in agricultural jobs came about largely through the conduit of the East India Company. These personal connections to India were less sensational than those stemming from the 'gang in The Tiers' and made an important contribution to the growth of the fledgling colony in the early decades of European settlement. Just two years after the 1836 arrival of Governor Hindmarsh, a naval officer and the first Governor of South Australia, Indian herdsmen worked on properties north of Clare. They had been recruited by a Mr Bruce who had previously lived in Calcutta. When Edward Gleeson, the founder of Clare, established a sheep station on the Hutt River in 1840 he employed these Indian herdsmen and brought out several more from India to work as shepherds. Other agricultural workers from India left their imprint in ways that today are largely unrecognised. For example, as the South Australian Migration Museum (1995, 218–9) explains:

The copper-mining town of Burra is connected with Indian settlement in South Australia. In the early 1840s, Indians working for pastoralist James Stein named the creek next to his property **Burra-Burra**, Hindustani for Great-Great, because the creek is the biggest in that section of the northern Mount Lofty Ranges.

Better known by far than the Indian herdsmen were the so-called 'Afghans', the camel handlers who were not really Afghans at all. Mostly they were Indians from the Punjab and Balochistan who were recruited by renowned South Australian businessman, pastoralist and public benefactor Sir Thomas Elder in the 1860s. Initially some 30 odd camel handlers were brought to South Australia, along with more than 100 camels, to provide transportation into the outback. But even though the Indian workers were in various specialised fields of employment, they were always a minor aspect of the connection between the two colonies. [6]

So too were new migrants from amongst the ranks of the old India hands. The flow was insignificant despite careful attempts to seductively woo those who dreaded returning to the leaden skies and cold winters of Britain. James Geo. Nash observed of the new South Australian colony in a letter to the *Calcutta Englishman* reprinted in the *South Australian Register* of 14 March 1840:

MY DEAR SIR— Having requested me to give you my opinion of the salubrity of our climate, and of its suitability to the constitution of Indo-Britons, I have much pleasure in being able to state that I consider the climate of South Australia admirably adapted to invalids obliged to leave either of the presidencies in consequence of repeated attacks of fever or hepatitis, or from a long residence within the tropics.

Here miasma is unknown, and I have not met with a single case of Patudal fever during a residence of more than twelve months in this colony. Our winter is sufficiently bracing without being too cold and our hottest summer days are almost invariably followed by cool and delightful nights. To those laboring under pulmonary affections, the purity of our atmosphere and the total absence of cold damp fogs offer peculiar advantages, and they would derive all those advantages from a residence amongst us which they might expect from a sojourn at Nice or the south of France, without having to encounter the inconveniences of a long sea voyage. (http://newspapers.nla.gov.au)

The flow of people from India through labour and migration was, however, a minor aspect of inter-colony contacts in the nineteenth century. The primary focus of this bilateral connection was always exports. But development of this trade from South Australia was by no means plain sailing. The difficulties in establishing firm export markets in India led to recurrent requests from businessmen for assistance from the state government (some things never change, perhaps). An editorial in *The South Australian* for 11 October 1869 complained 'We have so often directed attention to the vast importance of endeavouring to establish a trade with India that we feel it almost like useless repetition to renew those [requests] … [it is urgent] that the House will vote a sum not exceeding £250 for the purposes of such [assistance]' (http://newspapers.nla.gov.au). Ten days later it was reported that 'about 50 gentlemen men assembled at the Governor's … [to seek assistance in establishing] a trade with India for the products of this colony' (http://newspapers.nla.gov.au). Certainly, the commercial will was there, if not the practical and official infrastructure to promote and sustain it.

In early days, animals – dead and alive – and minerals were the export mainstays. An article in the *South Australian Register* of 18 May 1883 reported that in that year 'Horses and copper are the two principal articles which we sent to India' (http://newspapers.nla.gov.au). Other accounts (Westrip and Holroyde 2010, 211–212) have also noted horse exports. A decade earlier, an attempt in the early 1870s to establish an export market for preserved meat failed to secure a permanent arrangement (*Advertiser* 2 March 1870 http://newspapers.nla.gov.au).

A new commodity entered the export flow as grape growers established South Australia's wine industry and soon turned their attention to the British living in India as a promising market. Newspaper articles from the 1860s onward document efforts to export wine to India. For example, *The South Australian* of 11 January 1868 reported on 'efforts made … to open up a trade in colonial wines with India' (http://newspapers.nla.gov.au). Thirty five years later *The Advertiser* of 2 March 1903 presented an extended report on the visit to India by Mr W.G. Smith of Yalumba vineyards that included his attendance at the Delhi Durbar celebrating the coronation of King Edward VII and Queen Alexandra as Emperor and Empress of India.

> [Smith] said he attended nearly every gathering held in connection with the Durbar, which was a most magnificent spectacle. He had the good fortune to get Yalumba wines on the list at No. 1 camp, which was the Viceroy's guest camp. This meant for them a good advertisement. Australian wines, he says, are now circulating freely throughout, India.

Yet the report on Smith's marketing trip revealed one of the key problems for the export flow from South Australia:

> He had quite a number of enquiries in India, Burmah, and Ceylon for Australian compressed fodder for horses, and considers that a large export trade might be done in this product. Merchants in India complain of the uncertainty of shipments from Australia. Demand for many Australian products from this cause has fallen off.

After the end of World War I, references to attempts to develop export markets in India virtually disappear from South Australian newspapers. By the time of the Depression, linkages were reduced to South Australia only as the site of the closest ports for loading India-bound exports of silver from Broken Hill in New South Wales. But if the inter-colonial connection with India had become greatly attenuated by the end of the nineteenth century, by the time India achieved Independence in 1947 it had virtually disappeared. We can see signs of a small 'rediscovery' of India in the 1960s in the form of adventurous youthful travellers to India at a time when India had become fashionable for the young. Student interest in India in the late sixties was sufficient to support teaching by a Reader and a Lecturer in History at the University of Adelaide and later a Professor and a Lecturer in History at Flinders University. However, by the 1980s, teaching of Indian history was ended at the University of Adelaide, and by the middle of the first decade of the 21st century it was also ended at Flinders.

The engagement of South Australia with independent India remained rather weak. This is certainly true compared to, for example, Western Australia where a relatively large number of Indians (especially Anglo-Indians) settled in the late 1960s and early 1970s (Afsar 2004). The waning of South Australian interest in India was also evident in the business community. In the early 1990s, the Department of American Studies at Flinders University in association with the law firm Minter-Ellison organised a series of seminars on 'doing business in Asia'. There was only anaemic demand from South Australian firms for the sessions on India.

In this period, the Government of South Australia was also not interested in developing economic links with India. In 1995, planning and preparation were under way for 'Australia India New Horizons', a major national promotion of Australia in India undertaken by the Department of Foreign Affairs. However the South Australian Government, then led by the Liberal Party, declined to participate, stating that China and Vietnam were the state's primary export promotion foci and that funds were not available to support South Australian participation.

The Olsen government (1996–2001) maintained low interest in India during the five years when it held office, while none of the educational institutions in South Australia foresaw the potential of education with India that was already taking off in some other states. Asian studies at universities focused primarily on Japan and China with some interest in Southeast Asia. Today this situation has changed considerably, with Premier Mike Rann clearly interested in engaging India, as evident in his seven visits since taking office in 2002. His enthusiasm to engage South Australia with India was very clear in his interview with one of the authors in October 2010.[7]

CONTEMPORARY TRADE AND COMMERCIAL INTERESTS

The South Australian government under Rann has pushed its trade and commercial interests over the last several years but total trade between South Australia and India still remains quite low when compared with South Australia's trade with other major nations of the Asia Pacific.[8] In 2009, South Australia imported some A$185 million worth of goods from India comprising mainly electrical machinery, equipment and parts, and some pearls, precious and semi-precious stones and textile items. South Australia's exports to India that year were valued at A$356 million, comprising principally ores, slug and ash, followed by lead and lead articles, with some fruit, nuts and vegetables. In the overall economy and external trade of South Australia, trade with India is still a very small component. As we see in Figure 1, exports from South Australia have surged particularly since 2006, with a similar, if slightly lower growth in parallel imports.

By July 2010 South Australia's exports to India had reached nearly $600 million, an extraordinary leap from the previous year. Although concrete results in terms of greater investment and trade (especially imports from India) seem to be slow in taking off relative to the pace of commercial engagement with China, both sides have expressed interest in such areas as mining, infrastructure projects, water management, electronics and defence-related technology.

Figure 1: South Australia's trade with India

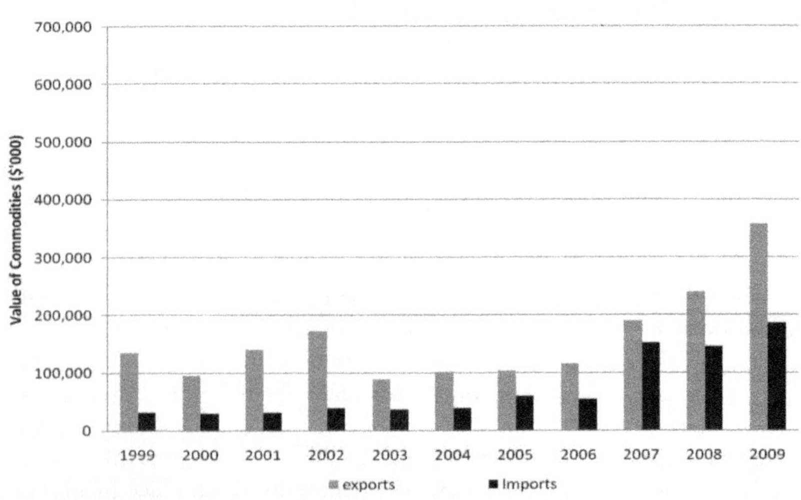

Source: ABS, Catalogue 5368.0 International Trade in Goods and Services

One area where trade links are expanding and diversifying is the non-traditional product of wine. While we have noted early attempts to stimulate wine exports to British colonisers in India more than a century ago, today the intended market is Indian people themselves. India has expressed some interest in this area through small investments in South Australia. Upper middle class India has expressed some interest in wine despite the small size of the wine market in India and the very high tariff on wine imports. Indian company Château Indage bought the Tandou winery (in the Riverland area) for A$10 million in 2007, and expressed interest in buying another (Loxton, also in the Riverland area) for A$60 million.[9] Now that wine production is gaining some momentum in India, Indage has tied-up with the University of Adelaide to establish a facility in the central state of Maharashtra for technical courses in wine production. In 2008, the University of Adelaide signed a Memorandum of Understanding to set up an Indian Institute of Vine and Wine near Mumbai. The University of Adelaide was chosen over competitors from Europe and North America.[10] And TAFE SA (the largest provider of vocational education and training in South Australia) has discussed the possibility of starting Wine Certification courses in India.[11]

One area where exports from South Australia could see a major boost is uranium; the state has huge deposits and India has strong demand to feed its nuclear fuel needs. Australia's Labor national government bans exports of uranium to nations that have not signed the nuclear non-proliferation treaty. Although opinion is divided even within the Labor Party, it seems that the current ban will remain in place over the short-term and perhaps at least as long as the current Labor Government remains in power in Canberra. Some Indian companies already actively explore for uranium, taking a broader view of the uranium sector's strength than simply securing supply for the Indian market. In 2008 a subsidiary of Reliance Industries Ltd, the largest private sector company in India acquired 49 per cent interest in four uranium exploration licences in South Australia (*The Hindu*, 28 May 2008).

The South Australian government has been keen to identify new areas where collaboration and further economic activities can be pursued. The defence industry is one such area. The Premier led a team of five defence company representative on his September 2010 mission to Delhi.[12] When signing a Memorandum of Understanding between the Confederation of Indian Industries (CII) and the Department of Trade and Economic Development of South Australia in New Delhi during the visit, Mike Rann welcomed future developments, claiming that 'South Australia is known as the Defence state of Australia, with over 200 defence companies now based in South Australia and a defence project pipeline of over $40 billion … Many of South Australia's defence companies are eager to work with Indian companies in developing defence products and services for India'.[13]

The South Australian government also seeks investment from India for a number of state projects. The Premier believes that since other Asian nations such as Japan, China and Singapore have invested in South Australian state projects, now India too should be actively courted to consider opportunities. Some of these are in 'green' industries. For example, there are opportunities for investment in environmentally sensitive waste management. India-based company Suzlon energy, which specialises in wind energy and is the world's fifth largest manufacturer of wind turbines, has been the biggest player in South Australia in wind turbines.

South Australia has also promoted itself as a location for shooting Bollywood movies. Bollywood's first commercial futuristic science-fiction feature film 'Love Story 2050' showcased Adelaide, where it premiered in July 2008. This Bollywood romance crosses time and space as it switches between present-day Adelaide and futuristic Mumbai. For Premier Rann, who had a cameo role in the movie, 'It is good for the film industry. It's great to have people spending money here for 55 days, using South Australia as a location, but it is also giving us worldwide publicity that money can't buy'.[14] Indian films shot in Australia have also had spin offs in other industries like tourism and education, as well as in the local economy and employment.

Trade relations so far have seen considerably higher value outflow to India than intake from India, producing a huge trade deficit in this sector. The South Australian government maintains that it is for India and Indian companies to explore possibilities of exports to South Australia, with Premier Rann claiming 'our doors are open for them to export and invest in this state'.[15]

INSTITUTIONAL AND POLITICAL LINKS

Both government and non-government bodies are at work to foster relations, particularly economic, between South Australia and India. The Rann government established a South Australian government office in Chennai in 2005 to support South Australian businesses in India, trading with India or seeking to trade with India.[16] This state office generally promotes trade ties and also helps to attract investment and migration to South Australia from India. It was originally co-located with the federal government's Austrade office in Chennai, but was made an independent entity in 2009 and was officially opened by Premier Rann during his September 2010 visit. The office is headed by a senior trade commissioner who is supported by four other full-time staff.

Premier Rann has visited India every year since his first visit in 2004 and has built strong and extensive personal links with Indian leaders at both state and national levels. Some state government ministers have also visited India, as have the Adelaide city mayor and senior managers of universities in Adelaide. However, we do not see similar enthusiasm from the Indian side. Very few high-ranking ministers, even from state governments in India, visit South Australia in an official capacity or at all. Links at senior manager level within the SA government remain extremely weak. Furthermore, there is little coordination between government departments to engage India comprehensively and strategically. The State Government has an India desk in the Office for International Co-ordination in the Department of Premier and Cabinet, but the resources provided are meagre and India knowledge within government shallow. For deeper, stronger, sustainable links, institutional-level support is essential. There is still no government–university–community linkage arrangement to engage India in a comprehensive fashion. While the importance of India is on almost everyone's lips, institutions are few, funding is weak, and a comprehensive strategic push is missing.

A private-sector organisation working specifically toward bilateral commercial links is the Australia–India Business Council SA (AIBCSA). Mr Brian Hayes QC who is a former national president of the Australia-India Business Council has been a major force behind making the SA chapter active. Premier Rann considers the AIBC 'an extremely important partner to the State Government in building an enduring and prosperous relationship between South Australia and India' (www.aibc.org.au/SA/). Testament to the AIBCSA's continuous efforts to build trade and other commercial ties, for the third time in succession, in 2010 it won the International Chamber of the Year award, sponsored by South Australia's Council for International Trade and Commerce. The AIBCSA was commended for its 15 per cent growth in membership from 2008–09, high-profile events throughout the year, and the momentum gained by its student chapter.[17] However, while this Business Council is a frontrunner in the South Australian state context, relative to India's national context, its contributions have enormous scope to cover.

MIGRATION FROM INDIA TO SOUTH AUSTRALIA

Migration has become a particularly important vehicle for bilateral ties since the federal government introduced the Skilled Regional Migration Scheme (SRMS) in 1999. The SRMS is to help regional areas attract and keep professional and other skilled migrants to fill skill shortages, boost development in regional communities, and counter the population decline in rural and low population growth metropolitan areas.[18] South Australia is the only mainland state as a whole to be included in the scheme, placing Adelaide as the only mainland capital city within the scheme – and thus a particularly attractive destination for many Indians seeking migration to Australia.

Data on Indian residents in South Australia over time reveal the incentive that the Scheme has provided. The 1986 Census indicates 2642 people of Indian origin living in South Australia. Indians in Adelaide were then one of the least concentrated birthplace groups, with an I_D of 13.8, indicating a highly dispersed population (Beer and Cutler 1995, 58). Indian-born residents then living outside Adelaide were relatively more concentrated; one quarter lived in the industrial area of Whyalla and another quarter lived in the irrigated farming areas of the River Murray around Renmark, Waikerie and Berri (Beer and Cutler 1995, 60). The 1991 Census reported a slight rise to 2891 Indians living in South Australia and like other South Australians, the majority (87 per cent) resided in Adelaide (Beer and Cutler 1995, 58). However the 2006 Census showed a leap in the Indian-born population to 8103, growth of 280 per cent on 15 years earlier and a sign of positive response to the Skilled Regional Migration Scheme (ABS 34120DO0006 Migration, Australia 2007–08). The Department of Manufacturing, Innovation, Trade, Resources and Energy have, however, prepared a 'Directions Paper' released in January 2012. This will be the foundation for an India strategy released later in the year.

We also see results of the SRMS in migration settlement statistics, which, we should note, do not account for further subsequent movement interstate and overseas. These statistics showed 10,388 people of Indian origin came to South Australia to settle between 2000 and the end of 2010. The annual number rose sharply after 2003–4, reaching a peak in 2007–8. At the 2007–08 peak, Indian migrants constituted some 40 per cent of all migrants coming to South Australia.

Figure 2: Indian-origin settlers in South Australia; India as % of SA migrant intake

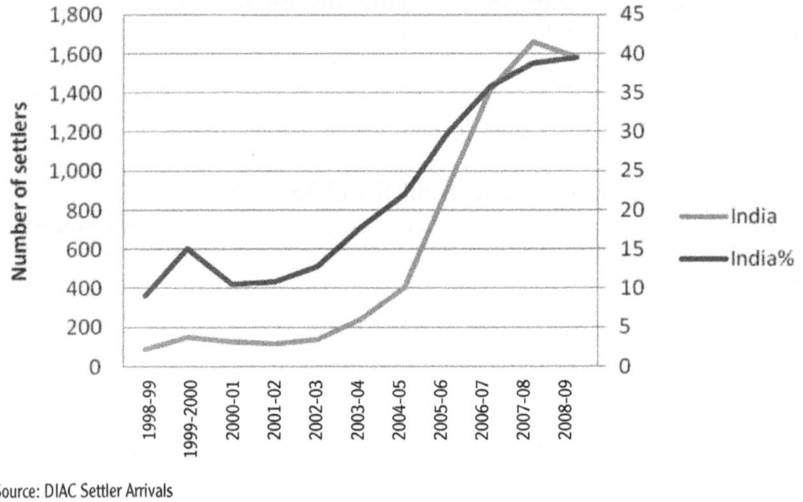

Source: DIAC Settler Arrivals

We get an imperfect glimpse of the regional origins of these settlers from the mother tongue information available for a minority (14%) of these migrants. In 2008–09, 23 per cent of the new settlers from India used English as their home language followed by Hindi (21%) and Punjabi (15%) and the rest spoke a variety of Indian languages.[19]

MIGRATION AND INDIAN STUDENTS

International education is now one of South Australia's largest export industries, injecting more than $1 billion into the state in the financial year 2009–10. The number of full-fee paying Indian students in South Australia has increased significantly since 2003 (Figure 3). In 2010, the roughly 6000 students from India were the second-largest cohort (after China) of South

Australia's total overseas student population of around 34,000 from more than 130 countries (Owen 2010). A major spur is the Regional Migration program. Through general 'skilled migration' pathways, the program facilitates higher education graduates who seek to remain in South Australia to live and work after graduating and those who seek to move to South Australia after graduating elsewhere in Australia. International students need to have studied full time at a campus in regional Australia or in a low population growth metropolitan area for at least two years before lodging a migration application. Adelaide is the only Regional Migration-qualifying mainland capital city and has three national universities, making it a very popular destination for Indian students seeking a longer term future in Australia.

Figure 3: Indian international students in South Australia: India as % of SA students intake

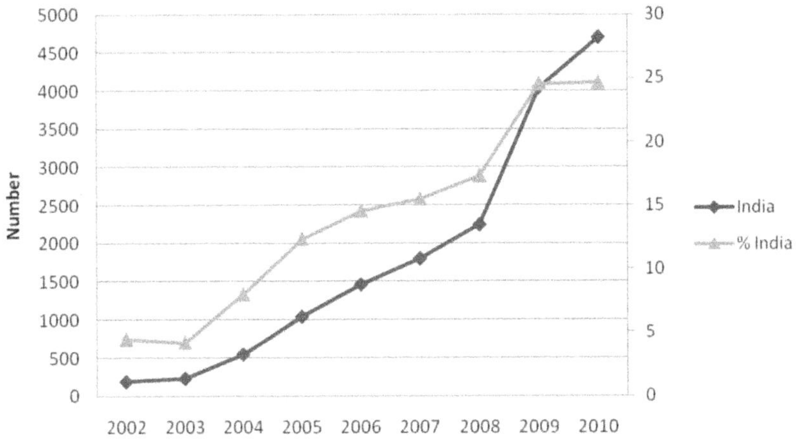

Source: Australian Education International 2010.

South Australia's continued significant uptake in Indian students defies a national trend showing some falloff in the flow of Indian students into Australia.[20] The major reason for the falloff has been attacks on people of South Asian appearance, both students and non-students, in some metropolitan cities, most notably Melbourne. Political leaders in South Australia such as the Premier and the Lord Mayor of Adelaide city, together with representatives from Education Adelaide, local universities and TAFE (Tertiary and Further Education) SA, have travelled to India to assure Indian authorities, parents, students and communities at large that Adelaide is a safe, welcoming city with world-class education services for international students.[21] South Australia clearly has much at stake in the continued flow of students from India and the premier's message has continued to affirm Adelaide's rating as the safest, friendliest and most affordable city in Australia, ready to welcome thousands more students from India (Rann 2010).[22]

ADELAIDE'S INDIAN COMMUNITY

The intended consequences of the Regional Migration program entail active involvement of people from India in community life across the state, particularly in Adelaide but also in the industrial and agricultural regions where Indians have settled. Indeed, growth of the Indian community is visible in many places through growing numbers of grocery stores, restaurants, Bollywood and Bhangra enriching the multicultural society of South Australia. It is not unusual to hear Hindi, Punjabi, Gujarati and other Indian languages in busy market places and on public transport. Apart from the professions such as medicine, teaching and engineering, in which some first generation Indian migrants have made their presence felt, a steady flow of Indian migrants is now employed in service sectors such as taxi driving, cleaning and public transport. The Indian Australian Association of South Australia (IAASA) represents the broader interests of Indian-origin residents in South Australia and a large number of regional and religion-based associations conduct their own activities independently of IAASA as the umbrella organisation. India's cultural and linguistic diversity are well reflected in these small community organisations across South Australia.

The South Australian government tries creatively to engage the state's growing Indian community. One vehicle is the South Australian Multicultural and Ethnic Affairs Commission (SAMEAC) headed by Lt Governor Hieu Van Le. Premier Rann and some government ministers themselves participate actively in cultural, religious and other festive events. To mark the opening of the September 2010 Commonwealth Games in New Delhi, Premier Rann sponsored a huge reception at the Adelaide Entertainment Centre with more than 500 people, mainly Indians, in attendance. The annual OZAsia festival in Adelaide in 2012 will be dedicated to the Indian theme.

PROMOTING SOUTH AUSTRALIA–INDIA RELATIONS

South Australia is working both in India and at home to further develop relations. In India advertising campaigns mostly coordinated through the Chennai office present South Australia as an attractive trade and investment destination, a world class education provider, and the 'Nobel Prize capital of Australia'. On the ground at home, more than any other premier, Mike Rann has successfully tried to draw on Adelaide's growing Indian diaspora to build links with India. In 2008 his government appointed a prominent local barrister of Anglo-Indian background, Brian Hayes QC, as the state's special envoy to India with a brief to promote South Australia–India ties. Mr Hayes believes that much more can be done through tapping the Indian diaspora to build stronger and comprehensive links between South Australia and India, and he is involved in various business promotions and cultural activities towards this objective.[23]

Present momentum to build wide-ranging ties with India depends on continuing the prerequisite political circumstances at both national and state levels. Nationally, it requires continuing current aspects of migration policy that give Adelaide special dispensation to attract students and other migrants from India. There are already signs that requirements for student visa and residency will be tightened, which will result in a drop – perhaps a significant one – in Indian students as permanent settlers in South Australia, particularly Adelaide.[24] At the state level, there is a need for the continuation of the style of political leadership that targeted India in a focused way,[25] and institutional scaffolding able to sustain and strengthen South Australia–India ties in a post-Rann government. The business and community links that Mike Rann has nurtured during his premiership may sustain the momentum. However significant growth is unlikely without strong political leadership underpinned by support at the top bureaucratic level within the state administration.[26]

Contemporary ties between South Australia and India are mainly rooted in short-term economic benefits. Subnational governments (at both state and local government levels) are essentially political actors with an eye on domestic politics. As long as politicians can convince voters that their international actions are in the local interest (particularly economic growth and filling needs for employees, especially in work and geographic areas where locals are unavailable), the politicians will cultivate relations with foreign countries. If they do not see such benefit, they will drop their engagement.[27] In the case of Indians in South Australia, however, the level of migration from India already may have secured a political voice for these constituents even if the current strategic momentum diminishes.

CONCLUSIONS

From early colonial connections in the nineteenth century, through decades of mutual disinterest across much of the twentieth century, through to vibrant, active and diverse linkages in the twenty-first century, South Australia's interest in India has surely been uneven over time. Personal ties have always been instrumental in developing South Australia's relations with India, whether economic, political or cultural. In recent years in particular, a range of institutional and other supports help to sustain and lubricate relations, particularly through the state government and with the imprimatur of the premier Mike Rann who has been a driving force here. The federal government's migration policy endowing Adelaide with special status as a 'regional' city and targeting India as a supplier of migrants and full-fee paying students has been especially prominent in greatly increasing the flow of new settlers to South Australia from India since the mid-2000s.

There is no doubt that today South Australia's engagement with India is deeper and broader than ever before. This is palpably evident in Adelaide from the city centre to the outskirts, through employment of Indians in front line service and retail sectors, increasing numbers of grocery stores and in Indian restaurants. Some regional towns where Indians have settled also have a visible presence. Clearly South Australia has given to and received much from the people who have come from India to share their knowledge, their culture and goodwill while pursuing commercial and other activities and some of them settling permanently.

India is therefore likely to remain an important partner country for South Australia for the foreseeable future. Some close associates of the current government who are officially responsible for promoting South Australia's ties with India are optimistic that even in the post-Rann government, interests in India will remain strong and effective strategies will continue to engage India deeply and comprehensively.[28] How far and how South Australia will proceed on this path remains to be seen. The institutional infrastructure, the commercial, political, cultural and personal linkages, and the bank of mutual knowledge and goodwill that are now in place provide a very valuable underlay for future links, however diverse and deeply they run.

NOTES

1 For example, Keating publicly opposed India's inclusion in the Asia Pacific Economic Cooperation forum (Keating 2000, 193).

2 Premier Mike Rann indicated that two Labor premiers before him had developed South Australia's relations in Asia: Don Dunstan with Penang in Malaysia and John Bannon with Shandong province in China. Premier Rann felt that it was time to engage India, given its rising importance and historical links with Australia. Through talks with a few other premiers such as Bob Carr of New South Wales, Geoff Gallop of Western Australia and Peter Beattie of Queensland, they agreed to engage with India at the sub-national level. Personal interview with Purnendra Jain, 8 October 2010.

3 Western Australia opened the first Australian state trade office, in Bombay/Mumbai in 1996, following many visits by Deputy Premier Hendy Cowan. (http://meacommunity.org/Documents/ANNUAL REPORT 1995.doc accessed 27/4/2011).

4 For example, the state of Victoria in 2010 launched a multi-million dollar four-year strategy to comprehensively engage India and the Indian community. See www.indianlink.com.au/melbourne-news/victoria-launches-multi-million-engaging-india-plan-to-boost-trade-ties/.

5 A recent book outlining bilateral colonial links is Westrip and Holroyde (2010).

6 There is an extensive literature on the Indian and Afghan camelmen. See for example (Brunato 1972), (Cigler 1986), (Jones 2007), (Rajkowski 1987), (Stevens 1989).

7 Purnendra Jain's interview with Premier Mike Rann in the Premier's office in Adelaide, 8 October 2010.

8 See chapters on China and Japan, for example, in this volume.

9 www.sommelierindia.com/blog/2008/03/sommelier_india_interviews_rt.html.

10 www.adelaide.edu.au/wine2030/news_and_events/events_2008/2008_6.html.

11 www.sommelierindia.com/blog/2008/03/sommelier_india_interviews_rt.html.
12 These are Codan (high frequency radios used in border patrols); Minelab (mine detectors); Lockheed Martin Australia (over the horizon radar); Daronmont (coastal radar systems) and Prism Defence Systems (helicopter guidance systems for ships).
13 www.india.embassy.gov.au/ndli/PA5110.html.
14 www.bollywood.com/adelaide-love-story-2050-mumbai.
15 Purnendra Jain's interview with Premier Rann.
16 During his visit to Chennai, Premier Rann also signed a sister-state agreement with the state of Tamil Nadu, of which Chennai is the capital city.
17 'AIBC wins CITCSA top award', *The Advertiser*, 3 September 2010.
18 www.loc-gov-focus.aus.net/editions/2000/january/reg.shtml.
19 www.immi.gov.au/settlement/.
20 Singapore/Indian trade mission', News Release, Premier Mike Rann, Government of South Australia, 27 August 2010.
21 'Singapore/Indian trade mission', News Release, Premier Mike Rann, Government of South Australia, 27 August 2010.
22 Also, see www.theaustralian.com.au/national-affairs/south-australian-premier-mike-rann-woos-indians-to-study-in-safest-state/story-fn59niix-1226030277943.
23 Jain's interview with Mr Brian Hayes, 18 April 2011.
24 On 12 November 2010 the Federal government unveiled new migration criteria that focus more strongly on English proficiency and high-level qualifications than on vocational skills and experience, a move likely to affect prospects of low-skilled Indian students seeking migration. http://indianlocal.com.au/tag/australian-universities/.
25 In an interview with Purnendra Jain on 18 April 2011, Mr Brian Hayes QC, who serves as South Australia's special envoy to India, confidently asserted that the political momentum built by Mike Rann will likely continue under any new Labor leader and also possibly under a Liberal–National government.
26 The Department of Trade and Economic Development, South Australia's principal institution in charge of promoting trade and economic links externally, suffered a major budget cut in the 2010 budget. Some of the Department's overseas offices, such as those in Singapore and Dubai, were merged within the Federal government's Austrade offices (Russell 2010).
27 Japan is a case in point. See Purnendra Jain's chapter on South Australia and Japan in this volume.
28 Jain's interview with Mr Brian Hayes, 18 April 2011.

REFERENCES

Afsar, Rita. 2004, 'Migration from Indian Sub-Continent to Western Australia: some Intriguing Issues of Religious Composition and Political Integration', paper presented to the 12th Biennial Conference of the Australian Population Association, Canberra, 15–17 September.

Beer, Andrew and Cecile Cutler. 1995, *Atlas of the Australian People—1991 Census* Canberra: Australian Government Publishing Service.

Brunato, Madeleine. 1972, *Hanji Mahomet Allum: Afghan Camel-driver, Herbalist, and Healer in Australia.* Leabrook, SA: Investigator Press.

Cigler, Michael. 1986, *The Afghans in Australia.* Melbourne: AE Press.

Dutton, Geoffrey, and David Elder. 1991, *Colonel William Light – Founder of a City.* Carlton, Victoria: Melbourne University Press.

Jain, Purnendra. 2004, 'Time to Take Advantage of a Booming Economic Tiger', *The Advertiser,* 8 September.

Jones, Philip, and Anna Kenny. 2007, *Australia's Muslim Cameleers: Pioneers of the Inland 1860s–1930s.* Adelaide: Wakefield Press/South Australian Museum.

Keating, Paul. 2000, *Engagement: Australia Faces the Asia-Pacific,* Sydney: Macmillan.

Martin, Robert. 1987, *Under Mount Lofty: A History of the Stirling District in South Australia.* Netley: District Council of Stirling.

Mayer, Peter and Purnendra Jain. 2010, 'Beyond Cricket: Australia-India Evolving Relations', *Australian Journal of Political Science,* 45:1, 133–148.

Migration Museum. 1995, *From Many Places: The History and Cultural Traditions of South Australian People.* Adelaide: History Trust of S.A. and Wakefield Press.

Owen, Michael. 2011, 'South Australian Premier Mike Rann Woos Indians to Study in 'Safest' State, *Australian,* 30 March.

Rajkowski, Pamela. 1987, *In the Tracks of the Camelmen: Outback Australia's Most Exotic Pioneers.* North Ryde, NSW: Angus and Robertson Publishers.

Rann, Mike. 2010, 'Indian Community Reception for Delhi Commonwealth Games', Adelaide Entertainment Centre, 18 September, copy of speech made available to Purnendra Jain.

Russell, Christopher. 2010, 'SA State Budget 2010 to cut $100m from Department of Trade and Economic Development', *The Advertiser,* 16 September.

The Crafers Centenary Committee. 1939, *A History of Crafers.* Adelaide: Webb and Son.

Westrip, Joyce and Peggy Holroyde. 2010, *Colonial Cousins: A Surprising History of Connections between India and Australia.* Adelaide: Wakefield Press.

Stevens, Christine. 1989, *Tin Mosques and Ghantowns: A History of Afghan Cameldrivers in Australia.* Melbourne: Oxford University Press.

CHAPTER 8

South Australia and The United States

DAVID F. MOSLER and SHARON A. MOSLER

HISTORICAL OVERVIEW: MOVEMENT OF PEOPLE IN BOTH DIRECTIONS

When the expansion of the British Empire reached the eastern shores of Australia in 1788 the new nation state of the United States had only been in existence for five years. But, with the world close to the first great wave of globalisation in the mid-19th century, commercial activities of Yankee traders in the South Pacific were already active and within six months American vessels appeared in Sydney Harbour. American whalers and sealers were enthusiastic to operate in the region and ties between Australia and America would be well established throughout the 19th century in commercial areas and exchange of peoples would be frequent in both directions.

The gold rushes in the American West, beginning with California in 1849, attracted Australians first to America and then those seeking wealth came back to Australia in the 1850s to Victoria and New South Wales. English-born Edward Hargraves went to the goldfields in California and returned to Australian colonies with the techniques of panning and cradling he had utilised in America. When he discovered gold in New South Wales in 1851 these discoveries started the Australian gold rushes and drew Yankees of all types—white, black and Hispanic—to Australia to seek their fortunes and many would stay.

By the end of the 19th century Americans made their mark in Australia in general and South Australia in particular as the exchange of peoples became more frequent. Concomitantly, American culture and ideas impacted on Australia in myriad areas such as the US Constitution which was used as a template for many aspects of the Australian Constitution in 1901 (American-style with a federal union, division of government into three branches of government with checks and balances between them, two chambers with equal number of senators from each state, a High Court and a federal capital but a British-style Westminster system without a Bill of Rights). The establishment of the Women's Christian Temperance Union (WCTU) in Australia in 1882 and then in Adelaide in 1886 spread the prohibitionist movement from America to South Australia. Coffee palaces were established in the city, including West's Palace in Hindley Street, and restrictive legislation followed which led to the famous 'six o'clock swill' in South Australian pubs until the Dunstan reforms in the 1970s.[1] The two Anglo-sphere nations were destined to develop as kindred cultures across the Pacific with strong business, geostrategic, migration and cultural ties down to the present as firm allies in peace and war (which were frequent).[2]

Most US contact in Australia has always been with New South Wales, which is very similar to California in climate and culture, but Americans have also made their mark in South Australia.[3] We are all familiar with famous US visitors in the 19th century such as Mark Twain, who toured Australia in 1895 and dined at the Adelaide Club, Henry George, the radical economic theorist who was greeted enthusiastically throughout Australia, President Herbert Clark Hoover (president 1925–1929), here as a young mining engineer in the late 1890s, and Walter Burley Griffin, the architect of Canberra. But among those American migrants of influence in South Australia in the 19th and in the early 20th centuries the most notable were John Greeley Jenkins (1851–1923), King O'Malley (1858–1953), and William Webb (1878–1936).[4]

John Greeley Jenkins was the only person of American birth ever elected to be premier of an Australian state (indeed, the only American-born premier until Kristina Keneally, niece-in-law of the famous writer Thomas, was made the first female Premier of New South Wales in a spill in December, 2009; she was born in Las Vegas, Nevada, grew up in Toledo, Ohio, of an American father and Australian mother). Jenkins was born in Pennsylvania of Welsh parents who had migrated to America in the 1830s. He was educated in a Wyoming seminary and came to South Australia as a publisher's traveller in 1878. He entered local politics in 1886 in Unley and was mayor in 1878. In 1887 he was elected to the South Australian Parliament as a protectionist and was considered to be a 'shrewd long-headed Yankee'. He became a minister in Thomas Playford's government in 1891 and Premier in 1901 and was elected in his own right in 1902. He remained Premier until 1905 and resigned from Parliament in 1908 to become agent-general in London, where he died in 1923 after a later career as a steel importer. In politics and in business he was agile; he is described by noted Flinders University psephologist Dean Jaensch as a 'political acrobat'.[5]

King O'Malley, born in America in 1858 (his place of birth is somewhat controversial for he also claimed to have been born in Canada in order to qualify for the federal parliament) and migrated to Australia in 1888. He was elected to the South Australian House of Assembly from Encounter Bay (Victor Harbor) and from 1896 he was a strong federationist. In 1901 he shifted to the federal sphere and was elected from the mining seat of Lyell in Tasmania. When Andrew Fisher became prime minister in 1910, O'Malley became Minister for Home Affairs, although Fisher had no great love for him.

O'Malley's career in federal politics is almost a caricature of Yankee behaviour. He was larger than life, garrulous, and a curious mixture of huckster, visionary, and, in the American vernacular, something of a 'screwball'. John Molony claims he 'fluctuated from the sane and wise to the flamboyant and unbalanced'. He was at the centre of many of the crucial issues in the building of the Australian nation, the most notable two being the selection and construction of Canberra and, as argued by his biography A.R. Hoyle, although the Commonwealth Bank was introduced by Prime Minister Fisher, O'Malley was the 'spiritual father' of the Commonwealth Bank. He achieved the highest political office of any American migrant. O'Malley supported his fellow American Walter Burley Griffin as the architect of Canberra and championed some strange names (obviously unsuccessfully) for Canberra such as Shakespeare or Myola. His career started on the decline when he lost his ministry in 1916 and after losing two more elections in the 1920s he faded from public life. He died in 1953 as the last surviving member of the first Commonwealth Parliament of Australia after a successful career in property.[6]

William Webb was a railroad engineer who was recruited as the commissioner of railways (1923–1930) by the South Australian government. Webb was born in Ohio in 1878 and was a prominent engineer with good political connections. Among those was a close relationship with Charles Evan Hughes who was the Republican (unsuccessful candidate against President Wilson) presidential candidate in 1916, Secretary of State in the Harding administration in 1921 and later Chief Justice of the US Supreme Court from 1930 to 1941. Webb's appointment as commissioner produced a political storm in South Australia. He was attacked by both the Left and the Right. Lionel Hill, Labour Premier in 1926, despised Webb's conservative politics and anti-Labour/union sentiments (as well as Hill's British imperial opposition to a non-British subject in the position). Webb distrusted and was dismissive of the Australian working man's work ethic and, according to his biographer Reece Jennings, 'was suspicious [of] the average Australian's idea of what constituted a fair day's work'. When Webb returned to America, after a period in which he greatly modernised and expanded the South Australian railway system, he enjoyed a successful career as an engineer (but the Labour movement was ecstatic to see him return to his country of origin).[7]

What these careers of Americans in Australia illustrate is a cross-fertilisation of ideas and people between Australia/South Australia and the US. However, the Australians have a great deal of transcendent ambivalence about Americans and American culture. The North Americans and their culture are appreciated for their levels of energy and commitment to work but they also are feared for allegedly right-wing political views and anti-egalitarian attitude in general and hostility to Australian working-class values in particular. The shift, therefore, during and after WW II from the tenacious and pervasive Australian-British imperial identity to being the Cold War ally of America was not done without a great deal of cultural and social anxiety and *angst* caused by the very British imperial and often anti-American prejudices of most Australians.[8]

In the 20th and early 21st centuries the exchange of peoples between the US and South Australia continued and escalated in many areas. Australia, after WW II, came increasingly within the American strategic and cultural orbit and was perceived globally and within Australia as firmly part of *Pax Americana*.[9] The best known South Australians in this period to work in the US were the Oliphants, father and son. Mark, who was a renowned physicist and worked in the Manhattan Project on the atomic bomb (1943), eventually returned to Australia to head up the physics department at the then new ANU (1950) and later to become Governor of South Australia (1971–1976). Pat is probably the most respected political cartoonist working in America today. Better known in Australia than America, but a celebrity in Adelaide, Andy Thomas has made a name for himself as an astronaut and still maintains his ties with the University of Adelaide and South Australia.

Among Americans coming to South Australia has been a steady stream of sportspeople, academics and professionals in medicine, law and business. Most notable among these are Mark Davis in his long and successful career with the Adelaide 36s basketball team and Roger Russell, Vice Chancellor at Flinders University in the heady days of 60s-style radicalism and protest in the early 1970s at the South Australian suburban university. Russell, like William Webb before him, had a reputation for aggressive and somewhat right-wing politics, characteristics by which Americans often been labelled over the past century by Australians.[10] Most South Australian American academics, however, like these authors, have lived quiet, uncontroversial and productive lives in the three universities of South Australia at Adelaide, Flinders and the University of South Australia.[11]

When Lord Casey presented his credentials to President Roosevelt in 1940, recognising the dramatic wartime shift from British imperial protection to the looming hegemonic power of the 'American century', full diplomatic ties with the US were formalised by his presence as the first Ambassador to the US. This would also usher in the exchange of diplomats between the two nations and many of these would be from South Australia. Prime Minster Chifley appointed Norman Makin, MP for Bonython, to be Ambassador in 1946 at a crucial time: the beginning of the Cold War and the close alliance between Australia and the US (ANZUS, SEATO, etc). He had a distinguished career in government including cabinet positions under John Curtin and Chifley prior to his foreign diplomatic appointment.

In the period since then numerous South Australians have followed: Chris Hurford (1988), MP for Adelaide and minister in several positions in the Hawke Labor Governments; John Olsen (2005), MP for Kavel, Premier of South Australia (1996–2001); and Philip Scanlon, (2008-), head of the Australian-American Leadership Dialogue (AALD), have served as Consuls-General in New York (Olsen also previously Consul-General in Los Angeles, 2001). Robert Hill, South Australian Senator who was a long-serving minister in many positions in Liberal governments, was Australian Ambassador to the UN (2006–2010) and is now (2010) Chancellor of the University of Adelaide; and Australia's longest serving foreign minister (1996–2007), Alexander Downer, formerly MP for Mayo, is presently (2009–) serving as the UN special envoy to the Greek-Turkish negotiations on Cyprus.[12] Thus South Australians have made a major contribution to foreign relations between the two Anglo-sphere allied nations.

COMMERCIAL RELATIONS AND DEFENCE OF THE REALM

Two things stand out in South Australia's commercial relations with the United States: one an export and the other an import. Adelaide was the starting point for the career of Rupert Murdoch as head of the now defunct tabloid the *Adelaide News* and until recently the headquarters of his global behemoth. The import of capital to South Australia from America has always been centred mainly on one company: GMH. Other large scale investment has taken place in mining and other extractive industries including gold, copper and uranium mining.

Trade between the US and South Australia reflects the historical trend for Australia to export commodities from mining, agriculture and other extractive industries. In 2008/09 the US was South Australia's largest export market worth $1.7 billion and the fourth-largest import source worth $620 million. The chief exports come from mining, wine and cars while the main imports are automotive parts, whiskey and fertiliser. US investment is significant with the main sectors attracting US capital being automotive, defence, information technology, financial and engineering services, food processing, wine and health. The largest US companies operating in South Australia are GMH, General Dynamics, Hewlett-Packard, Kimberley-Clark and Raytheon.[13]

Allied with these commercial activities has been defence and defence contracting. The most significant and controversial presence is at the Woomera Base with the US Nurrungar Project which came to an end in 1999. Nurrungar is connected in function with Pine Gap in the Northern Territory and have provided communication data to the US dealing with missile defence and crucial global communications systems. They have both aroused great debate in the Cold War era over the extra-territoriality status and Left opposition to the US alliance. Frequent demonstrations took place at these bases in the Cold War atmosphere but since the end of the great bi-polar conflict in the early 1990s, the Left opposition to US military activity in Australia has been relatively silent (even with occasional demonstrations against US policies in the Middle East and Afghanistan). US companies continue to invest in defence areas in South Australia including BAE Systems, Australian Aerospace, Raytheon, Tenix, ASC and Serco Sodexho Defence Services.[14]

The Premier of South Australia, Mike Rann (re-elected for a third term in May, 2010), views the US as a major trading partner of South Australia and thus has devoted a good deal of his overseas travel to cultivating US investment. He has undertaken three high level official visits to the US in the past four years including one to Governor Arnold Schwarzenegger of the largest US state of California. South Australian delegations attend trade shows in the US including the World Ag Expo, the National Restaurant Association, the United Wine and Grape Symposium and the Bio Conference. In 2009, Mike Rann appointed the former Premier John Olsen to be South Australian Government Special Envoy (Commercial) in the United States. He is to encourage trade with the US and to bring greater investment from the US to South Australia. He will also help with any interactions between Adelaide's sister city in the US, the capital of Texas and major university (the University of Texas) and high-tech town, the city of Austin.[15]

TOURISM

South Australia, with its wine regions, beaches and Kangaroo Island, is a major tourist destination for US tourists (although far less than the east coast of Australia). In 2009, 45,300 North Americans travelled to South Australia which was a 1% increase of visitor nights over the previous year even though the global financial crisis (GFC) caused in a 9% drop overall of US visitors to South Australia compared to 2008. The South Australian Tourist Commission is active in the US with representative arrangements in Los Angeles with a public relations firm.[16]

US IMPERIALISM: CULTURE AND SOCIETY

The importation of American culture, now pervasive in every aspect of life in South Australia, has always been viewed with ambivalence by both the Left and Right of politics. The Left, especially since the Vietnam War period sparked enormous hostility to US foreign policy particularly pronounced in the academy, have tended to view US cultural penetration as cultural imperialism deemed to be corrosive and smothering Australian culture in television, film, the arts in general, literature and in popular culture.[17] The Right, although embracing much of American-style economic theory of economic rationalism (that is, Friedmanite neo-classical, now called somewhat misleadingly neo-liberal, theory in the US) and anti-union ideology, is also suspicious of excessive American libertarianism and still has a smattering of old fashioned Tory Anglo-Australian contempt for all things American. Regardless of these attitudes, however, American culture has had an inexorable spread here sometimes to the dismay of Australians of all persuasions (exemplified by the extremely common pejorative phraseology 'we don't want that American [blank] here').

General Douglas McArthur, heading to Melbourne in wartime Australia, stopped at the then busy railway junction of Terowie, South Australia, to make a speech at the station (in which he uttered the immortal words 'I came out of Bataan and I shall return') to cheer up the Australian nation.[18] He did return to liberate the Philippines but he left a legacy of US culture and this famous speech symbolically launched a tidal wave of Americanisation (not just in Australia, of course, but around the world) of US cultural forms in Australia. With the massive infusion of American troops in the antipodes during and after WW II, the symbols and patterns of American culture would pop up everywhere: jazz music, on every corner with fast food chains, over the radio with American music, in elevators (formerly lifts) with American voices, in the Botanic Gardens of Adelaide, with memorials to US war dead and Elvis Presley. In short, it is ubiquitous and unavoidable.

American sports have taken off in South Australia with the most successful, until quite recently, being basketball with the popular Adelaide '36s (beset with financial problems but still going in 2010). Other American sports have not been so successful with on-again, off-again, leagues containing Adelaide teams in gridiron (called football, of course, in the US), baseball and ice hockey. These sports compete for Australian dollars with cricket and Australian football codes and at time have aroused resentment and fear of US sporting imperialism. Although some Australians have been very successful in the US sporting arena, such as the superstar Luc Longley who played for the National Basketball Association (NBA) champions the Chicago Bulls (1996–1998, with the greatest basketball player ever, Michael Jordan), there has been a steady but low-level criticism of US sporting penetration of Australian markets and television.[19]

In 2010 one would characterise the role of US sports in Australia as secondary to Aussie rules and cricket but still an important element in the Australian sporting scene. In Adelaide in early 2010 large crowds attended the suburban SANFL Norwood Football oval at the Claxton Shield national baseball league playoffs in which South Australia emerged victorious to go into the finals against Victoria in Melbourne (which, unfortunately for South Australian fans, Victoria won in a whitewash 2–0). The Adelaide General Manager for the Australian Baseball League is Pat Kelly former New York Yankee second baseman and member of the World Series Champion team in 1996. Australian teams in baseball have performed well at the Olympics with the winning of a silver medal in Athens in 2004 and the women's softball teams picking up three bronzes and a silver in the four Olympics from 1996 to 2008.

Australian basketball teams have also performed well at the Olympics making stars such as Andrew Gaze household names in Australia (he had a short career in the US NBA but here he remains a hero with a large presence in advertising). As in baseball, the women have been more successful in the international arena than the men with a bronze and three silver medals in the Olympics from 1996 to 2008; the last three attempts defeated by the mighty American team. The men have often been in contention but the best showing was fourth in the Sydney Olympics in 2000. Both basketball and baseball represent a permanent and important aspect of American cultural penetration in Australia and the ubiquity of globalisation American-style.[20]

Film and television have seen traffic from the US to and from South Australia. The most notable are Robert Helpmann and Anthony LaPaglia. Helpmann, born in Mount Gambier in 1909 and educated at Prince Alfred College in Adelaide, had most of his career in Australia and the UK but also had a great deal of success in America as a ballet performer, actor in US films and as a film director. His career has been recognised in Adelaide by the Helpmann Academy at the University of South Australia offering award courses for people seeking careers in the arts. Anthony LaPaglia was born in Adelaide in 1959 and has had a highly successful career in film and television in America. He has won three Emmy Awards for his television work which includes two for his television series *Without a Trace* in which he is the star actor, writer and sometime director.

The South Australian Film Corporation (SAFC) continues to have a strong focus on the US in promoting Australian films in North America and as a location for filming US productions and for post-production functions. The SAFC film, *The Boys are Back,* directed by internationally successful director Scott Hicks, had its premier in the US in November, 2009. Further interactions between the US and SAFC are planned and film media promises to be a most healthy cultural interaction between the US and South Australia in the future.[21]

US IMPERIALISM: EDUCATION AND IDEAS

The exchange of peoples and institutional ties between the US and South Australia have not always been strong but in the past decade the pace of interchange has picked up dramatically under the Rann Labor Government. In 2009, there were 257 students from the US enrolled in South Australian educational institutions about 2.4% of the national tally from the US. With the establishment of two American based mini-universities here by Carnegie-Mellon (the H. John Heinz III School of Public Policy and Management which opened I May, 2006) and Kaplan Universities, these ties look like increasing in the future. There are also regular exchanges of thousands of students at the secondary school level and from many American universities to universities in South Australia through programmes like the Study Abroad Programme (including one in which David Mosler taught with the second oldest college in America, William and Mary [1693] in Virginia, to the University of Adelaide). Fellowships from the American-Australian Association (based in New York City) and the Fulbright Fellowship bring Americans to Australia and take Australians to American for higher education study.[22]

CONCLUSION

The relationship between Australia and America has always been one of ambivalence from the Australian perspective. Historically subject to British Imperial disdain for most things American the dramatic shift caused by

WW II and the Cold War alliance system brought the enormous impact of US globalised culture to Australia in general and of course to South Australia. While embracing American cultural and economic forms, symbols, products and institutions there remains ambivalence and some outright hostility to these changes. Film producers struggle to get Australian films made and watched; writers struggle against American products and control of multinational book distributors and bookselling chains; and Australian television is flooded with US cheaply produced products. American sports compete with Australian sports for increasingly less disposable income in the post-GFC era and thus the debate about US cultural imperialism continues. No wonder the current historiographical penchant for pronouncing that American power is on the decline has received such a welcome audience in Australia especially amongst the Left in the academy and in the arts communities.[23]

But American academics working in South Australian universities have taken very different views on the declinist debate. David Mosler, writing in *Quadrant*, and teaching in international studies and history at the University of Adelaide, has argued that in the short to medium term there is unlikely to be a dramatic decline in US power. He argues that the rise of its competitors, specifically China and India, and decline of the US, have both been exaggerated in this polarised debate in which the strengths of the new rising powers are hyperbolically presented and their weaknesses understated and concomitantly the problems of the US are overemphasised. On the other hand, David Palmer, teaching in American Studies at Flinders University, has argued for a rapid decline of US power which in the '... twenty-first century [faces] decline, its symbolic 'last days' marked by the terrible recession that began in 2008 and indicated an economic shift to East Asia. Did the decline actually begin during the Vietnam War, a war the US had lost by 1975, followed by a decade of de-industrialisation and urban decay prior to the financial debacle in the next century?' Thus Palmer sees an end to the 'American Century' proclaimed in the triumphalism of Time-Life Editor Henry Booth Luce in the WW II era (*Life Magazine,* 1941).[24] This debate is now into its second decade around the world (launched by Paul Kennedy and Francis Fukuyama in 1987 and 1992 with their respective books *The Rise and Fall of Great Powers* and *The End of History*) but the future strength of the global reach of US power in general, and in the Asia-Pacific region in particular, will continue for some time and no doubt the robust debate about it will also continue among Australians and Americans resident in South Australia.

Globalisation now dominates the world conversation about the future in all the aspects of world social and cultural change. Migration, water resources, civil conflict, food production, fish stocks, piracy, global warming, AIDS, child labour, etc, etc. are all world problems and require world-wide solutions. The future interaction of South Australia with the US (presently there are 3,439 American-born residents in South Australia) is part of the general process of global change. The impact of Americanisation on South

Australia will continue as will the disputation over its benefits and consequences. It is hoped that this chapter has shed some light on the dimensions of this issue both historically and culturally and will stimulate further debate and research in the future.

NOTES

1 Susan Marsden, et al., *Heritage of the City of Adelaide* (Adelaide, 1996), p. 92.

2 The Australians have been enthusiastic allies with America in WW I, WW II, Korea, Vietnam, Gulf Wars I and II and now continuing along side American forces in Iraq and Afghanistan. George W. Bush frequently stated to his 'mate' John Howard (Prime Minister, 1996–2007) that no ally was a better friend of America than Australia with the possible exception of the Anglo-sphere mother-country of Britain. President Obama appears to have a similar view of his mate Kevin Rudd.

3 As illustrated by the developing 'California cuisine': a term now used for the generic cuisine in the Asia-Pacific which blends North American, Pacific and Asian flavours together in a syncretistic cuisine which reflects the common Asian-Pacific environment in cities such as Sydney, San Francisco and Hong Kong.

4 Two other Americans were also prominent in the mining industry in this period: James Rutherford in steel and Julius Kruttschmitt who was general manger of Mt Isa mines in the 1930s: David Mosler and Bob Catley, *America and Americans in Australia* (Westport, Conn., 1998), p. 20.

5 Dean Jaensch, 'John Greeley Jenkins', *ADB* (Melbourne, 1966–1991), pp. 478–479.

6 This section on O'Malley based upon Dorothy Catts, *King O'Malley:Man and Statesman* (Sydney, 1957); A.R. Hoyle, *ADB*, pp. 84–86; A.R. Hoyle, *King O'Malley: the 'American Bounder'* (Melbourne, 1981); and John Molony, *The Penguin History of Australia* (Melbourne, 1987), pp. 207, 209–211.

7 Reece Jennings, *William A. Webb* (Adelaide, SA, 1973), pp. 86, 87, 91, 161, 162.

8 These attitudes have always been pronounced among English Tory circles and the British academy has long been hostile to American higher education. In visits to America in the 19th century by English writers Charles Dickens (1842, 1867) and Anthony Trollope (1861–62), they both expressed contempt for American culture and distrust of its new democratic institutions: Charles Dickens, *American Notes* (New York, 1842); and Anthony Trollope, *North America* (London, 1862). These attitudes carried over to the colonial societies in Australia and New Zealand and have not entirely disappeared in the 21st century.

9 For a useful recent survey of the US in the Asia-Pacific see William Tow and Beverley Lake, 'Rules of engagement: America's Asia-pacific security policy under an Obama administration', *Australian Journal of International Affairs*, Vol. 63, issue 4 (Dec., 2009), pp. 443–457.

10 None more so as the notorious and ruthless 'Chainsaw' Al Dunlap who made a reputation as an international 'slasher' of companies including Kerry Packer's ANI and Consolidated Press. He eventually came to a sticky and scandalous end in

the US when he returned there after being fired by Packer in the early 1990s after controversial sackings and 'downsizing' in his companies.

11 There is no accurate account of the numbers but since WW II there would be approximately 1000–1500 American academics and related professionals who have worked in South Australia. In Australia as a whole the number would be several thousand and another American migrant who has gained prominence as an academic, and has something of a reputation as a conservative tough-talker, is the Vice Chancellor of Macquarie University Steven Schwartz (2006–). These authors migrated in the early 1970s which was the peak decade of post-WW II American migration to Australia as part of the world-wide exodus to Australia, Canada and Sweden, among many nations, prompted by opposition to the Vietnam War. See Mosler and Catley, *Americans, passim.*

12 The historiography of those Americans who are interested in Australian history, especially as a comparative field, is now fairly dense. Perhaps the Australian Ian Tyrrell of the University of New South Wales is the most prominent Australian scholar who has published widely on Australian-American comparative topics. The American 'father' of this comparative field, who published many books and articles on American-Australian topics, and lived and worked in Australia for long periods, is C. Hartley Gratton who taught at the University of Texas-Austin: for example see his classic *The Southwest Pacific to 1900* (Ann Arbor, Mich., 1963).

13 'The United States of America and South Australian Trade and Investment Relationship', The Office of the Premier of South Australia Mike Rann, 1/1/10 (private document held by the authors).

14 Ibid.

15 Ibid.

16 Ibid.

17 In November, 2009, the Australian literary community, writers and publishers, united to block the ending of protection of Australians from cheaper foreign books and successfully lobbied the Rudd government from changing these policies: *The Australian,* 15/11/09, p. 1.

18 Wilbur Besanko, *Historic Terowie* (Terowie, SA, 1977), p. 12.; *The News* (Adelaide), 21 March 1942. A plaque, at the now disused station, commemorates the occasion of Terowie's one brief moment on the world historical stage.

19 See the extended discussion of this in Mosler and Catley, *Americans,* pp. 129–133.

20 Another example of the exchange of athletes between the US and Australia is the college basketball team at St Marys in California in which seven of the starting twelve players on the team are Australians mostly recruited from the Institute of Sport in Canberra.

21 Office of the Premier, as above.

22 Ibid. The Heinz School offers a Master of Science in Public Policy and Management and the Master of Science in Information Technology as well as executive education programs.

23 For a thorough recent review of the literature see John Kane, 'US leadership and international order: the future of American foreign policy', *Australian Journal of International Affairs,* Vol. 63, issue 4 (Dec., 2009), pp. 571–592.

24 David Mosler, 'Is America really in Decline?', *Quadrant,* (July-August, 2007), pp. 32–38 and David Palmer, 'Last Days of Empire …', *Transnational Literature,* Vol. 2, No. 1(November, 2009), p. 1.

CHAPTER 9

South Australia and Japan

PURNENDRA JAIN[1]

INTRODUCTION

Early postwar, Australia's engagement with Asia focused primarily on Japan, principally for economic reasons, initially trade and investment and later tourism. From the 1990s, relations were especially expanded into political and strategic realms, particularly as the two countries collaborated in designing and implementing regional institutional architecture such as the Asia Pacific Economic Cooperation (APEC) forum (Rix 1999; Funabashi 1995). Stronger and more diversified engagement at the national level had a profound impact on bilateral engagement at subnational levels, providing the necessary groundwork in terms of institutional arrangements, mutual trust, personal connections and recognition of opportunities that subnational governments could take up within their own jurisdiction.

Some Australian state governments and local councils became recipients of huge amounts of Japanese direct investment. From the mid-1980s in particular, a steady flow of hundreds of thousands of rich Japanese tourists significantly boosted local economies, with Queensland a key beneficiary, especially through tourism and investment in tourism-related industry. Across Australia, interest in studying Japanese language and about Japan soared to an unprecedented extent; some called it a 'tsunami'. It helped to fuel development of cultural and educational ties at the subnational level through official 'sister' relationships between Australian and Japanese cities and between Australian states and Japanese prefectures, alongside exchange programs in universities, schools and other sectors. We see, then, that 'Japan as number one', the label popularised from the title of Ezra Vogel's 1979 hallmark study, made a strong impact on Australia in the late 1970s and 1980s in wide-ranging areas. Since the late 1990s, however, that impact has subsided significantly. Japan has experienced economic malaise from the so-called bursting of its bubble economy in the early 1990s, paralleled by the rise of other Asian countries, most notably China, which has pushed Japan several notches down on Australia's Asia radar.

South Australia's contemporary relations with Japan were steady and stable until recently, even if smaller scale than those of the states and cities along Australia's east coast which is geographically closer to Japan. But the ties have been on a trajectory of slow decline in recent years. Partly this is because of Japan's withdrawal and partly it is because of South Australia's growing focus on China and increasingly on India, a trend that is not vastly different from the national trend and helps to fill the gap created by a shrinking Japanese presence. Trade, investment, tourism and other connections such as educational links and migration are driving South Australia's greater interest in China and India, fuelled by institutional arrangements and political will, as discussed in other chapters of this book. Meantime Japan takes a significantly lower profile in the state's engagement with Asia and is unlikely to become anywhere near as important as it was only a couple of decades ago. Nevertheless South Australia–Japan ties will remain important in the overall context. Japan is still a major economic power with deep and wide-ranging ties rooted in relationships that reach over more than a century. These historical links were not particularly strong but nevertheless served to underlay the individual connections and institutional arrangements that provided solid foundations for contemporary ties to prosper in the closing decades of the twentieth century.

HISTORICAL TIES

Historical ties with Japan were built through two channels – individuals and institutions – although these ties were not particularly strong through either channel. Unlike South Australia's connections with India through colonial ties, its historical links with Japan were built through a number of individuals from Great Britain who had connections to South Australia and interest in Japan. Most did not develop into economic linkages, evolve into institutional form, or flourish into wider socio-cultural engagements across society. One deterrent was the White Australia Policy, the official policy of all governments and all mainstream political parties in Australia from the early 1900s to the 1960s, which excluded all non-European people from immigrating into Australia.

One family with an Adelaide connection that made a name for itself in Japan was the Black family who lived in Japan through both world wars. John Reddie Black (1827–1880) migrated from England to Adelaide where he married and his older son Henry was born in North Adelaide. After living in Adelaide briefly, when his business did not do well John decided to return to England in 1861, but his ship stopped in Nagasaki and he stayed (Morioka and Sasaki 1983, 135). He was soon appointed editor of the *Japan Herald*, publishing extracts from foreign papers, shipping lists and advertisements.[2] In 1867, he successfully started his own newspaper, the *Japan Gazette*, focusing on current events, and three years later he launched a fortnightly newspaper, *The Far East*, which became a major publication. Assisted by a Portuguese resident in Japan who could speak and read Japanese language, Black started a Japanese newspaper, *Nisshin Shinji shi*, which was widely read by politicians and students as well as bureaucrats in Tokyo. Yet it appears that John Black's connection with Adelaide did not provide a platform for linkages back from or over to Japan, and the family was identified by the country of his origin: England. Henry Black grew up in Japan and was the first Westerner to become a professional *rakugoka* (oral story teller). His contribution not only to public entertainment through *rakugo* but also in various other fields including law reform, education about democracy and so forth in Japan has been closely examined and recorded (Morioka and Sasaki 1983; McArthur 2008). There is no evidence of linkage back to the city of his birth, though contemporary Japanese resident in Adelaide Munetaka Umehara (2009) continues the memory of the Adelaide-linked father and son who contributed many 'first things ever' to Japan.

A number of individual men – from England, or from English families who returned to England – had passages through Japan that may have been vehicles for temporary cultural exposure and perhaps goodwill, but it appears these did not produce bilateral engagement.

John Daniel Custance (1842–1923) was appointed South Australia's first professor of agriculture in 1881. Before that he worked as professor of agriculture for four years from 1876 at the Imperial College of Agriculture located at Komaba in Tokyo, which later became a faculty in the University of Tokyo. In 1879, faced with numerous problems in agriculture, especially declining soil fertility, the South Australian government identified the need to establish an agricultural college and Custance was appointed professor of agriculture and director of the Roseworthy Agricultural College when it began in 1885 (Australian Dictionary of Biography). Records consulted make no mention of Custance introducing influences from Japan or maintaining connections with Japan after he migrated to Adelaide, which suggests that he was not a vehicle for bilateral linkages or if so, these were either insignificant or not enduring.

Wilton Hack (1843–1923) was born and raised in Adelaide and went to Japan in 1873 as a missionary. After his missionary work did not succeed, he took up a position teaching English but was soon dismissed. In 1876 he visited Adelaide from Japan and negotiated with the South Australian colonial government to accept a few hundred Japanese families to come and work in the Northern Territory (then administered by South Australia). Back in Japan he told the government that South Australia would provide free passage for the migrants but this was quickly denied in Adelaide and the Japanese authorities rejected the project.[3]

Another 'native' of South Australia, Mortimer Menpes (1855–1938), an artist and engraver from Port Adelaide, spent a short time in Japan studying Japanese house decoration. He used Japanese materials and decoration for a house he built in London.[4] Yet while Menpes's birthplace was Adelaide and he attended classes at the Adelaide School of Design, his family returned to England when he was aged 20 in 1875, and he began his formal art training at the School of Art in London in 1878. He never returned to Australia after his study experience in Japan to bring back the artistic influences or personal connections from Japan to South Australian soil.

An important bilateral link – one of the first in an institutional form – was the position of honorary Japanese consul in Adelaide. The Langdon Parsons family officially represented Japan in South Australia as Honorary Consul/Consul General across four generations for 69 years. The position was therefore kept by one single family who were South Australian locals – not Japanese – and was not paralleled by counterpart 'honorary consulate' positions with any other Asian country during this period. John Langdon Parsons was first appointee (1896–1903), succeeded by his eldest son Sir Herbert Angas Parsons (1903–1920), by Herbert Parsons' second son Frank Lancelot Parsons (1921–1941) and after a 22 year hiatus in response to World War 2, by Frank Lancelot's son Jeffrey Langdon Parsons (1963–1987) (Robertson 1993). The oral history presented by Jeffrey Parsons confirms that although members of his family were appointed over the years as Japan's official representatives in South Australia and the first two were honoured with an 'Order of the Rising Sun', bilateral trade, tourism or other sub-national linkages, including the presence of Japanese nationals in South Australia, were minimal. Until Japan's post-war economic resurgence from the 1960s, the perception that Japanese goods were of inferior quality discouraged international demand.

As minister in South Australia also controlling the Northern Territory, John Langdon Parsons travelled widely to East Asia on private and official business, notably in 1895 as honorary commissioner for South Australia.[5] During his visit to Japan, he explored the possibility of 'Japanese labouring-type people' emigrating to the Northern Territory for its development, an idea that Wilton Hack had tried to realise roughly two decades earlier. However, as before Japan rejected this idea (Robertson 1993, 6). Official representation through an Honorary Consul/Consul General was largely symbolic rather than instrumental as neither side had interest in the other nor reason to establish connections. One exception was the warm, ceremonious welcome given to members of a Japanese naval squadron of three cruisers that visited Adelaide in 1903, when officers 'were willing to discuss the strength of their navy, the wisdom of the Anglo–Japanese alliance, and all and everything relating to the land of their birth' (*Adelaide Advertiser*, 8 May 1903).

When Japan bombed Pearl Harbor in 1941, the prevailing sentiment in Adelaide towards Japan was 'disappointment', 'distrust' and even 'hatred', leading Frank Lancelot Parsons to hand in his appointment as Honorary Consul to then Premier Thomas Playford (Robertson 1993, 16). When approached by Japan for reappointment after the war, Lancelot Parsons supported the idea on advice from close military friends that accommodating and trading with Japan was important since the nation could otherwise drift to the communist camp. However, the institutional lineage was not officially re-established until 1963, with Jeffrey Langdon Parsons as Consul and later 'promoted' to Honorary Consul General.

Relations between Australia and Japan quickly began to prosper nationally through trade, and although less strongly than the east coast states, South Australia also began to develop commercial relations with Japan, which in time gave rise to other types of relations. Jeffrey Langdon recounts as a key achievement establishing the sister-city agreement between Adelaide and Himeji in 1982, on which Himeji gifted to Adelaide the Adelaide Himeji Gardens in the inner city south parklands, In 1986 Himeji Week in Adelaide brought 150 participants from Himeji and Adelaide Week in Himeji brought 200 participants from Adelaide. Sister-city weeks, sister-city exhibitions and other sister-city celebrations still continue to foster mutual knowledge and goodwill, some 25 years after the agreement was signed.

POSTWAR RELATIONSHIPS

Japan and Australia had fought the war from opposite sides but quickly restarted economic relations post-war, with Australia one of the first few nations to do so. Economic complementarities meant that Australia supplied a vast bulk of raw materials that the reviving Japanese economy used on its way to becoming Asia's new industrial giant by the late 1960s. The relationship also had a strategic dimension since both nations were tied to the US through security treaties and therefore shared many Cold War concerns. Like the US, Australia sought to keep Japan in the 'Western camp' lest it drift towards the Soviet side of the Cold War divide. Memories of Japanese wartime atrocities were fresh in the minds of the many Australians who had suffered cruelty directly at the hands of the Japanese war effort, but both nations saw the need to embrace a 'new vision' in their relationship for mutual benefit (Meaney 2007). The culmination point was the Australia–Japan Commerce Agreement of 1957 that laid a solid foundation for future bilateral economic relations (Rix 1986). Indeed, by the late 1960s Japan had already emerged as the most important market for Australian primary products such as wool, wheat, minerals and coal.

In this national context, South Australia too began to develop wide-ranging ties with Japan based on trade and investment. The office of Japanese Consul that was first established in the late 19th century provided historical foundation.[6] But whereas in the 1980s and 1990s in particular, relations strengthened, expanded and diversified, in the 21st century we observe a trend towards contraction of the economic links and to some extent of the strength and diversity of relations upon that economic basis. In surveying contemporary relations we observe how South Australia's relationships with Japan at the state–prefecture level and between cities remain deep and wide, but in recent years have become stagnant or begun to decline. South Australia orients more and more towards other Asian countries, particularly China and India, while Japan slips down in strategic priority and popular interest. Japan's sluggish economy has undermined the economic linkages, and lack of persistent effort to engage with South Australia in the face of weaker economic relations has contributed to the decline. Japan has a disadvantage here vis a vis China and India since unlike for those nations there is not a strong Japanese diaspora in South Australia to act as a lobby group and as a lubricant for cultural and political relations.

CONTEMPORARY LINKS

Contemporary South–Australia Japan relationships can be characterised as wide-ranging and deep-rooted. At their core are the strong economic ties through trade and investment, on which relations were expanded and diversified through the 1980s and 1990s. Tourism by Japanese that thrived in South Australia during the 1990s in particular has faded somewhat with Japan's economic decline, but formalised scientific, educational, cultural (sister-state and sister-city programs) and community links are still in place. Across the board, however, Japan has been overshadowed in recent years as South Australia's strategy of Asia engagement has responded to the emergence of other active international players that present fertile opportunity for mutual benefit with South Australia. Japan remains a significant player but with a lower profile. Fewer Japanese people pass through, or live, in South Australia for business, work, working holiday or tourism. Japan now receives less coverage by local media and recent reporting has been mainly negative, concerning closure of highly visible Japanese manufacturing units in the state and the negative consequences. In these circumstances Japan has virtually disappeared from the political radar of South Australia and exchanges at top political levels have effectively halted.

TRADE

Department of Trade and Economic Development (DTED) data indicate two-way trade in 2007–08 was worth A$1.77 billion, placing Japan in third place behind the United States and China. Consistent with the trend nationally, South Australia maintains a trade surplus with Japan, as it does to a much larger extent proportionately with India. Exports to Japan worth around $900 million in that yearly period comprised mainly resources derived from mining such as petroleum/bituminous oils, semi-manufactured or powdered silver and refined copper; primary commodities such as beef and seafood;[7] and $22 million worth of wine. Imports from Japan (worth $866 million) comprised mainly autos, auto parts and accessories, and processed petroleum products. Both exports and imports declined significantly in 2008–2009, with total trade falling 23 per cent on the previous year to $1.37 billion. Continued recession in Japan and the closing of Japanese manufacturing units in South Australia (Mitsubishi Motors, for example) contributed to this decline.

Half of the imports from Japan comprised vehicles other than railway or tramway rolling-stock, and associated parts and accessories, and the other half comprised machinery, equipment, mechanical appliances and electrical and electronic products. Exports from South Australia were mainly seafood, meat, beverages, mineral fuels and mineral oils, pearls and precious stones and uranium. Japan is the largest market for SA blue fin tuna.

Figure 1: South Australia's trade with Japan

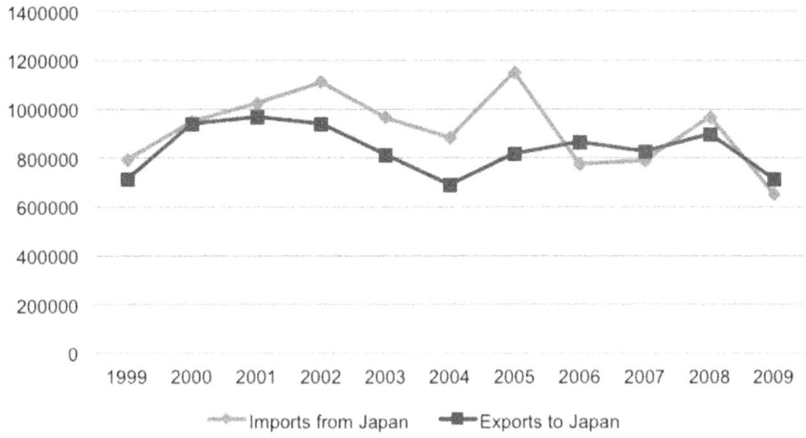

1400000
1200000
1000000
800000
600000
400000
200000
0

1999 2000 2001 2002 2003 2004 2005 2006 2007 2008 2009

Imports from Japan — Exports to Japan

Source: ABS, Catalogue 5368.0 International Trade in Goods and Services

Future prospects do not suggest a return to earlier peak trade levels. DTED expects that the ongoing economic recession in Japan will lower demand for exports from South Australia but identifies high-end technology and sciences such as nanotechnology, aerospace and environmental technologies as areas where trade is most likely to experience growth as South Australian exports to Japan. A Free Trade Agreement between Australia and Japan that is currently under consideration would bring both positives and negatives for South Australia. A study commissioned by the South Australian government indicates the state would gain in agricultural exports such as barley, beef, wine and citrus, at the expense of the automotive industry where further tariffs cuts would be required.

Meanwhile, in April 2011 South Australian Minister for Industry and Trade Tom Koutsantonis noted the success of the government's targeted campaigns in China (up $697 million or 61 per cent on the previous year), India (up $306 million or 74 per cent) and the ASEAN nations (up $575 million or 50 per cent), as these campaigns 'continued to pay massive dividends'.[8] Relative trade performance with Japan highlights how the economic underlay for South Australia's relations with Japan has been weakened as other nations in the region have overtaken Japan in trade performance, opening the way for more extensive relations with South Australia in other fields as well.

INVESTMENT

The two most prominent examples of Japanese direct investment in the manufacturing sector in South Australia are Mitsubishi and Bridgestone.

Mitsubishi began direct investment in South Australia in the 1970s through collaboration with Chrysler in automobile manufacture, but in 1980 Mitsubishi bought Chrysler and established Mitsubishi Motors Australia Limited. Although the state government poured huge subsidies into this industry, the company failed to remain competitive and closed its Adelaide production unit in 2008 after some 28 years of operations. The plant closure's negative impacts on South Australia's industrial sector were considerable, including unemployment for a large number of people and further weakening an already weak manufacturing base.[9] Even before its full shutdown, in 2004 the company had closed its engine plant, axing more than 600 jobs at the plant and another 350 jobs at the factory assembly line. In a bid to continue operating, the company developed a new model car in 2005 – the Mitsubishi 380 – forecasting sales of 30,000 a year. But when sales failed to pick up, it was only a matter of time until the plant was shut down. State political leaders criticised the closure since the state had heavily subsidised the company to keep this industry in Adelaide. The fallout through job and other industrial losses may have soured relations and mutual interest well beyond the ambit of Mitsubishi Motors Australia.

The other prominent Japanese company, Bridgestone, delivered a similar blow to the South Australian manufacturing sector in 2010 when it closed its tyre manufacturing factory. Claiming the Adelaide plant was no longer globally competitive, Bridgestone relocated its production overseas after more than 40 years of operation. Some 600 workers lost their jobs as a direct result of the closure and many more indirectly because their jobs depended on the plant's operation. The closure was received with mixed feelings. The company maintains its distribution, customer service and retail networks, employing about 1500 people, but the Bridgestone closure almost on the heels of the Mitsubishi closure is likely to have weakened mutual goodwill.

While the story of these closures made headlines in South Australia, new investment is hardly reported. For example, in 2010 Mitsubishi Corporation purchased a SA-based company, United Utilities through a consortium in which Mitsubishi has a share of 59 per cent. The other partners are the Innovative Network Corporation of Japan (30 per cent), Manila Water Company (1 per cent) and JGC (10 per cent). The company's name was changed to Trility in March 2011.[10] This shows that Japanese companies are looking for new opportunities for investment in South Australia, away from the manufacturing sector.

MULTI-FUNCTION POLIS (MFP): A STILLBORN PROJECT

Another development that began brightly but faded out completely was the multi-function polis (MFP). This proposal, which briefly put South Australia on Japan's map, was first floated by Japan's then Ministry of International Trade and Industry (MITI) in the heyday of Japan's economic boom. The plan was to develop a new city that would incorporate high-tech industry, education and tourism. Australia was seen as an ideal location given its vastness, industrial capacity, standard of living and growing bilateral relationship with Japan. When the concept was floated, many Australian states had their eye on this proposed city. The site of first choice was the Gold Coast in Queensland, but because of strong public opposition, the Queensland government withdrew from the project. In lieu, South Australia keenly raised its hand to provide a site for the project on the outskirts of Adelaide.[11]

The emphasis of the Bannon government (1982–1992) on expanding the Technology Park created in 1982 by the Tonkin government (1979–82) was important in inviting the MFP to Adelaide. The Bannon government anticipated that the MFP would establish SA as a technology hub in the Asia Pacific and by diversifying the economy would reduce the state's heavy dependence on the manufacturing sector (Minami 1997, 126–127). Some academic leaders such as the then Vice Chancellor of Flinders University, Professor John Lovering and a number of senior bureaucrats, especially the Head of Premier's Department, Bruce Guerin, supported the push (Patience 1991, 29–30). The Japanese proposal seemed particularly attractive for South Australia as reports suggested that out of the top 10 IT companies in the global market, six were American and four were Japanese. Launched as a joint project between the Federal and SA governments, in 1992 the SA government established the MFP Development Corporation under state legislation.

However the newly elected federal government under John Howard withdraw federal financial support in 1996, claiming it did not see the project would result in national benefit beyond benefits to SA. The MFP concept that had started as an international project then turned into a local project focused mainly on the development of South Australia (Parker 1998). With the future of the project on shaky ground, Rix observed: 'As of 1996, it would appear that the MFP has little future, at least as an Australia–Japan project' (Rix 1999, 112). In any case, Adelaide was not the first choice for the Japanese government and other Asian capital cities that were expected also to invest in the MFP were not seriously interested. Investment from Japan into Australia was drying up as Japan had turned investment attention towards East Asia, Europe and the US. With the loss of international interest and the Federal government withdrawing from the project, the MFP could not be successfully executed and the then Premier John Olsen wrote its official obituary in August 1997.

Although the MFP did not eventuate, South Australia established useful global connections during MFP negotiations with companies overseas. Several IT firms such as EDS and Motorola came to the state even without the MFP. It was estimated that more than 10,000 staff were employed in the IT field in Adelaide around the late 1990s, some 1.5 per cent of all jobs in the state at that time (Minami 1997, 129). This indirect result from the MFP was not of small consequence for South Australia and gave the state some longer-term advantage in the IT field.

With production units moving to more cost-effective destinations where labour is cheaper, Japanese investment in manufacturing units has declined. Nevertheless some new areas such as alternative energy have attracted Japanese companies to invest. For example, in 2009 Marubeni Corporation and Osaka Gas purchased 100 per cent of the shares in the Hallett 4 wind farm project in South Australia being developed by the major Australian energy company, AGL Energy Ltd.[12] However, the South Australian government is not actively seeking investment from Japan as it did in the 1970s and 1980s. It has the negative experiences associated with the MFP and plant closures by Mitsubishi and Bridgestone, but it also sees that the Japanese economy is stagnant and there are other interested players such as China, India and Southeast Asian countries that are more likely to be willing and able to partner with South Australia.

HUMAN FLOWS

Another trajectory of decline is the bilateral flow of people. One of the key areas of economic activity connecting Japan with South Australia has been study abroad. Here the fall off in students from Japan contrasts with the swelling numbers of Indian and Chinese students in South Australia in recent years. But it is consistent with the trend nationally and globally, as Japan's sluggish economy has lowered interest and financial capacity for international study.[13] The general decline after peaking in 2004 is evident in Figure 2.

Figure 2: Japanese international students in South Australia

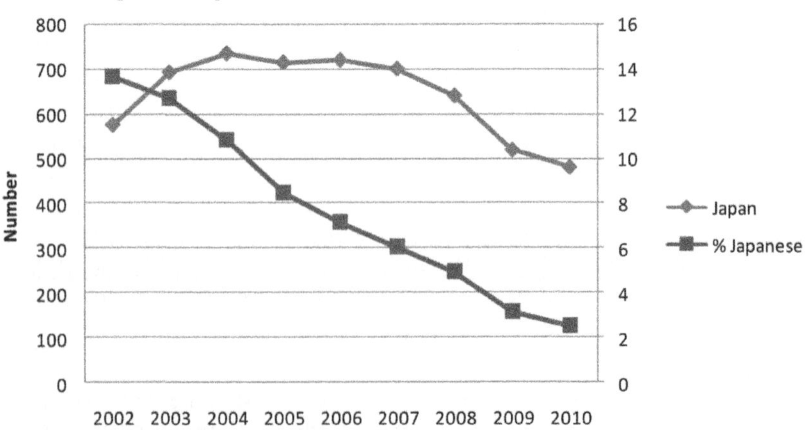

Source: Australian Education International 2010.

Tourism tells a parallel story with visitor arrivals from Japan to South Australia also in decline. Tourism Research, which surveys tourism in Australia, reveals that in the year to September 2008, roughly 11,000 Japanese visited the state, a fall of over 20 per cent on the previous 12 months and part of an overall downward trend in recent years.[14]. Another parallel is in the falling number of Japan origin settlers in South Australia, as evident in Figure 3. The number of these settlers is influenced by economic activity and study abroad that requires their residence in South Australia, and with trade, investment and study in South Australia by Japanese falling, the decline in Japanese settlers may well continue.

Figure 3: Japan origin settlers in South Australia

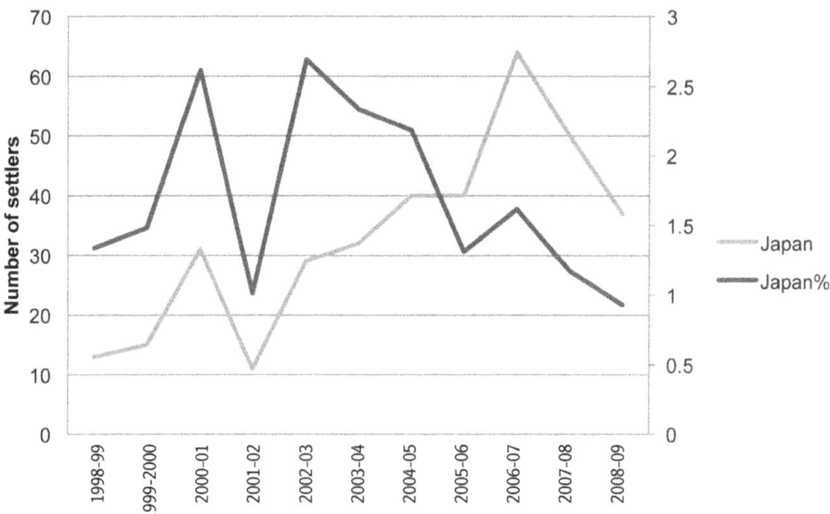

Source: DIAC Settler Arrivals

CULTURAL AND EDUCATIONAL LINKS

One official instrument used by governments below the national level to build ties with their counterparts overseas is official sister relationships. This instrument usually focuses on cultural and educational linkages. However, the increased bilateral flow of people and ideas that the sister relationship inspires usually has other flow-on effects, so indirect economic and socio-cultural impact is difficult to gauge. Usually the cities/states that take on sister relationships share geographic, industrial or other features that form the basis for unity. For example, Muroto city in Kochi prefecture is quite similar to its sister city Port Lincoln in that both are coastal cities with aquaculture as the main industry.

At the state level, South Australia signed a formal agreement to establish its first Japanese 'sister' relationship with Okayama prefecture in May 1993, following examples from around the world, particularly the relatively large number established between Australian and Japanese subnational entities (Jain 1991). This first formal state–prefecture agreement for South Australia was signed after intensive engagement between the two over a period of 10 years. Initial contact about the possibility was in 1984 through ties between

Ports Corporation South Australia and the port of Mizushima in Okayama prefecture. During the following ten years, delegations from Okayama came to Adelaide and vice versa, including trips by the governor of Okayama to South Australia and by SA Premiers Bannon and Arnold to Okayama (Minami 1997, 137–138). Nevertheless, Australian states and Japanese prefectures have had somewhat different expectations and priorities for these kinds of 'sister' arrangements. Minami (1997, 144) found that while the Japanese side was generally more interested in the 'softer' aspects of the relationship, that is cultural and educational dimensions, the Australian side was more interested in economic aspects. In the Okayama–South Australia example, Minami found that unlike the Australian side, the Okayama side had minimal interest in the explicitly economic dimension of the relationship.

One of the state's largest councils, Adelaide city, has a sister relationship with Himeji, symbolised by the Himeji gardens in downtown Adelaide. Adelaide city's website has a dedicated page for this sister city relationship, explaining its genesis in 1982 and listing achievements. These reveal both the strength of bilateral engagement during the 1980s and 1990s and a falloff throughout the 2000s.[15] The Japanese Council for Local Authorities for International Relations (CLAIR) lists nine sister relationships between local councils in South Australia and Japan (Table 3). Examination of websites of the nine councils with sister-city ties in Japan has revealed different levels and types of engagement. Some councils simply mention school exchange programs in council minutes, while others, like the city of Tea Tree Gully, are more forthcoming. Tea Tree Gully declares it is 'committed to the further development of this sister city relationship and encourages all community members and groups to visit Asakuchi City for a truly 'Japanese experience' based on friendship and mutual understanding'.[16] The Port Lincoln council states clearly the aims and purposes of its links with Muroto city in Japan and lists items related to the exchange program on council meeting agendas.[17]

Table 3: South Australia–Japan sister city linkages

S.A. local government	Japan local government, prefecture	Established
Adelaide	Himeji, Hyogo	19 April 1982
Barossa	Kumenan, Okayama	22 Aug 2002
Clare and Gilbert Valleys	Bizen (Yoshinaga), Okayama	18 Jan 1990
Holdfast Bay	Hayama, Kanagawa	15 Dec 1997
Marion	Kokubunji, Tokyo	2 April 1993
Port Lincoln	Muroto, Kochi	27 Mar 1991
Salisbury	Mobara, Chiba	25 May 2002
Tea Tree Gully	Asakuchi (Kamogata), Okayama	22 Oct 1997
Victor Harbour	Maniwa (Yatsuka), Okayama	26 May 2000

Source: http://australiahelps.gov.au/japan/business-and-community/sister-states-and-cities/, viewed 23 July 2011.

Councils recognise the need to carefully consider costs and benefits of such ties, as is evident in the response by the wine region's Barossa Council to a proposal for a sister program with a Chinese counterpart. Minutes of the

Council meeting where the proposal was discussed record acknowledgement that while significant cost is involved if trade and cultural delegations are exchanged frequently, the benefits of such relationships are difficult to quantify, as appropriate literature makes clear. The Council referred to its existing sister relationship with Kumenan Town in Okayama, noting 'the benefits (or lack of them) that this relationship yields'. The minutes record the assessment that 'much of Barossa's exporters, particularly in the wine industry, have well established links with a number of export destinations including China – would a sister city relationship augment this or duplicate existing effort?'[18] An outcome was not noted in the minutes.

South Australian councils were much more actively involved in sister-city programs when Japanese local governments had vast amounts of funds to spend on them. For now, with the Japanese economy in recession and local governments desperate for funds, programs are much less active than before. Nevertheless the sister ties with Japan from the 1980s and 1990s serve as useful precedents for South Australian councils, especially for informing Council decisions on whether or not to establish formalised sister links with cities in other countries, as is evident from the Barossa example with a Chinese counterpart.[19]

COMMUNITY ORGANISATIONS

South Australia's population of Japanese nationals is rather small compared to its populations from other Asian nations, as noted above both South Australians and Japanese are members of the four main community-type organisations: the Japan Australia Friendship Association of SA (JAFA), the Adelaide Nihonjin kai (the Japanese Society of Adelaide, JSA), the Australia Japan Association SA (AJA), and the Japan–Australia Business Council of SA (JABC).

JAFA aims to promote friendship between the two countries and showcases Japanese culture and exchange through cultural activities. One of the largest and most popular Japanese events in South Australia is the annual Kodomo no hi (Children's Day) celebration where thousands of visitors enjoy Japanese art, craft, music, dance and food. AJA presents a local radio program, 'J-Talk', every Friday evening on cultural issues, current affairs and music in English and Japanese. AJA also aims to promote friendship between the two countries and conducts a number of activities including Japanese conversation classes twice a month in downtown Adelaide. In 2011, it also helped organise the South Australia-based OzAsia festival whose national theme for 2011 was Japan.[20] AJA also actively promotes the annual Salisbury council Mobara Festival at Mawson Lakes. The Japan–Australia Business Council of SA, relaunched in 2006 after a brief hiatus, encourages South Australian businesses to refresh and renew its export interests with Japan. Invited speakers present talks to members on subjects related to economic and political issues.

While all four of these organisations promote Japan in various fields, none is especially influential in lobbying government and industry to forge ties with Japan. Nevertheless all four share concern that present Premier Mike Rann has not visited Japan during his more than nine years in office, even though he has visited India annually and China numerous times. And while South Australia has opened a number of new offices overseas including one in Chennai in India, it closed its Tokyo office some years ago, again signifying decline of Japan in South Australia's overall strategy of engaging countries of Asia Pacific.

CONCLUSION

Japan's absolute decline in South Australia – in exports and imports, and in number of tourists, international students and temporary residents – is largely symptomatic of Japan's economic downturn in the early 1990s and subsequent economic stagnancy. Its relative decline is accentuated by the exponential growth in South Australia of other economically ascendant Asian countries – China in particular, and India and other Asian countries more generally. The visible presence of students and workers from these countries, with retail catering to their needs, makes this 'other Asian' rise all the more visible and palpable.

Japan is, therefore, a source of valuable lessons for South Australia about the purposes, nature and possibilities of connections with other Asian subnational governments. In this instance, shared economic interests have been at the core of subnational bilateral relations. South Australia, like other Australian states, began to engage quite actively with Japanese counterparts since the early 1980s, which by now makes some 30 years of experience. We see that Japan's economic strength provided crucial underlay for other types of relations to develop. It created the capacity to engage in international trade and investment that inspired pursuit of local level engagements and it financed the costs of what became significant non-commercial cultural flows through visiting officials, cultural events and other programs that celebrate, foster and symbolise the local level engagement. We also see the flow on for these relations when economic relations weaken – when companies shift their operating units from high cost to low cost locations, and commercial and human flows reduce. It forces subnational governments, such as in South Australia, to move on towards different sources of trade, investment and other valuable connections where opportunities for its people and business prospects are strong. This is what we observe in South Australia's current economic and political strategies towards China and India, as Japan's capacity and will to engage with the state begin to fade.

Yet it is also important to remember that Japan is still, and will remain for many years, a key economic partner of South Australia. We need only recall the example of food exports where Japan is South Australia's largest market and its demand is rising further, to appreciate that the nature as well as the scale of economic linkage is changing. We also see interest of Japanese companies in new areas of the SA economy. Meantime, 30 years of connections at the subnational level have created an underlay of personal interest, understanding and goodwill that will not simply disappear as economic relations fade. Indeeed, these personal connections at local level are the real substance and long-term benefit of subnational relations. It takes two to tango and to have a bilateral subnational relationship. Subnational governments, their representatives and interested organisations on the ground on both sides will need to open their eyes further if they seek to bolster the waning relationships between them and re-establish Japan on the commercial, strategic and cultural map of South Australia. Some may see the current level of bilateral engagement being 'about right',[21] in my assessment there is scope for greater engagement given the potential of both sides.

NOTES

1 This chapter has benefitted from discussions with Gail and Munetaka Umehara who kindly provided me with information on a number of historical links between South Australia and Japan and directed me to some key materials. I owe thanks to Mr Adam Wynn, honorary consul general for Japan in South Australia, for drawing my attention to the Langdon Parsons family and their role in forging South Australia's official ties with Japan before any other colony in Australia. I am also grateful to him for reading an earlier draft of my paper and offering some very valuable comments. However, the normal caveat applies and I alone remain responsible for any errors.

2 www.mitsubishielectric.com/tasteofjapan/foreigners/black/index.html (viewed 5 April 2011).

3 http://adbonline.anu.edu.au/biogs/A040355b.htm (viewed 28 June 2010).

4 www.victorianweb.org/art/design/japan/menpes.html (viewed 5 April 2011).

5 http://adbonline.anu.edu.au/biogs/A110152b.htm (viewed 20 May 2011).

6 Even today Japan is represented by an honorary consul general in South Australia. While the importance of China and India are growing, neither has consular presence in South Australia.

7 A 2010 report by the Council of Trade and Commerce South Australia outlined rising exports of food items to Japan, which is already South Australia's largest food export market. In 2009 South Australia accounted for nearly 50 per cent of Australia's seafood exports to Japan. www.citcsa.org.au/content/citcsa-flash (No. 182, April 2010) (viewed 18 July 2010).

8 www.southaustralia.biz/News/2011/04/08/SA-export-market-continues-to-soar.aspx (viewed 7 June2011).

9 www.history.sa.gov.au/motor/mitsubishifilm.html (viewed 9 June 2011).

10 According to Mr Adam Wynn, the new CEO of Trility is a Japanese national and the company intends to make major investment in the water solutions area. Email correspondence, 1 August 2011.

11 Partly as a result of the memories of World War 2, Queenslanders regarded this project as another chance for Japan to 'colonise' Australia as rumours circulated that 200,000 Japanese wanted to settle in the Multifunction Polis. The debate on the left and right sides of the politics is briefly captured in Patience's essay (1991).
12 www.marubeni.com/news/2009/091001e.html (viewed 9 June 2011).
13 http://mdn.mainichi.jp/features/archive/news/2010/06/20100607p2a00m0na0180 00c.html (viewed 7 June 2011). One area that this paper does not address and for which data is hard to find is the flow of exchange students. Japan would figure here most prominently among its Asian peers.
14 Figures made available by DTED.
15 www.adelaidecitycouncil.com/council/programs/sister-cities/himeji.html (viewed 20 July 2011).
16 www.teatreegully.sa.gov.au/site/page.cfm?u=19 (viewed 12 May 2011).
17 www.portlincoln.sa.gov.au/site/page.cfm?u=550 (viewed 12 May 2011).
18 Minutes_from_Council_meeting_21_July_2009.pdf, http://ebookbrowse.com/minutes-from-council-meeting-21-july-2009-pdf-d142325156 (viewed 13 May 2011).
19 South Australia signed a new sister agreement with the Indian state of Chennai in 2005.
20 OzAsia started in 2007 that showcases multicultural heritage of South Australia.
21 Adam Wynn in an email correspondence, 1 August 2011.

REFERENCES

Advertiser (Adelaide), 8 May 1903, http://trove.nla.gov.au/ndp/del/article/4946412. Accessed 16 July 2011.

Australian Dictionary of Biography. 2011, 'Custance, John Daniel (1842–1923)', National Centre of Biography, Australian National University, http://adb.anu.edu.au/biography/custance-john-daniel-3305/text5033. Accessed 14 July.

Jain, Purnendra. 1991, 'Japan's Urban Governments, their International Activities and Australia–Japan Relations: An Exploratory Essay', *Policy Organisation and Society*, No. 4, Summer, pp. 33–44.

Meaney, Neville. 2007, *Towards a New Vision: Australia and Japan Across Time*, Sydney: University of New South Wales Press Ltd.

McArthur, Ian. 2008, 'Narrating the Law in Japan: *Rakugo* in the Meiji Law Reform Debate', *Electronic Journal of Contemporary Japanese Studies*. www.japanesestudies.org.uk/articles/2008/McArthur.html#r22.

Minami, Masaki. 1997, 'The Role and Policy of the South Australian Government in the Development of Economic Ties with Asian Nations', MA thesis, University of Adelaide, December.

Morioka, Heinz and Sasaki Miyoko. 1983, 'The Blue-Eyed Storyteller: Henry Black and His *Rakugo* Career', *Monumenta Nipponica*, 38:2, Summer, pp. 133–162.

Parker, Paul. 1998, 'The Multi-Function Polis 1987–1997: An International Failure or Innovative Local Project?' *Pacific Economic Paper*, No. 283, September.

Patience, Allan. 1991, 'Confronting a Terrible Legacy: Australia's Japan Problem and the MFP', *Policy, Organisation and Society*, Vol. 4, Summer, pp. 25–32.

Robertson, Beth M. 1993, 'Interview with Jeffrey Langdon Parsons', J.D. Somerville Oral History Collection, Adelaide: State Library of South Australia.

Rix, Alan. 1986, *Coming to Terms: The Politics of Australia's Trade With Japan 1945–57*, Sydney, London: Allen and Unwin,.

Rix, Alan. 1999, *The Australia–Japan Political Alignment: 1952 to the Present*. London and New York: Routledge.

Umehara, Munetaka. 2009, 'Unexpected Cargo – The Black Family in Japan: Transferring Democracy from Adelaide to Young Japan', paper presented at the Art Gallery of South Australia, 30 May (copy acquired from author).

Vogel, Ezra. 1979, *Japan as Number One: Lessons for America*, Harvard: Harvard University Press, 1979.

CHAPTER 10

South Australia–Southeast Asia Relations[1]

MING HWA TING

The Southeast Asian region consists of eleven states in various stages of development ranging from a first-world state such as Singapore to Timor Leste that only gained independence from Indonesia in May 2002. The Southeast Asian region is usually sub-divided into two primary categories: continental and maritime. States such as Cambodia, Laos, Myanmar, and Vietnam (CLMV) make up continental Southeast Asia and states such as Singapore, Malaysia, and Indonesia belong to the maritime category. Given the diversity of this region, this chapter has to be selective in its scope, and it will only be focusing on Singapore, Malaysia, and Vietnam to demonstrate South Australia's links with both maritime and continental Southeast Asia.

It may not be a well-known fact but contacts between modern-day Oceania and Southeast Asia have a very long history, and can be traced back to the Neolithic period, as evidenced by the spread of Austronesian languages from the former region to the latter (Bellwood 2004). In more recent times, maritime Southeast Asia has had more interactions with the outside world as Western travelers, sojourners, and settlers usually arrived in the region by sea. Consequently, maritime Southeast Asia has been the traditional conduit for Australia's interaction with the wider region as well, which explains why Singapore and Malaysia are chosen. These two states are chosen because they share many links with South Australia that can be traced back to when they formed the Straits Settlements during the period of British colonisation in the 1700s and 1800s; Vietnam is chosen because Australia played a direct role in the Indochina conflict in the 1960s and 1970s. Furthermore, the influx of Vietnamese into South Australia changed the state's demographic profile. However, what is significant to note is that the ability of the Vietnamese community to integrate with South Australian society as evidenced by the appointment in 2007 of Hieu Van Le as the state's Lieutenant Governor augurs well for the future of multiculturalism in South Australia. Through an examination of the historical, economic, and social interactions between these Southeast Asian states and South Australia, it will become apparent that the relations between the two regions, though frequently overlooked and obscured, are both multi-faceted and strong, which makes for a very positive outlook in the years to come.

HISTORICAL OVERVIEW

South Australia's links with maritime Southeast Asia harks back to the era of British colonisation when Singapore, Penang, and Malacca formed the Straits Settlements. For instance, Sir William Francis Drummond Jervois served as Governor of the Straits Settlements from May 1875 to April 1877 before taking up the position of South Australia's Governor in October 1877. His tenure as the Governor of the Straits Settlements made him sympathetic to the plight of ethnic Chinese there, and he was a strong champion of Chinese migration to Australia and New Zealand even though such a stance was considered rather unorthodox then (Winks, n.d.). In his role as South Australia's Governor, Jervois laid the foundation stone for The University of Adelaide in 1877, and the University would, in time to come, educate many Colombo Plan scholars from Singapore and Malaysia who later became the future leaders and captains of industry in their respective countries.

The historical links between South Australia and Southeast Asia do not stop there. Coincidentally, Colonel William Light, who was South Australia's inaugural Survey General and founder of Adelaide, was also linked to Southeast Asia. Colonel Francis Light, father of William Light, founded Georgetown, the capital of Penang in present-day Malaysia in 1786 as a Captain of the East India Company. In 1819, Sir Thomas Stamford Raffles founded Singapore. At that time, there was much opposition from the Dutch over the British control of Singapore. However, Warren Hastings, who was the Governor of Bengal, supported Raffles's actions, which meant that Singapore remained a British colony. As this chapter would go on and demonstrate, the links between Singapore and South Australia are arguably the most developed among all the other Southeast Asian states, which is why it is rather fitting for a mountain in South Australia to be named after Warren Hastings, even though he never set foot in South Australia!

SOUTH AUSTRALIA–SINGAPORE RELATIONS

Such oblique and little-known political links between Singapore and South Australia continue to the present day. For instance, Singapore's first elected President Ong Teng Cheong, who served in this position from 1993–1999, studied Architecture at The University of Adelaide and graduated in 1962. Prior to his accession to the Presidency, Ong was a long-time Deputy Prime Minister and headed the National Trade Unions Congress (NTUC) in Singapore. Similarly, the former First Lady Madam Ling Siew May also studied in Adelaide, and she was in fact the first Asian student admitted to Adelaide Girls High School. She graduated as Dux of her cohort and went on to pursue her tertiary studies in Architecture at The University of Adelaide as well.

The University of Adelaide can also lay claim to the current President Tony Tan Keng Yam. Elected in August 2011 as the city-state's seventh President, Tan received his doctorate in Applied Mathematics from Adelaide in 1967. Before becoming Singapore's Head of State, Tan was a Minister in various key ministries such as Finance, and he was also the Deputy Prime Minister from 1995 to 2005. After stepping down as a Member of Parliament in 2008, he headed the Government Investment Corporation in Singapore. Many Adelaide alumni have gone on to illustrious careers in Singapore, and the close links between Adelaide and Singapore are also reflected by the April 2006 publication of a commemorative volume titled *The Southern Light: Enlightening and Enriching* detailing the achievements of the Singaporean alumni from The University of Adelaide. At the book launch, Australian High Commissioner to Singapore Miles Kupa said he was 'heartened to acknowledge that a number of people featured in this book now hold senior positions in Singapore's public and private sectors and have made significant contributions to Singapore' (The University of Adelaide 2006). Education has therefore played a vital role in promoting links between Singapore and South Australia, and the future looks very positive.

In yet another sign of the close educational links between Singapore and South Australia, the Ngee Ann Kongsi and The University of Adelaide jointly set up the Ngee Ann-Adelaide Education Centre in 1998 to provide a range of undergraduate and postgraduate degrees and diplomas in a variety of disciplines (Ngee Ann Kongsi, n.d.). The fact that this initiative represents The University of Adelaide's first foray into setting up an overseas campus is indicative of the warm and mature ties between Singapore and South Australia, which are also present in the business sector.

As Singapore is the most economically developed state in South Australia, it is not surprising for South Australia to have good economic links with the city-state. The Government of South Australia maintains a number of overseas representatives offices that are under the purview of the Department of Trade and Economic Development. Currently, Singapore and Vietnam hosts two out of the eight overseas offices. In a very clear indication of the close economic links between South Australia and Singapore, the first such overseas office was set up in Singapore, ahead of the office in the United Kingdom (Ting 2011a). Set up in 1975 by State Premier Donald Dunstan, this office provides South Australian firms wishing to do business in Singapore and Southeast Asia with local market intelligence as well as with networking opportunities. Tay Joo Soon was the first Commercial Representative for South Australia in Singapore (Ting 2011c). Dunstan chose Singapore as the location of the inaugural office because he clearly recognised that healthy and vibrant trade relations with Singapore were vital to South Australia's then and future economic well-being. Given the high degree of complementarity between the two economies, it is hardly surprising that Singapore is South Australia's first port of call to the Asian region. This sentiment is also applicable to the national context. For instance, Australia's first Free Trade Agreement was also concluded with Singapore in July 2003.

As Austrade puts it:

Singapore is a natural first export market for Australian companies and a gateway to the growing markets in ASEAN. It is also a natural junction in trade flows between Australia and India, and between Australia and China. Australians are advantaged in doing business in Singapore because of close proximity, similar time zone, strong Australian reputation and SAFTA has guaranteed a more open and transparent environment. With the signing of the AANZFTA, Singapore is a natural hub for Australian business to expand into ASEAN (Austrade 2011).

Expanding on this point, Kirsten Sayers, Austrade's Senior Trade and Investment Commissioner in Singapore said:

Australia is Singapore's number 3 food supplier, and its number one in beef, lamb, pork, cheese and curd. You can even study at Curtin or James Cook Universities without leaving Singapore! This makes it a lot easier to do business in Singapore as compared to other destinations (Harcourt 2011).

South Australian firms also have a significant presence in Singapore, especially in the architecture sector. For instance, Woodside, which has offices in Adelaide and other parts of Australia as well as in Singapore, was responsible for Changi Airport's Terminal Three's and the National Library's interior design. Likewise, Singaporean firms are also present in South Australia. For instance, Sembcorp, which is a Government-linked Corporation (GLC), provides waste collection services in many Australian capital cities, including Adelaide.

At the same time, South Australian firms in the tourism and hospitality sectors have also been regular participants in the Food and Hotel Asia trade show held in Singapore on a biennial basis. Given the nature of Singapore's economy and the city-state's lack of natural resources, the majority of foodstuff consumed there are imported. Singapore's lack of self-sufficiency in this area therefore makes it a viable export market for South Australian produce. Furthermore, through the collaborative efforts of the Australia-Singapore Business Council SA, Council for International Trade and Commerce South Australia Inc, in association with the Department of Primary Industries and Resources of South Australia, organised a market awareness mission to Singapore for South Australian food exporters. Although Australian produce are more expensive than imports from other countries, consumers are willing to pay a premium for quality. For instance, during the outbreak of avian influenza in 2007, consumer demand for Australian eggs and poultry in Singapore increased significantly (Ting 2011a). The increased demand lends credence to Austrade's Maurine Lam's belief that 'Australia's strong reputation as a quality supplier of food and beverages, our geographic proximity ... have given Australian exporters a major competitive advantage' (Austrade 2008).

Singapore's increasing receptiveness towards Australian produce also extends to the wine sector as well (Ting 2011a). For instance, MP International, which is headquartered in Singapore, has been organising 'Wine for Asia' annual trade show, which is the largest wine convention in the region, and provides South Australian wineries with a good opportunity to showcase their products to an emerging Asian market. South Australian wineries such as Burton Estate, Ceravolo, Lavina Wines, Linda Domas, Murray Street Vineyards, Nookamka, Normans, Peter Lehmann and Yaldara appear in the 2010 edition (Wine for Asia 2010). Even though South Australian wineries are well-represented at this event, more could be done to encourage other wineries to participate in the premier wine convention in Asia. This is because Singapore is an ideal launching pad for South Australian wineries. As Maurine Lam, Austrade's Senior Trade Commissioner, puts it:

> With Singapore positioning itself as the lifestyle capital of Asia and influencing trends in consumption across the region, Australian wines served in Singaporean restaurants have a better chance at success in Asia.

Furthermore, Lam also states that, 'Australian wine producers could almost make no mistakes in Singapore. The proximity, the business culture, the English-speaking community, the international palate – everything is perfect for a new exporter' (Austrade 2007).

The aerospace and defence industry is another area that presents many promising opportunities for closer relations between Singapore and South Australia. The Singapore Airshow is the largest of its kind in Asia and ranks in the top three of aerospace and defence events in the world. As South Australia is the 'Defence State', closer collaboration and increased investment in this sector is likely to result in a win-win situation, and should be actively encouraged by the State Government (Ting 2011a). On the civilian aviation sector, the links between Singapore and South Australia have been very strong. Singapore Airlines have been flying to Adelaide since 1986, and it now accounts for more than 30 per cent of direct inbound and outbound international passengers to Adelaide (Crouch 2009). Yet, given the close private sector links between Singapore and South Australia, it was only in August 2010 that Mike Rann made his inaugural visit to Singapore (Wills 2010). Given the geographical proximity between the two regions, it represented a rather curious development.

Bilateral relations between Singapore and Australia have been good, but they were temporarily affected by the execution of Van Nguyen on drug trafficking charges. Despite Federal Labor's calls for the capital sentence to be commuted, Rann supported Singapore's tough stance on matters law and order. In fact, he was very vocal in voicing his opposition to the Australian public's call for a minute's silence when Nguyen was hanged. Rann stated very forcefully that even though he was personally against capital punishment, nevertheless, he supported Singapore's tough stance on law and order:

> Van Nguyen is not Florence Nightingale. Van Nguyen is one of a number of people who want to peddle death to our young people and make money out of it and it doesn't come much lower than that. He is … I mean, drug dealers in my view are murderers, therefore should get life sentences for their actions.

> I find it deeply offensive that people have called for some kind of minute's silence for the death sentence if it's actually passed in Singapore. I also find it offensive that people are talking about trade embargoes.
>
> I mean, the fact of matter is that we in Australia have two minutes silence a year – one minute at Anzac Day and one on Armistice Day for those who sacrificed their lives to give us our freedom. And we have to put into perspective that Van Nguyen shouldn't be idealised in terms of what he's done. (ABC 2005)

Rann's support of Singapore's zero tolerance on drug trafficking was not unexpected because he was very keen in projecting an image of being tough on crime during his tenure as the State Premier.

SOUTH AUSTRALIA–MALAYSIA RELATIONS

Just like Singapore, Malaysia's relations with South Australia can also be traced back to the period of British colonisation discussed above. In a further sign of the close links between them, Donald Dunstan proposed that Adelaide and Georgetown, the capital of Penang become sister-cities, a move that came into force in December 1973. For Georgetown and Adelaide to become sister-cities is very significant because it draws attention to the historical ties between them as they were both founded by the Light family in the 1700s and 1800s respectively. Since becoming sister-cities, there have been increased interactions between them as evidenced by the introduction of direct flights from Adelaide to Malaysia, as well as the increased exports of South Australian fruits and produce to Malaysia (Adelaide City Council, n.d.).

Education has also played a major role in enhancing the links and contacts between Malaysia and South Australia. Many eminent Malaysians studied at the University of Adelaide as Colombo Plan scholars. For instance, Datuk Dr Gopal Ayer Sreenevasan, Malaya's first urologist in 1955, was made an Honorary Fellow of St Mark's College, the University of Adelaide in April 2009 (Colombo Plan Secretariat 2009). Today, Adelaide continues to attract many Malaysian students, and these links are set to continue into the future. As evidence of the growing presence of the Malaysian community in South Australia, a Malaysian Carnivale and Malaysian Festival were held in Adelaide in 2010. The event showcased various aspects of Malaysian culture and history to South Australians. It was so well-received by the local population that the event was awarded the 'Community Event of the Year Award' at the City of Adelaide Australian Day awards (Department of Foreign Affairs and Trade 2011). A similar event was held at Victoria Square in September 2011, and it was also very well-received by the local community. Furthermore, more and more South Australians are becoming increasingly familiar with Malaysian cuisine through MasterChef's finalist Poh Ling Yeow's enthusiastic promotion (Yeow 2010), which provides another easily accessible avenue for South Australians to become acquainted with Malaysian culture.

Despite the close people-to-people links between Malaysia and South Australia, the latter still lags behind New South Wales. For instance, the Australia-Malaysia Institute [AMI] launched a sister school program to promote and increase collaboration between Australian and Malaysian schools. At the time of writing, 26 Victorian schools have partnered with their counterparts from various parts of Malaysia such as Kuala Lumpur, Kedah, and Perlis (Department of Foreign Affairs and Trade 2011). There are no such arrangements in place in South Australia at the time of writing in September 2011. However, on a more positive note, Arts SA, in conjunction with AMI and Asialink, have provided funding that made it possible for Daniel Jaber to undertake his Artist Residency at Rimbun Dahan in Malaysia. During his tenure, Jaber has already two new dance works involving both Malaysian and Australian dancers (Department of Foreign Affairs and Trade 2011), and it is a good example of the close artistic collaborative efforts between South Australia and Southeast Asia.

There are also many other good examples of the artistic and cultural interactions between South Australia and Southeast Asia. For instance, the Art Gallery of South Australia successfully staged the 'Crescent Moon: Islamic Art and Civilisation' between November 2005 and January 2006. This was a significant milestone for the Gallery because it represented the first time such an exhibition was staged anywhere in the world. Furthermore, many of the pieces on display for this exhibition were permitted for the first time to leave their respective home countries (Art Gallery of South Australia 2005). In June 2010, the Art Gallery of South Australia staged a one-day event to introduce Southeast Asian culture to young South Australians. The South Australia Art Gallery, which has one of the world's leading collections of Thai ceramics, staged 'Reflections of the Lotus' between May and July 2010. These various art exhibitions are important because they expose South Australians to the art and culture of Southeast Asia, and increase their awareness of their neighbours in the region.

On the business front, South Australia's relations with Malaysia have also been very good. The Australia-Malaysia Business Council SA branch, which was established in 1994, has been facilitating closer links between South Australia and Malaysia on a number of diverse fronts ranging from medical to business. In conjunction with the Australia-Malaysia Institute that was established in 2005 by Alexander Downer, these organisations have created links between the Malaysian Ministry of Health and the Women's and Children hospital that made it possible for Malaysian doctors to receive specialised training in South Australia. Furthermore, AMBC (SA) also estimates that since its 1994 inception, it has taken part in various trade missions to Malaysia which brought in export sales and inbound investment of approximately $25 million (Australia Malaysia Business Council (SA) Inc 2006).

However, there are some potential obstacles that might undermine the economic relationship between Malaysia and South Australia. For instance, foreign companies investing in Malaysia need to abide the country's bumiputeras policy which requires ethnic Malays to hold 30 per cent equity. In brief, this policy is similar to the affirmative action. However, the distinguishing trait is that the bumiputeras policy as practiced in Malaysia provides ethnic Malays, who constitute the majority of the population, with positive discrimination in areas such as housing, education, and business, regardless of income levels. Ethnicity is the only criterion, which excludes the Chinese and Indian minorities in Malaysia. As a result, the continual implementation of this policy might act as an additional barrier of entry for South Australian firms into the Malaysian market, thereby making it a less attractive investment destination. Although, there are signs that this policy is easing, Malaysian Prime Minister Najib's decision in June 2011 to retain the bumiputeras policy in the 10th Malaysian Economic Plan showed that any progress in this area is likely to be slow and protracted. Nevertheless, South Australia still enjoys a trade surplus with Malaysia, indicating that local businesses have not been that adversely affected by the bumiputeras policy.

SOUTH AUSTRALIA–VIETNAM RELATIONS

South Australia's interactions with Southeast Asia are not solely confined to the maritime region; it has interactions with the continental region as well, most notably Vietnam. The Korea and Southeast Asia War Memorial, which is located at the Port Road median at Hindmarsh, is a continuing physical reminder of Australia's military involvement in Vietnam, Borneo, Korea, and Malaya. The South Australian connection is especially evident in the display depicting the Vietnam conflict. The display featured a Canberra bomber piloted by Michael Herbert from Glenelg, and navigated by Robert Carver. The aircraft was on a bombing mission in Da Nang when it disappeared from the radar screen, and all contact was lost. The two airmen were reported as missing, and presumed dead (Vietnam Veterans Association of Australia, n.d.). The Indochina conflict was a brutal and protracted conflict that led to the displacement of many Vietnamese, especially from the South. Many Vietnamese sought refuge in other countries, and Australia was one of them, and the influx of Southeast Asian refugees expedited the end of the White Australia policy in 1977, the same year Hieu Van Le arrived in Australia as a refugee. With the abolition of this restrictive immigration policy, many Southeast Asians now call South Australia home. As of December 2010, there were 11,474 Vietnamese, 7,664 Filipinos, 6,483 Malaysians, 2,229 Thais, and 2,070 Singaporeans (Multicultural SA 2011). There are also migrants from other Southeast Asian states, but the numbers are lower. There is arguably no better indication of the multifaceted interaction between South Australia and Southeast Asia than the appointment of Hieu Van Le as South Australia's Lieutenant Governor in August 2007. Significantly, he is the first person of non-European origin to hold this office. He was also one of the first boat people to arrive in Australia, and his successful integration to the

South Australian society shows that multiculturalism is an ideal that can be achieved.

There are also growing trade links between South Australia and Vietnam. As mentioned, Vietnam plays host to the second overseas representatives office. It was set up by the Department of Trade and Economic Development in August 2009, and its establishment showed that Vietnam is becoming important to South Australia. As Huyen Nguyen puts it, the 'South Australian Government maintains commercial representation in key target markets to provide export assistance to South Australian businesses and help attract business investment and migration to the State' (Ting 2011b). This positive outlook and assessment is more than warranted. As shown in the graph below, not only does South Australia enjoy a trade surplus with Vietnam, there is also a general upward trend as shown in the graph below:

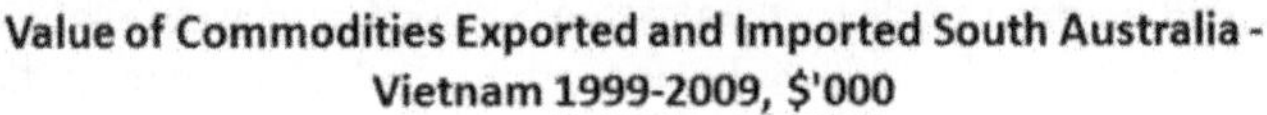

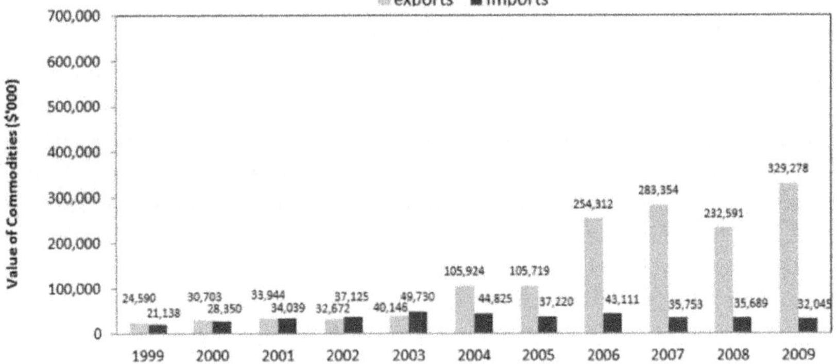

Since this office came into operation, it can be expected that various South Australian companies will experience much success in exporting to Vietnam in the years ahead (Austin 2010).

CONCLUSION

With the concurrent rise of India in South Asia and China in Northeast Asia, it is not unexpected that South Australian policymakers and the general public pay more attention to developments there. Even though India and China are powering the global economy, and South Australia has also benefitted greatly from the rapid economic growths of these two countries, it is arguably equally important to pay attention to Southeast Asia. After all, South Australia only constitutes a minor part of the Chinese and Indian economies. Consequently, South Australia is not that important to these two rising powers. On the other hand, the size of the South Australian economy is generally more comparable to those of Southeast Asian states, which makes for a far more equitable relationship. Furthermore, as this chapter has shown, South Australia shares many historical, economic and social links with the Southeast Asian region. From the period of European colonisation in the 1700s and 1800s to the present, South Australia has played a part in the region. Although these links may not be that apparent and have been obscured by South Australia's interactions with more prominent states such as Britain, China, and India in the present, it is still necessary to be aware of developments in Southeast Asia. This is because events unfolding there can have a direct impact on South Australia. It is therefore important for Southeast Asia to remain on the radar of both South Australian policymakers and the public alike.

NOTES

1 The author would like to acknowledge the assistance provided by Dr Ernie Teo, President of the Australia-Singapore Business Council (SA) Branch, Ms Huyen Nguyen, South Australian Business Development Officer, Austrade Vietnam, Ms Serena Xie, Commercial Representative, South Australian Government Singapore Office, and Associate Professor Peter Burns in drafting of this chapter. The usual caveat applies, and I am responsible for any errors or omissions.

REFERENCES

ABC 2005, No sympathy for Nguyen from Rann. *The World Today*. ABC.

Adelaide City Council (n.d.) George Town, Penang, Malaysia. Adelaide, Adelaide City Council.

Art Gallery Of South Australia 2005, 180 Southeast Asia treasures in Adelaide for world-first exhibition. Adelaide, Art Gallery of South Australia.

Austin, N. 2010, South Australian exports to Vietnam set to surge, export ambassador says. *Adelaide Now*. Adelaide.

Austrade 2007, Singapore's Love for Aussie Wine Tempts Asia. Austrade.

Austrade 2008, Tastes of Australia to invade South East Asia. Austrade.

Austrade 2011, Singapore Profile. Australia Government.

Australia Malaysia Business Council (SA) Inc 2006, Inquiry into Australia's Relationship with Malaysia. *Joint Standing Committee on Foreign Affairs, Defence and Trade Foreign Affairs Sub-Committee.*

Bellwood, P. 2004, The Origins and Dispersals of Agricultural Communities in Southeast Asia. in Glover, I. and Bellwood, P. (Eds.) *Southeast Asia: From Prehistory to History*. London and New York, RoutledgeCurzon.

Colombo Plan Secretariat 2009, The Colombo Plan-University of Adelaide Alumni Gathering. Colombo Plan Secretariat.

Crouch, B. 2009, Adelaide welcomes Singapore Airlines comfort class. *Adelaide Now*. Adelaide.

Department of Foreign Affairs and Trade 2011, Funded Projects. Department of Foreign Affairs and Trade.

Harcourt, T. 2011, Singapore Slings Plenty of Trade Australia's Way. Australian Government.

Multicultural SA 2011, Arrivals in South Australia at and since 2006 Census. Adelaide, Government of South Australia.

Ngee Ann Kongsi (n.d.) Ngee Ann-Adelaide Education Centre. Singapore, Ngee Ann Kongsi.

The University Of Adelaide 2006, Singapore alumni celebrated. *lumen.* Adelaide, The University of Adelaide.

Ting, M.H. 2011a, Personal interview with Dr Ernie Goh, President of Australia-Singapore Business Council (SA) Branch.

Ting, M.H. 2011b, Personal Interview with Huyen Nguyen, South Australian Business Development Officer, Austrade Vietnam.

Ting, M.H. 2011c, Personal Interview with Serena Xie, Commercial Representative, South Australian Government Singapore Office.

Vietnam Veterans Association of Australia (n.d.) City of Charles Sturt, South Australia. Vietnam Veterans Association of Australia.

Wills, D. 2010, Rann on a tight Budget schedule. *Adelaide Now.* Adelaide.

Wine for Asia 2010, WFA 2010 Participant Listing. Singapore, Wine for Asia.

Winks, R.W. (n.d.) Jervois, Sir William Francis Drummond (1821–1897). *Australian Dictionary of Biography.*

Yeow, P.L. 2010, Poh's Blog. *Poh's Kitchen.* ABC.

Contributors

Jennifer Bain is a postgraduate student in Politics at the University of Adelaide. Her doctoral dissertation is on the genealogy of peak oil. She has also conducted research on green policies and climate change in Australia.

Associate Professor Barry Burgan is Head of the University of Adelaide Business School and researches and teaches in the area infrastructure financing and financial and economic evaluation. As Head of the Business School, and as a member of the Pre-Accreditation Committee of the preeminent international Business School accrediting body AACSB, he has an ongoing engagement in the directions of international education, and ensuring that the University of Adelaide Business School is maximising opportunities for all stakeholders. He has extended experience in applied and academic research in regional economic development policy.

Dr Gerry Groot is Senior Lecturer in Chinese Studies at the Centre for Asian Studies, University of Adelaide where he teaches Asian studies and Chinese politics. His research interests include united front work and corporatism but also extend to Chinese folk religion, ghosts, soft power, social change as well as Asian influences on Western and Australian culture.

Professor Graeme Hugo is ARC Australian Professorial Fellow, Professor of the Discipline of Geography, Environment and Population and Director of the Australian Population and Migration Research Centre at the University of Adelaide. His research interests are in population issues in Australia and South East Asia, especially migration. In 2002 he secured an ARC Federation Fellowship over five years for his research project, 'The new paradigm of international migration to and from Australia: dimensions, causes and implications' and in 2009 an ARC Australian Professorial Fellowship over five years for his research project 'Circular migration in Asia, the Pacific and Australia: Empirical, theoretical and policy dimensions'.

Professor Purnendra Jain is Professor in Asian Studies at the University of Adelaide. Author and editor of 12 books and numerous scholarly articles on contemporary Asian politics and foreign policy issues, his latest co-edited books are (with Brad Williams) *Japan in Decline: Fact or Fiction?* (Global Oriental 2011); (with Takashi Inoguchi) *Japanese Politics Today: From Karaoke to Kabuki Democracy* (Palgrave Macmillan 2011) and (with Lam Peng Er) *Japan's Strategic Challenges in a Changing Regional Environment* (World Scientific, forthcoming 2012). A former President of the Japanese Studies Association of Australia, he is currently President of the Asian Studies Association of Australia.

Professor Greg McCarthy is Head of School, Social Sciences, at the University of Adelaide. His research interests are on the politics of change with a special focus on comparing transitional changes occurring in Australia and China, a comparison that includes politics, climate change and public administration.

Dr Julian Morison is Managing Director of EconSearch. He has over 25 years experience in applied economic analysis, particularly related to primary industries, natural resources and regional economic development. Julian has undertaken many projects investigating socio-economic, institutional, policy and business dimensions of natural resource management issues such as planning for reduced water allocations in the Murray Darling Basin and the establishment of marine parks in the state waters of South Australia.

Dr Sharon A Mosler was born in the United States and educated at Wayne State University (BA, English). After migrating to Australia, she completed a PhD at the University of Adelaide (PhD, History). She has published numerous articles on heritage history and in 2011 published a book entitled *Heritage Politics in Adelaide.* She resides in Adelaide and is presently a Visiting Research Fellow in the School of History and Politics in which she continues to teach Australian and European history and undertake research on heritage politics.

Dr David F Mosler was born in the United States and educated in History at Stanford University (BA, PhD) and Georgetown University (MA). He has taught History and Politics in Australian universities for forty years and has published four books and some twenty articles on US and Australian politics, history and international relations. He lives in Adelaide and is presently a Visiting Research Fellow in the School of History and Politics at the University of Adelaide where he continues to teach and research.

Associate Professor John Spoehr is the Executive Director of the Australian Workplace Innovation and Social Research Centre at The University of Adelaide. He is a political economist specialising in research on work, inequality and society. His previous books with Wakefield Press include *Beyond the Contract State: Ideas for social and economic renewal in South Australia*, *Power Politics: The electricity crisis and you*, *State of South Australia: Trends and issues* and *State of South Australia – from crisis to prosperity.* He is currently working on a new edition of *State of South Australia.*

Dr Glen Stafford returned to the University of Adelaide to complete his doctorate in Chinese Studies after studying, working and travelling throughout Asia. His research interests are education, social change and social mobility in China, as well as international education and globalisation. Dr Stafford is currently Executive Officer of the Confucius Institute at the University of Adelaide.

Dr Ming Hwa Ting was formerly an Associate Lecturer at The University of Adelaide. A published poet, he is currently researching on the international competition for rare earths. His works in this area have been published in outlets such as *Global Asia, The Australian*, and *The Diplomat*. He now works for the SA Department of Further Education, Employment, Science and Technology.

State of South Australia
From Crisis to Prosperity?

Edited by John Spoehr

Will South Australia emerge from the global economic crisis relatively unscathed and enter a period of unprecedented prosperity? *State of South Australia* tackles this and many other questions, offering the most comprehensive analysis of the major social, economic, cultural, environmental and political trends and policy challenges facing this state.

ISBN 978 1 86254 865 7

For more information visit www.wakefieldpress.com.au

Turning Points

Chapters in South Australian History

Edited by Robert Foster and Paul Sendziuk

South Australia has often been represented as 'different': free of convicts, more enlightened in its attitudes toward Aboriginal people, established on rational economic principles, and progressive in its social and political development. Some of this is true, some of it is not, but mostly the story is more complex.

In this book eminent historians explore these themes by examining some key 'turning points' in South Australia's history. Henry Reynolds considers the question of Aboriginal rights to land. Bill Gammage illustrates the nature of Aboriginal land management. Paul Sendziuk unravels the myth of the colony's convict-free origins, while Robert Foster and Amanda Nettelbeck reveal a surprisingly strong sense of 'nationalism' in colonial South Australia. Susan Magarey traces the histories of two crucial events in the advancement of women. Neal Blewett examines the political innovations of Don Dunstan. Jill Roe looks at life in the country in twentieth-century South Australia, and Mark Peel life in the city, in particular the migrant experience after World War Two. Finally, John Hirst asks: 'How distinctive was South Australia after all?'

ISBN 978 1 74305 119 1

For more information visit www.wakefieldpress.com.au

Out of the Silence

The History and Memory of South Australia's Frontier Wars

Robert Foster and Amanda Nettelbeck

When South Australia was founded in 1836, the British government was pursuing a new approach to the treatment of Aboriginal people that it hoped would avoid the violence that marked earlier Australian settlement. The colony's founding Proclamation declared that as British subjects, Aboriginal people would be as much 'under the safeguard of the law as the Colonists themselves, and equally entitled to the privileges of British subjects'. But could colonial governments provide the protection that was promised?

Out of the Silence explores the nature and extent of violence on South Australia's frontiers in light of the foundational promise to provide Aboriginal people with the protection of the law, and the resonances of that history in social memory. What do we find when we compare the history of the frontier with the patterns of how it is remembered and forgotten? And what might this reveal about our understanding of the nation's history and its legacies in the present?

Robert Foster and Amanda Nettelbeck's *In the Name of the Law: William Willshire and the Policing of the Australian Frontier* was described as 'a book that deserves to be on the reading list of any guide to essential reading in Australian history'. Their first book with Rick Hosking, *Fatal Collisions*, was described as 'groundbreaking' and 'an important contribution to current thinking about frontier histories'.

ISBN 978 1 74305 039 2

For more information visit www.wakefieldpress.com.au

Great Central State

The Foundation of the Northern Territory

Jack Cross

The Northern Territory's first European decades were an extraordinary mixture of grand vision and human folly, peopled with larger-than-life characters.

In *Great Central State,* Jack Cross tells the story of South Australia's ambitious – or foolhardy – plan to become the premier colony of Australia using its own unique experience in planned colonisation, and its bid to develop the north coast as an integral part of South-East Asia. Bitter feuding abounds alongside admirable efficiency, while tales of courage and sacrifice are matched by episodes of sad ignorance and abuse. This is a history strange but true.

Great Central State is a result of the most sustained historical research on a South Australian subject since Douglas Pike's *Paradise of Dissent* published in 1957. In his wry, meticulously researched book, Jack Cross demonstrates that already before 1911 when the Northern Territory was ceded to the Commonwealth, it had a sophisticated history of its own. He looks forward to the day when it will become the seventh Australian state.

> 'From its murky beginnings during the 1860s, the Northern Territory became the exotic locus of South Australia's best utopian dreams and worst administrative nightmares. Jack Cross has trawled through the record of this extraordinary colonial venture, sorting folly from foresight and identifying pioneers and villains, opportunists and adventurers. He has given us a frank, unrestrained history of Australia's own frontier colony.' – Philip Jones

ISBN 978 1 86254 877 0

For more information visit www.wakefieldpress.com.au

GREEN AUSTRALIA
A Snapshot

Steve Lancaster

Green Australia: A Snapshot examines the ways in which Australians are attempting to reduce their ecological footprint both at home and at work.

In 2009, the CO_2 Energy Emissions Index found that Australia had overtaken the USA to become the largest per capita emitter of greenhouse gases in the world – a legacy of dependence on coal-fired power stations, the widespread adoption of conventional farming techniques, heavy reliance on vehicles powered by fossil fuel, 'dirty' industrial practices and a growing mountain of waste. Yet, in recent years, there has been a growing awareness that climate change is beginning to bite, the recent drought and devastating floods suggesting that more extreme weather patterns are likely unless significant steps are taken to combat global warming.

Using case studies and up-to-date research, this book demonstrates that, although much more needs to be done if Australia is to secure a carbon-neutral future, some Green shoots are beginning to emerge.

ISBN 978 1 74305 013 2

Wakefield Press is an independent publishing and distribution company based in Adelaide, South Australia. We love good stories and publish beautiful books. To see our full range of books, please visit our website at www.wakefieldpress.com.au where all titles are available for purchase.